INTEGRATING WORLDS

INTEGRATING WORLDS

How Off-Campus Study Can Transform
Undergraduate Education

Scott D. Carpenter, Helena Kaufman, and

Malene Torp

Foreword by Jane Edwards

STERLING, VIRGINIA

Published by Stylus Publishing, LLC.
22883 Quicksilver Drive
Sterling, Virginia 20166-2019

Library of Congress Cataloging-in-Publication Data
Names: Carpenter, Scott Dominic, 1958- author | Kaufman, Helena, 1962- author. | Torp, Malene, 1973- author.
Title: Integrating worlds : off-campus study in undergraduate education / Scott D. Carpenter, Helena Kaufman, Malene Torp.
Description: Sterling, Virginia : Stylus Publishing, [2019] | Includes bibliographical references and index.
Identifiers: LCCN 2018051269|ISBN 9781620360002 (cloth : alk. paper) | ISBN 9781620360019 (pbk. : alk. paper) | ISBN 9781620360026 (library networkable e-edition) | ISBN 9781620360033 (consumer e-edition)
Subjects: LCSH: Foreign study. | American students--Foreign countries | International education--United States. | University extension--United States. | Education and globalization--United States. | Higher education--Aims and objectives--United States. | Higher education--Curricula--United States.
Classification: LCC LB2376 .C34 2019 | DDC 370.116--dc23 LC record available at https://lccn.loc.gov/2018051269

13-digit ISBN: 978-1-62036-000-2 (cloth)
13-digit ISBN: 978-1-62036-001-9 (paperback)
13-digit ISBN: 978-1-62036-002-6 (library networkable e-edition)
13-digit ISBN: 978-1-62036-003-3 (consumer e-edition)

Printed in the United States of America

All first editions printed on acid-free paper
that meets the American National Standards Institute
Z39-48 Standard.

First Edition, 2019

CONTENTS

FOREWORD   vii
Jane Edwards

ACKNOWLEDGMENTS   xiii

1   OFF-CAMPUS STUDY   1
Multiplying Impact

2   AN INTEGRATIVE EXPERIENCE   21
Off-Campus Study and Liberal Education

3   THE LONG RUNWAY   45

4   BRINGING IT BACK   61

5   A WORLD OF DIFFERENCE   79
The Culture Question

6   ENGAGED GLOBAL CITIZENSHIP   97

7   MEASURING CHANGE   111

8   PRESSURE POINTS   129
The Future of Off-Campus Study

9   SUSTAINING INTEGRATION   149

REFERENCES   165

INDEX   177

FOREWORD

This book appears at a time when questions about the nature and effectiveness of undergraduate education in the United States trouble us at every level. The validity of the liberal arts model in fostering skills and qualities necessary for young people to make their lives productive and worthwhile in this new era of globalization is routinely challenged. Issues of access, curricular and cocurricular structures, cost, and value are debated with a new level of energy.

Because globalization is at the center of this maelstrom of anxiety, those of us who work in international education, a key zone in which the U.S. educational system intersects with the rest of the world, have new opportunities to contribute to these often contentious discussions. The value of this timely book lies in this arena. If we believe that international experience really does have a great impact on our students' ability to contribute cheerfully and productively in today's complex globalized world, then we can no longer think about study abroad and domestic study away as a costly marginal frill for the privileged. We must instead rethink institutionally our educational propositions, and this book is structured to help us do just that.

The authors of this book suggest a radical shift, that we turn our thinking about the place of off-campus study in the undergraduate liberal arts experience upside down. Working from an analysis of the ways that dislocation—moving away from the familiar campus environment—can affect learning, they suggest that the well-designed off-campus experience should be not an optional extra but one of the foundational building blocks of our curricula in all areas. If we can accept this radical proposition, then we can revitalize and renew our students' learning.

A rethinking of this kind can be transformative for the community of faculty and administrators who work together to structure the educational experience we all seek for our undergraduates. The authors of this book suggest that their primary goal is to fuel and support discussions among our institutions' often segregated groups of faculty, senior institutional planners, and study abroad professionals. To facilitate such conversations, the authors address a broad audience. This book can introduce faculty and educational administrators who may have no experience at all with off-campus study to current thinking and practice in the field but can also serve as a rich resource for international education professionals. If these constituencies decide to bring together those who oversee off-campus experiences in the United States with those who work in other countries, new and productive synergies can emerge.

Integration is the key concept; this book is structured to explore how the off-campus experience can best be conceptualized as part of a curricular initiative and then implemented in ways that maximize all aspects of student learning. Thus, preparation on campus inside and beyond the classroom, the design of the off-campus experience, and the work of reintegration of that experience after the students return to campus are all essential components. Integration of the work of faculty, institutional planners, and program designers and implementers should also be our goal; in many institutions this remains aspirational. Such efforts at collaboration can be energizing for everyone involved and sometimes little short of revolutionary. If this book is read by those involved as a prelude to discussion, new avenues might lead to collaborative initiatives building on a shared recognition of effective pedagogies and program design.

The claims made here for the value of the off-campus experience, which are supported by a body of research well used and documented in this book, are founded on the premise that the pedagogical bases of well-designed off-campus programs are those we know to be effective in all our teaching and cocurricular programing, on campus or off. Study abroad and study away are, at best, an aggregate of what are now best known as *high-impact practices*, those pedagogical strategies the higher education community has come in recent years to recognize as most effective with our students. These practices, as catalogued by the Association of American Colleges & Universities (Kuh, 2008) and discussed in chapter 1, are familiar to many educators. Together they provide a springboard for the discussion of ways we can best achieve the integration of curricular and extracurricular experiences, whether our students are on campus in our classrooms or roaming the world beyond our borders.

The single most striking and useful concept may be *intentionality*. Too often we design course components and cocurricular experiences because of a general sense that they are a good thing. We can do more. The authors lay out a route map for conceptualizing and implementing experiences ranging from research field trips embedded in science courses to semester or year-long off-campus experiences that go beyond the traditional idea of language and culture. If we embrace a broad understanding of how our students are now structuring their own educational aspirations, we can include in our teaching many of the innovations described in these pages. To provide specific examples, anticipating issues that we all struggle with, the authors examine in chapter 3 the ways language acquisition is experienced by students today, clarifying many of the vexing questions that are raised by the spread of English globally as a language of instruction in higher education. Another of the great campus debates of international education focuses on the imperatives and problems of models of what is called *global citizenship*, and the concise and clear exploration of a way of thinking about this is provided in chapter 6 and offers an excellent platform for the conversations we need to have with our students and with each other.

Many innovative and highly effective program design strategies are detailed here, some originated by faculty and others growing out of the observations of program managers. Underlying all is the recognition that the clear definition of goals and intentional and conscious planning for student experiences are the best foundation for this work. Engagement of the students themselves in establishing expectations and in self-assessment are essential to achieving the progress—academic and personal—for which these programs are designed. The road map provided here is based on a recognition of the need for a coherent and, indeed, integrative approach to this work. This is far more effective than the opportunistic and sometimes almost random mode so often driven by our sense of urgency and our isolation from our colleagues. This is the integration that will fulfill the goal of giving students opportunities to develop their ability to understand cultural variables and global systems and prepare them to seek grounds for empathy rather than rationales for judgment.

As we all understand, students' goals and expectations about what constitutes a valuable educational experience have changed radically in recent years. Experiential learning is a hallmark of this new era. We place great value on field-based team research led by a faculty member. We support and foster, and sometimes even finance, practica in nongovernmental organizations where students learn how to apply what they have learned about health care delivery, microfinance, or sustainable energy. We support students who seek work experiences where international teams focus together on problem solution, we help them find apprenticeships in the arts, and we guide them to structured internships in every imaginable sector all over the world. We know that through daily life in unfamiliar environments—through dislocation—students learn things they cannot learn in a classroom. Student voices are included throughout this book, testifying to the good and the less successful outcomes of their own experience. The inclusion of these testimonials serves as a preface and a reminder of the third foundational principle the authors draw on besides integration and intentionality, namely, reflection.

In the past decade we have established through research what many of us knew intuitively through our work in advising students: The unexamined experience, whether abroad or in an unfamiliar region of the United States, often has little impact. The structure of this book allows the reader to accompany the student through the preparation for this experience and then enter the phase of dislocation, the physical movement to an unfamiliar place. In chapter 1 the authors argue that this dislocation is crucial: "By taking students to a significantly different environment—one of overwhelming novelty—they learn to observe differently" (p. 13). In the not-too-distant past we could all rest comfortably on our understanding of what this meant, but this age presents new challenges in thinking about what dislocation means for our students.

The changes in communications technologies, which have slammed us all so relentlessly over the past decade, have fundamentally changed the nature of international experience for everyone. But those of us who focus specifically on internationalization are by definition operating not only in different locations around the globe but also in global collaborations through new digital systems, and we are acutely aware of the ways that our work, and our students' experience, are affected by these changes. As I write at home in central Connecticut following a conference call at 7:00 p.m. to accommodate colleagues in Beijing (for whom this was a prebreakfast 7:00 a.m. call), my husband is in the next room delivering a lecture on Skype to an audience in Indonesia. Tomorrow I will be immediately reminded as I open my laptop that my students are connected with each other and with me across the country and across the globe, through blog posts and half a dozen social media platforms, through Skype calls across the world with faculty advisers, and through Internet access to the library resources of their home campuses. The significance of this for our students' learning cannot be overstated. Their understanding of *immersion* is fundamentally different from our own because of the constant accessibility of multiple culturally varied domains through handheld devices. And yet we understand that actually spending physical time in a new environment remains a human experience of profound and often transformative educational value, and one that has arguably become essential. This is a foundational proposition of this book and is perhaps the one that will spark the most interesting and productive debate.

The final three chapters address those institutional issues we all face and possible structures that can have a positive impact on curricular integration, which is the core topic. Assessment and accountability are part of the campus landscape in ways some find distracting and wrongheaded, and others regard as a necessary step in creating a climate of mutual trust and transparency in the campus community. If in our discussions we can follow the guiding principle of this book—that is, that we should maintain our focus on student learning—then we can together use tools proposed in these pages to help us understand what is really being learned and how. If we can agree on the principle, then we can also agree that the technologies that challenge us also provide new tools like ePortfolios, discussed in detail in chapter 7. This will assist students as they think about their career exploration as part of their educational experience (rather than an alarming hurdle to be faced in their final semester) and will help address another of the criticisms we regularly encounter by guiding students in their next steps after graduation.

This book is an invitation to us as educators to set aside our own agendas and preferences and to focus in a spirit of collaboration on the integration of the rich array of experiences that are now possible for our students in and beyond the classroom, wherever that classroom may be.

Jane Edwards
Dean of International and Professional Experience
Yale University

ACKNOWLEDGMENTS

We owe a great deal to many people for this book. One of them is Anders Uhrskov, former director of the nonprofit foundation DIS Study Abroad in Scandinavia, whose career, leadership, and contributions to the field have guided all three of us in various ways over the years. Indeed, the idea for *Integrating Worlds* sprang from a series of far-ranging conversations with Anders several years ago.

We could each cite the many faculty, administrators, and study-abroad professionals who have shaped our thinking, but special thanks are due to a few. Beverly Nagel, of Carleton College, supported this project from its infancy, making it possible for one of us to teach at DIS Study Abroad in Scandinavia for a semester. Several colleagues provided critical readings of the manuscript, in particular, George Shuffelton, professor of English and former associate dean at Carleton College, and Martin Hogan, deputy executive director of DIS and well known for his service with the Council on International Educational Exchange and the Forum for Education Abroad. We're deeply grateful to Jane Edwards, dean of international and professional experience and senior associate dean at Yale University, for tackling the foreword.

Furthermore, we'd like to thank John von Knorring of Stylus Publishing, for his patience and keen eye; without him, this work would never have seen the light of day. Alexandra Hartnett guided us expertly through the editorial hoops, and Sean Green's sharp pencil saved our prose at many turns.

Finally, we owe a special debt to our program assistant, Mikaela Auerbach, who not only served as an eagle-eyed reader but also proved to be an indefatigable and unstumpable chaser-down of facts and citations. Mikaela's assistance with editing, proofreading, and formatting was invaluable.

Like so many debts, those mentioned here are destined, sadly, to go unpaid, except in the currency of friendship and collegiality.

OFF-CAMPUS STUDY

Multiplying Impact

*To make correct decisions about your future in this now global world, you need to see
what the world has to offer. This doesn't mean that I will end up living somewhere
outside the U.S. It means that I am more confident in the decisions that I make because
I have a more informed, more complete understanding of how the world works.*

—Participant from off-campus study program in Nepal[1]

W hat if the most powerful education our students ever receive occurs when they leave campus behind for study abroad or domestic study away? If this admittedly humbling proposition proved to be true, wouldn't we want to structure our curriculum to facilitate and even enhance such experiences? Shouldn't we work to make them available to all? Wouldn't we strive to harness our students' learning once they return to their home campus, using their experience away to fuel their education and inspire their careers?

Such an approach requires rethinking undergraduate education. Rather than considering off-campus study as a pleasant supplement, we should focus on sending our students away, plunging them into difference.

Why should anyone consider putting study abroad and study away at the heart of undergraduate education? First, because today's world requires broad understanding. People, goods, and capital stream across borders and oceans with the same ease as ideas, images, viruses, and pollutants. Natural and man-made disasters demonstrate the fragility of the networks linking our local existence to remote cultures and economies. In our own communities, political, cultural, and linguistic differences divide us as effectively as seas. Although global forces press in the direction of homogenization, people with other practices and ways of living struggle to maintain their autonomy, sometimes violently. In short, our lives are now inextricably tied to elements that are intercultural, cross regional, and cross disciplinary.

Second, we find the greatest personal growth in situations of extreme difference. Students who are linguistically or culturally decentered learn about themselves as they encounter strangeness. The dislocation they experience makes culture suddenly perceptible, leading to reflection, learning, and evaluation. This growth, which is important and satisfying in its own right, prepares and motivates students for the academic challenges we need them to undertake.

Third, because if we fail to do this work, or fail to do it well, we're sacrificing one of the greatest educational opportunities our students will ever have.

However, the benefits of an off-campus experience are not automatic. It takes forethought, which is to say intentionality, to produce an effective curriculum, whether in a particular course or a program, and naturally the same holds true for the curricular and cocurricular experiences students have during study abroad or domestic study away. This means that effective off-campus study actually begins and ends on the home campus. We need to entwine on-campus and off-campus experiences, plan their progression, and make them mutually reinforcing. It is far from simple to connect diverse cultures, disciplines, pedagogies, objectives, and languages. The work is hard, yet consequential. For better or worse, its effects and repercussions can resonate throughout a student's undergraduate degree.[2] This work—that is, the integration of off-campus work with the curriculum of the home institution—is the focus of this book.

In the following pages we aim to show how *off-campus study*, an umbrella term covering study abroad and domestic study away (important differences between these are discussed later), is more than a desirable educational supplement; rather, it is crucial for education today. To meet the challenges of an increasingly interconnected world, students in all fields need to learn more and better, integrate their learning across disciplines, and blend academic and experiential practices. It has never been more urgent for higher education to equip students with the tools needed for understanding and addressing complex global issues like infectious disease, access to clean water, food security, immigration, human rights, and climate change. All of these require expertise in multiple disciplines, and each demands a profound understanding of the local entanglements of general, often global, challenges.

Why should you care? It's tempting to think that the work of integration is being handled by somebody else. After all, many colleges and universities have some kind of senior international officer, whose job description presumably includes managing the demands and opportunities of off-campus study. In fact, however, as organizations like the Association of International Education Administrators (AIEA, 2016) have emphasized, the real work of senior international officers is to enlist "the support and actions of individuals and campus units across the institution" (para. 11). (See chapter 9 for more on AIEA standards.) In short, if off-campus study is to become a central component of the undergraduate experience, it depends on the understanding and involvement of many stakeholders across campus, including faculty, administrators, and staff. Not everyone needs to be an expert, but a basic familiarity with the goals and trade-offs involved will help each person determine how or if off-campus study is relevant for a particular department or office. The hot potato can't simply be handed off to others.

We are hardly the first to champion the integration of off-campus study into the undergraduate curriculum. Burn (1991) published the results of eight institutional case studies on the obstacles to curricular integration and proposed solutions. The following decades saw increased interest in this topic, ranging from Anderson's (2005) work at the University of Minnesota to Brewer and Cunningham's (2009b) theory and practice collection of essays. Off-campus study is so important that NAFSA (Association of International Educators) maintains a best practices page on the topic (Parcells & Woodruff, 2016).

However, most of these earlier efforts sought to draw the asteroid of off-campus study into the gravitational field of undergraduate education. Our proposal is more Copernican: We maintain that off-campus study should be central to this education, acting like the sun around which much can or should revolve. Such an approach invites a rethinking of the way undergraduate education operates. In many ways our approach dovetails with the work of the American Council on Education's (n.d.-b) Center for Internationalization and Global Engagement, which proposes a model of "comprehensive internationalization" (para. 2–5) that permeates all aspects of an institution, including the mission statement, leadership, curriculum and cocurriculum, faculty and student experience, and connections with other entities.[3]

We thus propose to go beyond the small tactical ways individual faculty or departments may link on-campus curricula to off-campus experiences. Although such efforts are crucial, we hope to illustrate something larger and more systemic, namely, the idea that off-campus study often exemplifies the integrative learning that lies at the heart of American liberal education. It is no longer sufficient for us as educators to think only about predeparture work, which typically occurs in the weeks or months before a student leaves for an off-campus experience, or reentry activities, which typically occur shortly after the student's return. To realize all the potential of off-campus study, it is incumbent on us to consider the ways such experiences are threaded throughout the entire undergraduate degree and beyond.

No American college or university administrator can afford to ignore this issue, for the urgency of this work is signaled nearly everywhere and not just by organizations dedicated to furthering it. As Ungar (2016) put it,

> The almost universal failure of the broader U.S. public to know and understand others, except through a military lens, is not just unfortunate but also dangerous. It severely hinders the creation and implementation of a rational, consistent, and nuanced foreign policy that reflects American values and enjoys public support.
>
> Luckily, there exists a disarmingly simple way to help address this problem and to produce future generations of Americans who will know more and care more about the rest of the world: massively increase the number of U.S. college and university students who go abroad for some part of their education and bring home essential knowledge and new perspectives. (p. 112)

Ungar speaks specifically of study abroad, but the same could be said for domestic study away, or even outreach into local communities.[4] His call is reflected in a number of national initiatives. The Senator Paul Simon Study Abroad Act (2017) sets a goal of sending one million American college students abroad every year, representing a nearly fourfold increase over current levels. In 2014 the Institute of International Education (IIE, 2018) launched Generation Study Abroad, an initiative to double study abroad participation by 2020. During his presidency, Barack Obama called for study abroad participation to China to be doubled (Mulholland, 2011). The Department of State formed a partnership with NAFSA and others as part of the 100,000 Strong in the Americas project (see www.100kstrongamericas.org), which supports educational exchanges among 25 countries in the Western Hemisphere (see also NAFSA, 2018). Many institutions are also promoting domestic study away opportunities. Campuses everywhere scurry to incorporate words like *internationalization* and *global* into their mission statements, even if the terms remain more aspirational than descriptive. Finally, students themselves are clamoring for these opportunities. According to a student survey in 2008, 55% of college-bound students said they fully intended to study abroad, and 35% hoped to participate in an internship abroad (American Council on Education, Art & Science Group, & College Board, 2008). Demand was also high for service-learning (or civic engagement)[5] in students' local communities and in other countries (American Council on Education, Art & Science Group, & College Board, 2008).

Although nearly everyone agrees that American students should develop some kind of global awareness, studies show that our students actually hunger for it. Off-campus study can be highly motivating for students and is connected to the high-impact practices reported by the Association of American College & Universities (AAC&U) to help "increase rates of student retention and student engagement" (Kuh, 2008, p. 9).[6] Prominent among the 10 high-impact practices is diversity and global learning. According to Kuh,

> Many colleges and universities now emphasize courses and programs that help students explore cultures, life experiences, and worldviews different from their own. These studies—which may address US diversity, world cultures, or both—often explore "difficult differences" such as racial, ethnic, and gender inequality, or continuing struggles around the globe for human rights, freedom, and power. Frequently, intercultural studies are augmented by experiential learning in the community and/or by study abroad. (p. 10)

It's one thing to urge a better understanding of the world and its complexities, but it would be another to insist that students need to leave campus to accomplish this. Of course, at least some of this work can be accomplished on the home campus. Coursework in race studies, women's and gender studies, world religions, and foreign languages, for example, can catalyze this learning, as can the cocurricular realities of a campus that brings together students of different ethnicities, social classes, religions, genders, and nationalities. Even far-flung international connections can be introduced on the home campus, thanks to practices such as collaborative online international learning (COIL; Landorf, Doscher, & Hardrick, 2018; State University of New York, n.d.-a).

However, on-campus learning has its limitations. Just as a geology professor eventually needs to move students from the classroom into the landscape, students of global learning in all disciplines benefit from their own extended field trips.

Off-campus study, when properly designed and implemented, can have a multiplier effect on learning. Given the vast range of models for programs (discussed later), it's impossible to provide a universal template. Nevertheless, many instances of off-campus study provide the conditions for a uniquely powerful educational experience thanks to their layering of high-impact practices, which take place more or less simultaneously. Thus, in addition to diversity and global learning, several of the AAC&U's high-impact practices may be found in a single off-campus study experience:

1. Common intellectual experiences. In some programs students take many of their courses together, but even when this is not the case, the

cocurricular components alone often unify them in their intellectual endeavors.

2. Learning communities. AAC&U advocates for groups that "encourage integration of learning across courses . . . to involve students with 'big questions' that matter beyond the classroom" (Kuh, 2008, p. 10). In many programs, students benefit from just such integration (discussed further in chapter 2).

3. Writing-intensive courses. Not all programs are writing intensive, but many engage students in journaling and reflective writing that helps them record their experiences and examine their reactions. Off-campus programs create an ideal environment for such work.

4. Collaborative assignments and projects. Team-based work is frequently an aspect of off-campus study, made easier by the fact that the students are engaged in a common intellectual experience and are often part of a learning community.

5. Undergraduate research. Many programs include research components, which range from scientific fieldwork to cultural observation exercises, or even academic research in otherwise inaccessible libraries or archives.

6. Service-learning, community-based learning. Because students are typically eager to connect with the communities in which they find themselves, many programs offer service-learning components.

7. Internships. Although often difficult to arrange, internship opportunities are growing in importance during off-campus study. In addition to the preprofessional experience they provide, they establish connections to the community and provide opportunities to practice cultural skills, which often include foreign languages. Overall, they are powerful motivators for student work.

8. Capstone courses and projects. Because they tend to be intense experiences, many programs lead to a culminating project. Alternatively, at some institutions, students may continue their off-campus work once they return to the home campus where their work evolves into a senior thesis or capstone project for their undergraduate studies.

Granted, no single off-campus program will include all of these practices, but many include three or more—and often in ways that are not possible on the home campus. (The reasons for this are discussed in chapter 2.) The layering of high-impact practices in a single program helps explain how such experiences strike students in the solar plexus, producing the kind of transformative experience they so often describe. Time and again we see how well-implemented off-campus study can provide students with the social and cultural understanding they cannot acquire elsewhere. It can provide access to complex cultural and scientific problems in their natural context, adding practical and experiential components to classroom learning. Moreover, it can serve as a springboard for more advanced study and research when students return to their home campus.

Curiously, though, the very experiences that so often figure as the highlight of a student's academic career are often managed as an ancillary component of college and university curricula, sometimes handled by offices tangentially connected to the academic loop. Moreover, relatively few professors, deans, and provosts have direct experience with study abroad themselves. They are not fully prepared for the discussions that are already charting important parts of the future of their institutions and their disciplines. The problem is made more daunting by a university establishment that thrives on specialization. The division into departments and majors, where students are encouraged to drill deeper as they progress, exists in tension with the broader work that straddles boundaries, as off-campus study so often does. Furthermore, the firewalls between curricular and cocurricular elements of campus life leave many of us with a poor understanding of the possible synergies between the two, despite the more porous models experienced during off-campus study.

In the meantime, participation in off-campus study continues to increase, with more than 325,000 American students studying abroad each year (IIE, 2017a).[7] (Figures for domestic study away are not centrally collected.) This means that whether we want it to or not, off-campus study has a growing role in our institutions, touching nearly every major and influencing many aspects of our students' undergraduate and graduate lives.

And yet the benefits of off-campus study are not automatic. It's not as if shipping students anywhere and anyhow will suffice. Nor is it possible to apply a one-size-fits-all approach; programs need to be envisioned, implemented, and approved in ways that mesh with each institution's goals and culture. The topic calls for discussion on our campuses, and the goal of this book is to fuel those conversations.

Framing the Discussion

I think the most important learning outcome . . . was that they went down to [New Orleans] with lots of ideas about how to "fix" the city's problems, and they had to abandon most of those ideas once they started talking to people. They learned to see these issues from the point of view of the people living there—they learned just how much they don't know, and how important it is to listen with respect to the people they're trying to help.

—Study away program director and professor of political science

We hasten to note that this is not primarily a book for specialists in international or intercultural education. On the contrary, we seek to broaden the discussion. Although our frameworks will be familiar to study abroad professionals, we are also addressing faculty and "administrators" (directors, deans, provosts, vice presidents, and other members of campus leadership) who will in varying ways define the role that off-campus study plays at their institutions. In addition, we hope our work will be useful to program providers—those third parties who receive so many of our students at off-campus (often foreign) locations, and who might well benefit from a deeper understanding of the system from which their students have come, and to which they will return.

At most colleges and universities nothing characterizes off-campus study more than a lack of definition. The role of such experiences is rarely developed in the institution's mission, often because local policies and practices for off-campus study have evolved in a piecemeal way, thanks to historical contingencies or forceful personalities. For a long time such programs were considered the purview of a few departments, especially in foreign languages, and usually contained in one academic division (typically the humanities). In many cases, this kind of educational opportunism served the institution well and even contributed to its identity. However, such a model is by and large outdated; the proliferation of senior international officers on campuses, often guided by the work of AIEA, suggests that off-campus study is becoming an all-campus concern.[8] Moreover, given today's world, where local and global issues are so tightly entangled, it is crucial for us to reflect more deeply and explicitly on the role off-campus study should play. The continued success, and even the relevance, of our institutions may very well depend on it.

Moreover, any increase in off-campus study can fuel anxiety. In an era of fierce competition for institutional resources, off-campus study may appear to some to be an expensive luxury. *Integrating Worlds* seeks to show, to the contrary, how it is an affordable necessity that must be designed to match each institution's needs and resources.

Making decisions about this practice requires a deep understanding of the field. A great deal of specialized work exists already in the many subcategories of off-campus study, such as pedagogy, program models, intercultural competence, assessment, and much more. But these writings often focus on highly technical knowledge for specific and increasingly professionalized groups. The nonspecialist has little access to, or time for, this information. Our task in this book is not only to clarify definitions but also to provide tools for thinking about how off-campus study might evolve. Only then can we meaningfully address the difficult questions facing our own institution. How does off-campus study fit with our educational mission? What is our plan for using it appropriately? What materials do we need? What will it cost? How will we know when it's done, and how can we tell if it works?

These are complex and important issues, and readers might well wonder whether we are qualified to moderate the discussion. If nothing else, our backgrounds shape the way we think. Because *Integrating Worlds* does not address an intimate specialist audience, we should say a few words about ourselves and our approach. Because this book emphasizes the role of experience, our own experience matters.

Scott D. Carpenter is the Marjorie Crabb Garbisch Professor of French and the Liberal Arts at Carleton College in Minnesota. He is the chair of French and francophone studies, director of cross-cultural studies, and the founding director of Carleton's Center for Global and Regional Studies. His education and career have been shaped deeply by experience abroad, ranging from childhood years spent in the United Kingdom; three different university-level off-campus programs in England, France, and Germany; a number of years working in France; and his position as a regular director of Carleton's own term-length program in Paris. He has also held a visiting position in Denmark, and he participated in faculty study programs in Japan, Turkey, and elsewhere. A frequent speaker on the topic of off-campus study, he also serves on the academic board of an independent study abroad program in Paris, the Center for University Programs Abroad.

Originally from Poland, Helena Kaufman is director of off-campus studies and a lecturer in Latin American studies at Carleton College. In addition to her studies in Poland, Portugal, and the United States, she has broad experience teaching on the topics of national and cultural identity. In off-campus studies she is involved in everything from curriculum planning to risk management for a vast array of off-campus study programs of nearly every kind: term-length and short-term faculty-led programs, consortial and third-party provider programs, and more. She is a member of and a frequent contributor to NAFSA and the Forum on Education Abroad, where she works as a member of the Outcomes, Assessment, and Research Committee.

Malene Torp is the executive director of DIS Study Abroad in Scandinavia, headquartered in Copenhagen and one of the largest nonprofit, independent programs for American students in Europe. Trained as a political scientist, she has a deep understanding of American higher education, having been a Fulbright scholar at New York University and a visiting scholar at the University of Virginia's McIntire School of Commerce. She is a member of AIEA's Leadership Development Committee and a frequent contributor to NAFSA and the Forum on Education Abroad, especially on topics such as short-term programming, faculty development, experiential learning practices, and strategic planning.

No group of contributors can represent all facets of off-campus study, but we hope to provide a reasonable cross-section. All of us have experience teaching on-campus and away, we all have some administrative background, and we are all involved in high-level discussions about curricula at our institutions. Carleton sends students on more than 100 programs worldwide in more than 60 countries, and DIS receives students from more than 140 different U.S. colleges and universities. Although our collective specialties lie principally in Europe and the Americas, we each have extensive knowledge of and firsthand experience with programs in many other parts of the world including Asia, the Middle East, Africa, and more. Finally, we share considerable experience with service-learning and internships, which are becoming increasingly important in off-campus study. In the areas where we have less experience, we rely more heavily on input from relevant colleagues and from the vast and growing literature.

It is perhaps useful to note what we are not: theoreticians of intercultural or international education—a field that has become increasingly specialized over the past two decades. However, we participate actively in the scholarship of these fields, and as informed generalists, we are in a good position to present the current thinking of the discipline as it applies to our work.

In these pages we avoid purely theoretical discussions. Rather, our goal is to draw on practices (and, with luck, on best practices) that are shaping the field. One technique for illustrating the impact of these practices is through the comments of students and faculty that appear throughout the chapters. We do not base our arguments on anecdotes; however, stories can serve as powerful illustrations of broader principles. They are manifestations of experience, some qualities of which cannot be fully captured by more quantitative means. Indeed, by including these experiential accounts, *Integrating Worlds* seeks to blend theory and practice.

Our goal is to discuss a certain kind of field trip—the kind that typically lasts for weeks or months, usually under the label of off-campus study. For us, the term *off-campus study* refers to educational experiences occurring away from the home institution in domestic or international venues; they are of sufficient duration and structure that they result in the granting of academic credit.

The flexibility of this description reflects the considerable variety of models for off-campus study adopted by different institutions, and we hasten to underscore that the spectrum of possibilities is vast (some definitions are provided in the next section). The two-week, faculty-led excursion that complements an on-campus class lies at one end of the spectrum, and at the other, individual students directly enroll in a foreign university for a year-long course of study, tending to their sundry living and social needs entirely on their own. Although we acknowledge special circumstances when appropriate, our primary focus is on short- and medium-term programs that are the mainstay of off-campus study, running from a few weeks to a few months, domestically or abroad. Our goal is to show how such programs can be a crucial component of an undergraduate degree, especially when it is enmeshed with the curriculum.

A Few Definitions

Off-campus study is a wilderness of models, goals, assessments, and vocabularies. Because it has only recently become recognized as a specialty in its own right, many institutions have homegrown vocabularies for the practices that have evolved on their campus. For this reason, we begin with the following small set of general terms:

- *Off-campus study* refers to credit-bearing academic experiences that are conducted away from the home institution's campus and includes study abroad and domestic study away; it may also include embedded internships or service-learning.[9] Off-campus study programs may be short term or long term and are of various kinds.
- *Island* programs are designed to cater primarily to American students, often using primarily American faculty. Usually they have no contact with local institutions on the off-campus site, and they do not include local students in their classes. Typically, island programs seek to replicate the American classroom and American pedagogy in off-campus environments.
- *Hybrid* or *peninsula* programs are organized and run by the home institution in collaboration with local partners, usually including at least some local faculty, sometimes blending students into local classrooms.
- *Faculty-led* programs, which may be island or peninsula programs, are organized and run primarily by the home institution, typically for the students of that institution. These programs are often shorter in duration and operated in collaboration with a partner institution or provider that customizes its services to accommodate the goals of the faculty-led program.
- *Third-party* programs, which may be island or peninsula programs, are organized and operated by entities independent of the home institution. These entities are called third-party providers.
- *Consortium-based* programs, which may be island or peninsula programs, are organized by a consortium of U.S. colleges or universities, typically accommodating students from the member institutions.

- *Direct matriculation* refers to the direct enrollment of a student in a different, usually foreign, university, without the support of a third party.
- *Short-term* programs are defined by IIE as summer programs, or programs of eight weeks or less. Most of these programs are much shorter, from three to six weeks (Hovde, 2002). Short-term programs accounted for 63% of all students studying abroad in 2015–2016 (IIE, 2017a).[10]
- *Medium-term* programs last one semester or one or two quarters; they accounted for 34.6% of students in programs abroad in 2015–2016 (IIE, 2017a).
- *Long-term* programs, which last an entire academic or calendar year, accounted for less than 3% of study abroad students in 2015–2016 (IIE, 2017a).
- *Embedded* programs, which can be island or peninsula, are short-term programs of one to four weeks, led by faculty, and connected to an on-campus course before or after the program. They usually take place during breaks in the academic calendar, such as January terms, Maymesters, or winter and spring breaks.

These definitions are somewhat fluid. For example, our conflation of study abroad with domestic study away is imperfect: although an off-campus experience in Beijing shares many similarities with a program in Chicago or New Orleans, the two are also different in substantial ways. In this book we do not seek to erase this difference, and when we discuss resources that pertain to only one category or the other, we split off-campus study into its constitutive branches. Moreover, it's important to note that the body of research available for domestic study away is much smaller than for its study abroad counterpart. In chapters 6 and 8 we deal more fully with the tension between these two forms of off-campus study.

There is also room for interpretation in the definition of program models. Some hybrid or third-party programs are nearly indistinguishable from so-called island programs, whereas others do little more than provide a safety net for direct matriculation. Durations vary considerably, as do curricular structures, cocurricular components, and connections to local communities. In short, it's best to look beyond the labels.

Most crucially, we would like to deflate, at least provisionally, the prejudices that exist on many campuses about what the ideal model is for off-campus study, which often aligns with whatever one's own institution currently does. We contend that meaningful reflection about off-campus study will require current assumptions to be set aside. Moreover, there are multiple variables to consider; many models can be effective in one configuration or context and yet ineffective in another. The success of a particular program will depend on how it has been conceived in the broad context of a student's undergraduate experience and on how well it supports the educational goals of the institution.

Dislocation

Given the panoply of models for off-campus study, one might reasonably wonder what, if anything, such experiences share. In what way, for instance, can one meaningfully compare a two-week, faculty-led trip focusing on renewable energies in India to a direct enrollment experience in an art history program at the Universidad de Chile in Santiago? How about the student who spends a semester in Washington DC, instead of grappling with courses in Chinese in Beijing?

What links these different cases is the experience of dislocation, which we understand as a kind of decentering that is not merely geographic. It is related to what some have termed *dissonance* (Brewer & Cunningham [2009a] discuss the role dissonance plays in learning during study abroad; see also McKeown, 2009; Wexler, 2006). Dislocation implies a shift in perspective. Typically it involves a change of physical venue, although there is no necessary connection between physical distance and cultural difference. Just as one student might remain in a cultural cocoon while studying in Asia, another can experience revelations during an urban service-learning experience close to home. Fruitful dislocation occurs when students engage with the novel and unsettling contexts where they find themselves.

The importance of dislocation in off-campus study is not specific to any discipline, although it is perhaps most obviously exemplified wherever cultural engagement is foregrounded. For instance, students often find themselves especially challenged by foreign languages or radically different cultural practices. In such situations, they typically experience particularly intense learning.

This principle of dislocation is key to off-campus learning in many fields—even in the hard sciences, as a Carleton biology professor reported in one of our surveys: "When I take students abroad, it's in order to hone their skills of observation." This doesn't mean that students cannot see things at the home institution; however, the familiar has a way of becoming invisible. By taking students to a significantly different environment—one of overwhelming novelty—they learn to observe differently.

Dislocation offers the additional advantage of introducing comparative study. After all, people who study foreign languages often develop a profound understanding of their mother tongue, those who travel abroad understand their homeland better, and people who cross socioeconomic boundaries have a better understanding of their own starting point. As we show in later chapters, the binocular perspective provided by off-campus study is a key benefit in all disciplines.

Dislocation fosters dissonance, introducing radical difference in the lives and studies of our students. Some experience of this dissonance may be available locally. Indeed, many institutions seek to integrate forms of difference on the home campus, as when one strives for cultural, ethnic, and socioeconomic diversity among the faculty and in the student body. We applaud such efforts, but also acknowledge their limits. Not all colleges and universities have the resources to realize their aspirations in the area of on-campus diversity, and in any case, few can match the radical shift associated with a different cultural environment. Leaving campus is a crucial component of the experience.

But so is the return. After dislocation, relocation; after departure, the homecoming. Since the advent of the field trip, educators have understood that the benefits of departure are not exhausted at the end of the excursion; indeed, preparation and follow-up are both crucial. Field trips are designed to integrate theory with practice: after weeks of classroom preparation, geology students hike out to a hill and chip away at fossils, history students visit an archive, or a religion class meets with community representatives at a local place of worship. In each case students enter environments where they can try out previously acquired learning in circumstances that are less controlled than the classroom. In the process, they typically encounter the messiness and unpredictability of real life: It rains on the geology students, sinking them into a bath of mud; the historians arrive to find the archive closed because of a power outage; and the religion majors are stifled by a format that separates them from their hosts. As frustrating as they may be at the moment, such complications are lessons on their own, and if the teacher is clever, they become important raw material for future reflection and training in the classroom. Moreover, despite all these challenges, certain goals are typically achieved and often in unexpected ways—for example, when a fossil specimen of less than textbook clarity is identified as a rare find, a helpful director treats the apprentice historians to a behind-the-scenes visit of the museum, or the religion students converse meaningfully with hosts after the formal program is over and coffee is served.

Not all complications will have silver linings, and sometimes a field trip results in failure. Not all dislocations are profitable, and this too requires careful consideration. At different points in their personal or academic development, different students will benefit from different degrees of dislocation. One student may find a short-term program to California daunting, whereas another may be ready to embrace direct enrollment at the Freie Universität in Berlin. The key is to identify what might be called the Goldilocks zone—the distance of the personal, academic, cultural, linguistic, and emotional leap that will prove optimal for any given student.[11]

The Order of Events

If *Integrating Worlds* begins with the assertion that off-campus study holds real and urgent promise for higher education, it does not do so uncritically. Not all forms of off-campus study are equally successful. Fundamentally, in an era of scarce resources it is crucial to evaluate which forms are best suited to an institution, and which departments or disciplines stand the most to gain. Furthermore, it's important to consider how one moves beyond the *bracketed* off-campus study adventure, where students' transformative experiences feel largely disconnected from the rest of their academic career. How can we better prepare them for these experiences, and how can we help them deepen their new understanding once they return? Finally, what are the institutional obstacles to study abroad beyond the (admittedly crucial) question of finances? Finally, how might one evaluate and address these impediments? Each chapter of this book addresses one of the key issues.

As discussed in chapter 2, "An Integrative Experience: Off-Campus Study and Liberal Education," many institutions adopt inspirational and aspirational language in their mission statements, especially for undergraduate degrees. Administrators of these institutions want their students to learn how to master important fields of knowledge, challenge assumptions, think critically, collaborate with others, and blend disciplines as they work to solve complex and abstract problems. These skills are linked to the notion of *integrative learning* (Palmer & Zajonc, 2010) that underlies American higher education.[12]

On our campuses, the aspiration of integrative learning is often difficult to achieve: Strict departmental curricula discourage interdisciplinary learning, haphazard advising results in missed opportunities for synergies among courses, and the division between curricular undertakings and cocurricular lives hampers the reinforcement of connections. However, profoundly different structures are sometimes available in off-campus experiences, and these can bring the elusive goals within reach. In particular, we show how the components of off-campus experience add up to the best-integrated and most holistic learning experience students ever have. Moreover, off-campus study helps produce what AAC&U (2002) calls *intentional learners*—a topic we return to in chapter 2.

Paradoxically, we can sometimes accomplish our institutional goals better when students are away from the institution, especially when departure has been adequately prepared. Drawing on examples in various divisions (humanities, social sciences, natural sciences) and contexts (study abroad and study away, including service-learning and professional training), this chapter demonstrates how off-campus study does not just follow effective learning practices, it exemplifies it, illustrating what can be the purest realization of the ideal of integrative learning.

Off-campus programs are often integrated learning experiences on their own, but they are also part of a larger whole—the four-year undergraduate experience. In chapter 3, "The Long Runway," we examine how early on-campus work can prepare students for their off-campus experience and even lay the groundwork for their successful return to the home institution.

So-called predeparture activities for students gearing up for off-campus study are sometimes little more than health and safety meetings. However, preparation for study away implicitly begins much earlier—often before students' arrival on the home campus, during the recruitment phase when off-campus study may feature prominently in admissions materials and presentations. For many students arrival on campus will already be a kind of study away (or even study abroad) experience, and it typically introduces all of them to a rich medley of groups, nationalities, ethnicities, classes, sexualities, and religions. Our campuses and their surrounding communities thus become their own introductory courses into global and local entanglements that many professors are exploring in on-campus work. In this chapter, we thus examine how on-campus curricula can prepare students for their off-campus experiences. Moreover, we will examine how curriculum integration can intersect with different dimensions of globalization as it is understood and practiced today.

Too often students shelve their experience once they return, partly because there is no obvious "next step" for them on campus. In chapter 4, "Bringing It Back," we examine strategies for students to further the work they undertook while away, and we help faculty and staff consider frameworks for this work. This is not just a so-called reentry problem, where one needs to ease reverse culture shock or assist students with credit transfers. Because the off-campus experience is complex and multilayered, as shown in chapters 2 and 3, the same holds true for the work following their return. If students know that relevant courses and opportunities await them, this will sharpen their focus while they are away. Certain classes or units can help students process personal growth (or personal difficulties). A course in global issues, for example, on immigration and refugees, would today resonate with students returning from many parts of the world, including certain locations in the United States, and such a course could include collaborative learning using overlapping knowledge from various disciplines. Courses in travel writing can help students distill issues of personal growth. The use of ePortfolios can draw together disparate aspects of an experience that don't neatly fit in existing categories on campus. Fellowship and internship opportunities that build on their experiences (or even allow them to return to the site of the study away program) can be invaluable. Moreover, research projects undertaken during off-campus study can be an excellent starting point for advanced work on the home campus and lead to senior projects or other research opportunities.

Beyond disciplinary understanding, off-campus study teaches important lessons about different cultural practices that are necessary for operating successfully in a globalized society. This principle holds for study abroad and study away, and in chapter 5, "A World of Difference: The Culture Question," we examine the importance of location, that is, the geographic, historical, political, and social contexts where an off-campus experience takes place. The connection between a program and its context is often crucial, with implications that are ethical and educational. In many cases, the culture question may be regarded through the metaphorical lens of discourse. Students will benefit from learning to interact with their host community on its own terms, recognizing its local knowledge and logic, its complexities and tensions. This doesn't mean every student going to China needs to study Chinese. Indeed, it is possible to learn much about a foreign culture without learning the language—and vice versa. However, a deep understanding of other cultures enriches and motivates other forms of learning while at the same time demonstrating respect. Such learning does not happen automatically on its own. Administrators of some programs, especially very short-term programs or programs in locations where English is widely spoken, often view the cultural connection as an unnecessary complication. We strive to demonstrate the importance of addressing this topic deliberately and thoughtfully in the design, assessment, and approval of off-campus experiences.

We need to consider not only how to increase the number of American undergraduates who study abroad but also how to develop new strategies for accomplishing these goals ethically and sustainably. In chapter 6, "Engaged Global Citizenship," we discuss best practices that prioritize reciprocity and balance between the goals and outcomes of different stakeholders: students, sending institutions, local partners, host families, and communities. Already recognized as a catalyst for academic and personal growth, off-campus study can also play a crucial role in preparing students for ongoing engagement across cultures. Many programs go beyond typical classroom learning to include opportunities for independent research, service-learning, and internships. Such endeavors help students to learn about the entanglements between local issues and the global context, engaging them also in reflection about ethical issues of global citizenship. Among these is the key question of reciprocity, or lack thereof, in many forms of off-campus experience. We often refer to the communities we join temporarily as *hosts*, a term with a dangerous double valence, making us either guests or parasites. Helping students reflect on their relationship with the host community requires considerable scaffolding.

We should only engage in off-campus study if it provides the outcomes we seek. However, the measurement of these outcomes is bedeviled by many complexities. Chapter 7, "Measuring Change," shows that study abroad and study away professionals have developed a number of methods for measuring certain qualities, such as *intercultural competence*; however, many benefits of study abroad, as with other practices in education, prove resistant to direct and quantifiable assessment. Also, some effects of off-campus study may require time and maturity to come to fruition, showing their effects more plainly years later. While avoiding an overly technical discussion, we provide some overview of the issues and make common sense suggestions about what steps one might usefully take to frame further discussion. In particular, we identify four major areas ripe for assessment: academics, cultural learning, personal growth, and synthesis.

The first seven chapters focus on the educational and personal benefits of off-campus study. However, chapter 8, "Pressure Points: The Future of Off-Campus Study," addresses the many hurdles institutions face when implementing and integrating such experiences. Off-campus study costs money, there may be programmatic or institutional constraints, and some students or faculty or administrators may be resistant. Moreover, there is the question of how much of the home culture can or should carry over into off-campus study situations. Issues of political correctness, pedagogical styles, and student identities (sexual, racial, ethnic, religious) have emerged as important topics. Moreover, what of the ongoing questions about the ethics of off-campus experiences, perhaps because of the lack of reciprocity with host communities? Finally, what is the role of personal growth in off-campus study? Few would deny that students encounter challenges, such as dissonance, difference, and discomfort, which can have a powerful effect on their understanding of their own identity, but there is disagreement about how central this development is to the academic mission. All these issues are evolving quickly, and it's often a challenge to imagine and address their effect on off-campus study.

In chapter 9, "Sustaining Integration," we seek to provide frameworks to guide discussion in and among those who currently seek to rethink the role of off-campus study at their institution. In particular, we examine different ways of institutionalizing the practices discussed throughout the earlier chapters. Integration of the student experience requires close coordination among entities that typically have few preexisting channels of communication and often cross well-policed institutional borders, say, between academic and cocurricular entities whose different budgets, reporting lines, and priorities can create tension. Without an institutional commitment to integration, which means money, time, personnel, and sometimes even changes to administrative structures, commitments to integration are likely to go the way of other unfunded enterprises on our campuses: They will wither.

Our ambition is to illustrate how central off-campus study is to undergraduate education, and how its integration can be achieved. The good news is that this goal is within reach for most of our institutions. With this book we endeavor to demonstrate why it's worth the effort.

Notes

1. Unless otherwise indicated, comments by students and professors are taken from surveys conducted at Carleton College and DIS Study Abroad in Scandinavia. We typically provide participants' field and program location, but responses are otherwise anonymous.

2. This book focuses on the role of off-campus study in the four-year undergraduate degree; nevertheless, many of its arguments are relevant for other elements of American education including graduate programs or vocational degrees.

3. The American Council on Education has provided extensive materials for its model, many of which can be found at www.acenet.edu/news-room/Pages/Center-for-Internationalization-and-Global-Engagement.aspx. The Internationalization Toolkit (American Council on Education, n.d.-b) is an especially useful resource.

4. Many works cited in this book focus specifically on one topic, such as study abroad, study away, service-learning, or internships. Often, though, the argument presented can be applied more generally to most or all components of off-campus study.

5. The term *civic engagement* is increasingly preferred over *service-learning* in the field. However, AAC&U uses service-learning in its description of high-impact practices (Kuh, 2008). We use these terms interchangeably.

6. Declaring something a high-impact practice isn't sufficient to make it so. The research on what constitutes a high-impact practice is ongoing. Although the standard reference is to Kuh (2008), Brownell and Swaner (2009) provide a review of the literature. Another useful source is Brownell and Swaner (2010), and perhaps Hubert, Pickavance, and Hyberger (2015).

7. According to IIE (2017a), 325,339 students studied abroad in 2015–2016. Participation has increased by an average of 3.5% annually over the past five years.

8. In addition to its conferences and publications, AIEA (n.d.) runs a number of boot-camp-style academies for new senior international officers, offering training for positions that are nearly unique in the academy, given how they reach across divisional lines.

9. Some institutions use *study away* as an umbrella term for domestic and international programs. See Braskamp (2009).

10. IIE study abroad data includes only U.S. students studying outside the United States. Statistics for domestic study away are not available in a similar form.

11. Sanford (1966) advocates for a balance of challenge and support in learning environments, asserting that too great a challenge may cause students to retreat from learning, whereas too little limits students' opportunities for development. See Vande Berg, Connor-Linton, and Paige (2009) for an analysis of Sanford's challenge-support hypothesis in the context of study abroad.

12. AAC&U typically uses the term *integrative* learning, although some refer to *integrated* learning. It may be useful to think of integrative learning as the process that produces integrated learning. In most cases, however, we do not distinguish between these terms. See AAC&U (2009b). We address this issue in more detail in chapter 2.

2

AN INTEGRATIVE EXPERIENCE

Off-Campus Study and Liberal Education

The trip was my first time visiting a developing country, and [it] certainly left a lasting impact on me in a way that my visits to developed countries did not. I left with a deep appreciation for how fortunate I am. Additionally, the trip helped me understand that conservation is not a simple procedure, but rather an incredibly complex process that mixes biodiversity, human rights, and economics.

—Economics major, program in Tanzania

Americans have gone abroad for their studies for a long time, and in the beginning they didn't just leave for a January term or even a semester or two. They went for years, hungry for experiences and learning not available in their homeland. When—and if—they returned, they were changed souls. Some embraced foreign ways, and others rejected them; most struggled with difficulties in language and culture; many formed emotional, professional, and even romantic attachments; and many of them were down to their last dime. In short, they had typical off-campus study experiences.

These adventures of American artists, writers, doctors, or politicians date from a couple of centuries ago, and their tale is told by historian David McCullough (2011). Ambitious, and generally privileged, Americans traveled to France throughout the nineteenth century to further their education in medicine, law, and the arts. These travels were a more focused version of the world-broadening and oat-sowing adventures that young European gentlemen used to enjoy under the name of the Grand Tour (see Hoffa, 2007; Lewin, 2009; McCullough, 2011). The voyages McCullough described, however, had a definite academic bent, and many of the travelers returning from their journey used their hybrid learning to redefine the disciplines back home.

Study abroad professionals already know how today's off-campus stud-ies rose from travels of this sort, but for those outside the field it is useful to review the history. Study abroad and study away entered the American academic model late and through a side door, and this marginal status helps explain some of the peculiar ways we have developed for running, financing, and imagining off-campus study in our curricula.

It's telling that these early experiments in academic travel as described by McCullough were the result of personal rather than institutional initiative. At the time, staff of American universities neither organized the trips nor formally recognized the achievements of those returning. Since the begin-ning, off-campus study has been held at a distance, often regarded with a blend of fascination and suspicion, especially by those with little direct expe-rience of it. Perhaps that's not surprising. After all, colleges and universities labor to champion their own institutional identities, and academic depart-ments promote the integrity and inviolability of their curricula; according to what twisted logic might one serve students by sending them away?

Institutionalization started slowly. In 1902, for example, 32 Americans began traveling to attend Oxford University every year as Rhodes scholars. These departures were especially easy to accommodate because the schol-arships were a postgraduate experience, requiring no coordination with an American curriculum. It took another two decades before fledgling U.S. undergraduate programs abroad began; the University of Delaware is cred-ited with the first, inaugurated in 1923, and Smith College followed in 1925. American universities experimented with such programs tentatively and in select disciplines, the most common of which were also the most obvious: foreign language and literature (Hoffa, 2007, pp. 71–86). (Walton [2009] discusses the Delaware program in detail; other programs in France in the 1920s are discussed in chapter 3.) History students couldn't undertake field trips to the past, and astronomers remained sadly earthbound, but French and German and Spanish majors could travel to Paris or Austria or Madrid, which some of them did. In select cases, administrators of universities con-ceded that off-campus study might be a useful supplement to on-campus work, at least for those who could afford the considerable expense (Hoffa, 2007, pp. 80–95; Walton, 2009).

For many years, even after the hiatus triggered by World War II, off-campus study represented the thinnest sliver of educational opportunities, overwhelmingly associated with language departments, which themselves were sometimes marginalized. By no means were such programs part of the central mission of the university. Generally speaking, off-campus study at most institutions remained primarily the bailiwick of modern languages well into the 1980s, and domestic study away went mainstream much later.[1]

There were some exceptions. Even in the 1920s and 1930s, opportunities cropped up in subjects like world issues and music (Hoffa, 2007). After the war, more opportunities were created in international relations and economics. The Fulbright U.S. Student Program, founded in 1945, aimed to promote "international goodwill through the exchange of students in the fields of education, culture, and science" (Fulbright U.S. Student Program, n.d., para. 4), and national defense interests sought to support the study of the "critical languages," that is, critical for national security (Kuenzi & Riddle, 2005, p. 8).

In addition to geopolitical concerns, academic motivations began to fuel the growth of programs in the United States and abroad. Europe's Erasmus Programme, for instance, began in 1987.[2] In the 1970s and 1980s, *interdisciplinarity* became a buzzword. Structuralism linked disciplines as far apart as literature, anthropology, religion, linguistics, and psychology. The new porousness among disciplines helped make other borders more permeable too, especially the invisible fence that surrounds most university campuses. At about this time, the first domestic study-away programs began, in recognition of the fact that considerable cultural, racial, linguistic, and economic diversity could be found close to home.

Many of these initiatives received funding from foundations or the federal government, but they were not necessarily aligned with institutional mandates or strategic plans, where international or intercultural learning rarely figured as part of the institutional mission. Rather, in most cases, off-campus study arose thanks to isolated (and some might say "rogue") professors who operated makeshift programs the way a woodworker might pursue projects after hours using the company's woodshop.[3] This benevolent disregard allowed programs not only to survive but also to flourish, and after decades of honing their craft, academic do-it-yourselfers produced some results handsome enough to inspire other colleagues to crack their knuckles and try their own hand at it.

We know the rest: Programs began springing up in new disciplines, such as political science, religion, and history. Soon they involved science, technology, engineering, and mathematics (STEM). Departments practicing fieldwork from anthropology to geology hopped onto the bandwagon, and by the end of the 1990s students were clamoring for service-learning and internship opportunities, domestically and abroad, a trend that has continued (see DeWinter & Rumbley, 2010, on the rapid spread of study abroad). Originally a supplemental, or even ornamental, experience in a restricted number of disciplines, off-campus study was turning into a central component of a variety of departments.

In addition to the multiplication of fields, total enrollments swelled. In 2015–2016, some 325,000 American students participated in programs abroad, more than triple the number of just 2 decades earlier (IIE, 2017e).[4] The traditional European destinations now account for barely half of study abroad, and the number of destinations has burgeoned, with countries in Asia and South America figuring much more prominently than before (IIE, 2017b). Domestic study away has continued to be a presence in the field as well, although these numbers are harder to measure.[5]

Although minority students are still greatly underrepresented in study abroad (NAFSA, n.d.-c), the diversity of study abroad participation has increased in recent years. More financial aid is available, and some institutions have made off-campus study a graduation requirement. A few have even turned it into a threshold experience for entering freshmen.

Of course, this growth has not been universal. Although some institutions, especially elite colleges and universities, boast of participation rates ranging from 50% to 100% (IIE, 2017c), the numbers nationally are far lower, with only 1 undergraduate in 10 pursuing studies abroad at some point during the undergraduate experience (IIE, 2017a). Here, as elsewhere, domestic study away numbers are harder to obtain.

Nevertheless, the overall shift has been dramatic. In a span of a few decades, off-campus study has moved from a modest enterprise into a powerful, sometimes central, position in many institutions of higher learning. Thanks to the U.S. government's efforts to multiply participation—for example, through the Senator Paul Simon Study Abroad Act (2017) and the Lincoln Commission Fellowship Act (NAFSA, n.d.-d)—off-campus study may become the most commonly shared experience in undergraduate liberal arts education.[6]

In addition to the growth in participation rates, we have witnessed the development of different models of off-campus study, which can be traced through history. In the early years the driving forces behind off-campus initiatives were idiosyncratic at best, with predictably variable results. Because no set model existed for such experiences, they evolved in disparate ways, conforming to the needs of small groups or the aspirations of the faculty members who designed, sponsored, and ran them. The early decades of experimentation led to a proliferation of options, a multitude of curricular approaches, and a host of (usually shaky) methods of financing the experience.

The legacy of this messy beginning is still evident today. Although off-campus study has become institutionalized, usually including full-fledged offices staffed with study abroad professionals and supported with polished websites and brochures, beneath this glossy surface a measure of chaos churns. Nearly every study abroad office advertises a smorgasbord of options, including the institution's own semester programs abroad, short-term faculty-led programs, consortia programs, third-party-provider programs, direct enroll-ment options, international internships, exchange programs, and more. Why do we tolerate such a proliferation? Would it not be wiser to determine which model works best and limit ourselves to that? The answer: probably not.

Granted, the assortment is not always perfect. Some of the overabun-dance can be attributed to faulty work processes, departmental territorialism, or even a reluctance to terminate legacy programs that are deemed part of the institution's character. But even if some judicious pruning occurred, most of the complexity would remain, and for good reason: A certain amount is an irreducible reality in off-campus study. It reflects the need to customize an institution's offerings to match a specific educational mission with the broadly disparate needs of the students. In this way, each of the various spe-cies arising in the ecosystem of off-campus study occupies its own niche. Not all are equally effective, but overall the plurality of options is a positive.

Many institutions run a number of programs, and many operate suc-cessful exchange programs directly with foreign universities. But perhaps the most puzzling aspect of off-campus study, at least for outsiders, is the role of third-party providers—organizations that are not colleges or universities but help facilitate or even create opportunities in study abroad or domestic study away. And the role of these providers is considerable: At least 25% of U.S. study abroad students participate in programs operated by a third-party (Heyl, 2011). Some of these providers have become educational institutions in their own right.

Why would an American college or university outsource this work, plac-ing its students in the hands of an organization that might have a financial rather than purely academic incentive? The reasons for this are largely prag-matic. As Hoffa (2007) tells us, decades ago, students and administrators looked for assistance to affordably transport students across the ocean. The first providers, then, were in the business of securing passage to Europe—leasing ships so students could make the transatlantic journey (Hoffa, 2007, pp. 200–207). Third-party providers quickly expanded to supply other ser-vices as well, such as preparatory coursework (onboard language and culture classes), affordable accommodations in Europe, assistance with visas, and more. As crossing the Atlantic became less cumbersome and more afford-able with the emergence of accessible commercial airlines, third-party pro-viders turned their attention to tailoring and delivering educational add-ons (Hoffa, 2007). From the start, providers demonstrated a useful nimbleness, often thanks to their knowledge of and connections in the host countries. They adapted rapidly to provide services matching the changing needs of institutions and students. Sideli (2010) points out that a new type of all-purpose provider emerged, especially in the 1990s, changing the landscape and providing new ways for how off-campus study could be delivered and structured:

> Some of these new program providers began to offer services to campuses to assist them in setting up overseas programs. They offered help in logistics and travel, in leasing facilities, in finding overseas faculty to teach courses, and the like. (p. 392)

These days, most U.S. universities and colleges rely on providers for logistical and educational services. Although transatlantic passage on converted freighters or battleships may no longer be in high demand, assistance with on-the-ground logistics as well as tailored academic offerings are. In our era of global connectedness, where communications, discount airlines, and hotel reservations are only a click away, one might wonder why American colleges and universities have not reabsorbed this work.

The reasons for this are multiple. Operating their own programs abroad can be too costly for many institutions, especially if this entails owning properties or paying for permanent on-site staff. Such arrangements may not even be legal for institutions with no official presence in the host country, and learning how to pay rent, expenses, and salaries in accordance with the host country's laws presents a challenge. Going it alone may thus be unattractive to administrators of American colleges and universities, which leads them to create consortia with other institutions to spread out the financial and technical burdens. As Heyl (2011) pointed out, they may outsource the off-campus activities altogether: "Going forward, the reduction of fixed asset programs (i.e., those with campus-funded resident directors and staff abroad) due to campus budget cuts might well encourage universities to rely more on provider organizations for semester-length study" (p. 4).

Another option might be for U.S. institutions to bypass third-party providers by forming partnerships with foreign universities, allowing their students to enroll directly, sometimes independently, sometimes through institutional exchanges. Although there is no doubt that direct enrollment can be a worthwhile and valuable educational experience for the right student, it's a difficult model to bring to scale. For one thing, the differences in institutional cultures, practices, curricula, and bureaucracies may be difficult for many students to navigate. Foreign universities often operate on a different schedule and provide fewer student services than is typical on U.S. campuses (especially regarding health and safety or learning accommodations), and they are often unable to provide tailored courses, such as local language instruction. A more fundamental challenge is that the U.S. undergraduate model remains to a large extent incompatible with foreign educational systems, especially if the ambition is to truly integrate what happens when the student is abroad with the institution's mission-driven educational goals. As DeWinter and Rumbley (2010) point out, there are often "radically different pedagogical approaches in U.S. and, say, European education" (p. 65). This results in a "clash of expectations" that "is making it difficult for many undergraduates to successfully enroll in foreign universities, be it the more independent study environment or the lack of a syllabus readily available to guarantee course approval prior to departure" (p. 65).

Another compelling reason for the involvement of third-party providers has to do with the Fair Trade Learning movement (discussed in more detail in chapter 6). Although early study abroad tended to favor one-off or irregularly scheduled programs, this lack of consistency can be exploitative of local communities that rely on long-term economic and cultural involvement. If we care more about reciprocity and fair treatment of community partners (e.g., foreign universities, homestay providers, or community organizations), we should work to ensure continuity.

Finally, the persistent involvement of third-party providers is explained in part by the way students are beginning to sidestep institutional offices. Increasingly, they conduct their own research about which study abroad programs are available and desirable. Department chairs, academic advisers, or off-campus offices may still act as gatekeepers for actual enrollment (and credit transfers), but they no longer control the flow of information. Third-party providers now have more direct communication with students than ever before. As Sideli (2010) reports, nonprofit as well as for-profit providers also gained momentum with the emergence of the Internet. Students now have ready access to information about study abroad opportunities around the world. Providers can communicate directly with students, and students now arrive at the study abroad office knowing all the details about programs the study abroad adviser may never have heard of (Sideli, 2010).

The patchwork of models in off-campus study is thus reflective of the complexity of the field's entanglements with the outside world. On the home campus the institution can set its own rules and guidelines; however, off-campus study necessarily involves compromises and negotiations with other entities. At the same time, it needs to match opportunities with students who have different levels of preparation, autonomy, education, and maturity. The result is the surprisingly varied and yet efficient system we know of as off-campus study.

Professionalization of the Field

The previous section shows how off-campus study has moved from the periphery of undergraduate education toward its heart while paradoxically maintaining its outsider status. Off-campus study is now often included as a component of the undergraduate experience; however, mere inclusion does not guarantee mindful integration. On our campuses we spend little time thinking about how off-campus study interacts with other elements of undergraduate education. Moreover, the components of undergraduate education are interconnected in ways that recall complex systems: The parts often interact in a nonlinear fashion, and small changes in inputs may have disproportionately large repercussions on outputs, often triggering feedbacks that will themselves affect the system.[7] Thus, it's not simply by doing *more* off-campus study in the same old way that one necessarily does it *better*. Instead, it's crucial to understand how off-campus study is connected to the other cogs and pulleys of education; only then can we determine which levers of the machine to pull.

It would be helpful to review how well off-campus studies align with each institution's goals and mission, but even this step is harder than one might suppose. Because most colleges and universities outsource all or some of their off-campus study offerings to third-party providers, relatively few representatives on the home campus have any direct or even indirect knowledge of what these offerings truly consist of. This alone makes it hard to understand or evaluate a program's suitability. Moreover, a third-party program can rarely adhere to a single institution's needs, for it usually caters to students from many colleges and universities—each of which has somewhat different goals.

Therefore, third-party and consortia programs typically aim for a compromise, striving to conform to guidelines or principles established by their partner institutions, in the case of a consortium, or to what might be considered industry standards set by large organizations like the Council on International Educational Exchange, AIEA, NAFSA, or the Forum on Education Abroad. These external bodies have typically created a buffer between off-campus programs and the faculty (or institutional administrators in charge of academic decisions at home institutions). Thus, the very experience we now consider part of the undergraduate core is the one that faculty and administrators, who are typically in charge of their institution's curricula, often know the least about.

Moreover, off-campus study has ramifications that require input from many nonacademic offices. For instance, are off-campus opportunities the privilege of the few, or a right (or even a rite) for all? How does one facilitate a student's departure and reentry? What becomes of financial aid? How does the institution manage fluctuations in on-campus enrollments? What are the insurance liabilities? How does one manage health and safety? Finally, how are material concerns like these to be weighed against the perceived educational benefits?

These financial, technical, and practical aspects of off-campus study can be so overwhelming that they eclipse academic objectives and the means for attaining them, at least from the institutional point of view.

If off-campus study is to become a central experience of undergraduate education, academic professionals on campus need to craft the objectives and evaluate the practices that will lead students to achieve their goals. In short, although the off-campus experience may and usually must be largely outsourced, the guidelines structuring those experiences need to be articulated in-house by faculty and institutional leadership. For these decision-makers to establish appropriate educational parameters, they will need a deep understanding of the off-campus experiences their students are having, which takes into consideration the idiosyncrasies of the institution. In short, each college and university will need to customize, to some extent, its approach to the practice.

The good news is that this work is already happening successfully at many institutions, and the process for accomplishing it is not difficult. Because off-campus study has long been subject to a kind of academic Darwinism—only flourishing where it was fit to survive—it has succeeded precisely where it resonates best with the preexisting mission of many institutions. Although there are many reasons that off-campus study is valuable for undergraduates, perhaps the most powerful argument in its favor is the way it aligns with the principles of liberal education and integrative learning.

Integrative Learning

> *The cultural experience we had was a very significant part of my program. We were taught a song in Māori (the language of the native people of New Zealand) and we sang both it and a traditional American folk song as part of a ceremony welcoming us into a* marae. *We were all greeted by the traditional Māori greeting of touching noses and spent the night in the Hall of Ancestors. This was a really significant experience because while we were there on a science program to study the land of New Zealand, the people who inhabit that land have a deep connection with it and are profoundly impacted by the geology of their home, so it would have been wrong to never meet the people who call the land we were studying home.*
>
> —Geology major, program in New Zealand

Liberal education, which we might summarize as a commitment to form the whole person, lies at the heart of American higher education (for more on this point, see Palmer & Zajonc, 2010). The idea doesn't apply only to so-called liberal arts colleges; far from it. With the exception of certain vocational schools, for example, most institutions include some commitment to general education. Even a school as technically inclined as the Massachusetts

Institute of Technology (MIT; 2017) reflects this practice, as illustrated in this excerpt from its academic catalog:

> MIT provides a substantial and varied program in the humanities, arts, and social sciences (HASS) that forms an essential part of the education of every undergraduate. This program is intended to ensure that students develop a broad understanding of human society, its traditions, and its institutions. The requirement enables students to deepen their knowledge in a variety of cultural and disciplinary areas and encourages the development of sensibilities and skills vital to an effective and satisfying life as an individual, a professional, and a member of society. (p. 38)

Just how an appreciation of culture might benefit a software engineer, for instance, or why universities should worry about preparing students for a satisfying life are mysterious to educators in many other countries.[8] General education requirements (or encouragements) of different stripes appear in the majority of undergraduate catalogs in the United States, applying to majors as diverse as business and biology, or design and dance. Some institutions have done away with general education requirements altogether, although this doesn't always narrow the course selections students make. Although some educators may complain that the gestures toward liberal education by technical schools are too limited, it's worth noting that they remain extravagant by the standards of many other nations. In most European countries, for instance, it would be hard enough to explain why a sociology student might benefit from a history course, let alone why a physicist might be allowed, or even encouraged, to take a course in poetry. Meanwhile, in the United States a student's major requirements typically constitute between a quarter and a third of the total number of classes. The wager is that breadth of study will more than compensate for the lack of additional depth in a specialty. Indeed, the learning will be all the stronger because the various strands of a student's education are entwined.

More significantly, AAC&U (2002) attempted to specify the goals of modern liberal education, emphasizing in particular the training of "intentional learners":

> To thrive in a complex world, these intentional learners should also become: *empowered* through the mastery of intellectual and practical skills; *informed* by knowledge about the natural and social worlds and about forms of inquiry basic to these studies; *responsible* for their personal actions and for civic values. (p. xi)

The report explains in some detail the skills associated with each of these qualities, which might be summarized as interpretation, integration, and communication of knowledge; appreciation of historical, natural, and global contexts; and development of moral, civic, personal, and interpersonal understanding. (For more on the role of international experience in liberal education, see Brockington & Wiedenhoeft, 2009).

In many respects, the notion of intentional learners drives what AAC&U (2009b) has come to refer to as integrative learning, which it has identified as an especially important goal for higher education, characterizing it as "an understanding and a disposition that a student builds across the curriculum and co-curriculum, from making simple connections among ideas and experiences to synthesizing and transferring learning to new, complex situations within and beyond the campus" (para. 2). Among the AAC&U (2009b) VALUE rubrics (sets of criteria for evaluating learning outcomes), integrative learning has been accorded special importance, evident in its framing language:

> Fostering students' abilities to integrate learning—across courses, over time, and between campus and community life—is one of the most important goals and challenges for higher education. Initially, students connect previous learning to new classroom learning. Later, significant knowledge within individual disciplines serves as the foundation, but integrative learning goes beyond academic boundaries. Indeed, integrative experiences often occur as learners address real-world problems, unscripted and sufficiently broad, to require multiple areas of knowledge and multiple modes of inquiry, offering multiple solutions and benefiting from multiple perspectives. Integrative learning also involves internal changes in the learner. These internal changes, which indicate growth as a confident, lifelong learner, include the ability to adapt one's intellectual skills, to contribute in a wide variety of situations, and to understand and develop individual purpose, values and ethics. Developing students' capacities for integrative learning is central to personal success, social responsibility, and civic engagement in today's global society. Students face a rapidly changing and increasingly connected world where integrative learning becomes not just a benefit . . . but a necessity.

Many teachers and students are familiar with the difficulty of connecting learning from one class session to another, from one semester to another, and from one discipline to another. But it's important to recognize the AAC&U's emphasis on connections that bridge the divide between curricular and cocurricular. Increasingly, we seek to develop curricula that can weave multiple skills into a complex fabric of understanding. Palmer and Zajonc (2010) describe it in this way:

> A truly integrative education engages students in the systematic exploration of the relationship between their studies of the "objective" world and the

purpose, meaning, limits, and aspirations of their lives. The greatest divide
of all is often between the inner and outer, which no curricular innovation
alone can bridge. The healing of this divide is at the heart of education during the college years, rightly understood. (p. 10)

Although the integration advocated by AAC&U (2002) emphasizes
primarily connections across disciplines, Palmer and Zajonc (2010) go a
step further. The inner and outer distinction they describe has largely to do
with the split not only between objective and subjective learning, as well as
between theory and practice, but also between the intellectual endeavors of
college and the personal growth we hope students will achieve. Many educators now urge us to recognize the potential connections among these areas,
and this more holistic view of education is gaining traction, extending well
beyond liberal arts colleges and even beyond the borders of the United States.
In part it encourages us to recognize that our students lead lives outside the
classroom. More important, it encourages us to take advantage of the links
between academic pursuits and our students' inner, personal development.
It also points to the importance of another kind of connection, notably the
intersubjective ties students have with other people in a decidedly extracurricular way.

Although it can be challenging to pull off, many U.S. colleges and universities attempt to integrate curricular and extracurricular education, for
example, by engineering the residential components of the undergraduate experience. This practice is based partly on the belief that institutions
of higher education should create communities that can "help [students]
develop leadership and communication skills, explore career interests, and
apply what [they] are learning in the classroom" (University of Wisconsin
Office of Residential Life, n.d.). Other efforts on campuses work to connect
clubs or sports to the academic mission.

Although each institution interprets these values differently, there is
considerable agreement about the importance of integrative education. The
commitment stands out in institutional mission statements, where even a statistical rendering of keywords (the size of words reflects the frequency of their
appearance) demonstrates a considerable overlap in goals (see Figure 2.1).

A word cloud like the one in Figure 2.1 is a blunt instrument, but it's
perhaps not far from the mark when it links liberal education with certain
key concepts, evoking a *student*-focused experience in an *intellectual* and *residential community* where students *engage* with *knowledge, scholarship,* and the
world in *committed* and *ethical* ways. (Parents of these same students may
identify more strongly with some of the finer print in Figure 2.1, such as
financial.)

Figure 2.1. A word cloud generated from the mission statements of five selective liberal arts colleges.

Note. The word cloud is not statistically significant on its own, nor should much be read into the juxtapositions of terms, which do not necessarily reflect syntactic or semantic connections in the mission statements. It is important to note that the mission statements for liberal arts institutions do have some striking differences from other types of institutions (see Hersh & Schneider, 2005).

Many of us admire the aspirations of such goals. But do we realize them? It's curious that so many of our institutions proclaim the centrality of our engagement with the world, often evoking directly or indirectly a commitment to study abroad, at the same time that we administer off-campus study as an essentially marginal operation. Although a few institutions have embedded off-campus study as an expected or even required component of the undergraduate experience (Soka University of America and Goucher College, for instance, require study abroad for all their students), most do nothing of the sort. Indeed, on most of our campuses, off-campus study is treated unlike any other academic entity. It is subject to different financial constraints, for study abroad offices are often expected to be at least self-sufficient and sometimes even revenue generating. Also, its credits may not transfer seamlessly throughout the institution, its curricular rules are different, and its advising services are largely disconnected from standard academic advising. Most surprising of all, the offices focused on this supposedly central aspect of undergraduate education, contributing to what many institutions refer to as *global citizenship*, have limited dialogue with the personnel of departments and programs that chart so many of the educational priorities on our campuses.

Institutionally, these peculiarities suggest that off-campus study is somehow different from and perhaps secondary to the on-campus curriculum. It is worth examining the validity of this implicit claim.

Integrative Education On Campus

More importantly, at [our home university] we live in a bubble. In Peru, too, we lived in that bubble, but it was harder to reenter every time. When you left El Agustino you were relieved and exhausted, but the fact of the matter is that most people will never leave El Agustino. . . . I think it's easy to forget that—but once you stare poverty and struggle in the face, it's hard to leave it behind completely. . . . Most importantly, my closest relationship in Peru was with my boss, Sara. We spoke in Spanish, English, and Spanglish. She taught me about Peru. She related to me as an extranjera *[foreigner]—she was from Spain. She, too, was a stranger. She was an excellent mentor and I learned much from her, in addition to her coworkers, who each told me their story with the organization. They are not stories I will soon forget.*

—Cinema and media studies major, program in Peru

If fully integrative learning—merging related disciplines and blending academic and personal growth—is the core goal of liberal education, how is it best achieved? Thanks to small class sizes and innovative pedagogies, colleges and universities have proven themselves adept at transmitting knowledge and skill sets, including those needed for the next generation of professors. (See Bourdieu & Passeron, 1990, on the reproductive function of education.) However, the integrative learning that Palmer and Zajonc (2010) advocate remains somewhat elusive. In a sequence of courses in a major, students often have difficulty transferring skills from one class to another, and that difficulty can be compounded when they need to translate across disciplinary lines. Even harder to traverse is the boundary between academics and one's personal life. Most professors know very little about the lives of their students beyond the classroom, despite occasional field trips or social interactions. Conversely, students often think of their professors as nothing more than teacher-scholars who work 24-hour shifts. What professor has not received an e-mail with a 1:00 a.m. time stamp, followed by a reminder from the same student at 3:00 a.m.?

Over the past two or three decades the divide between academic pursuits and personal life has grown on many campuses, often for understandable and even laudable reasons. At Carleton College, which like many liberal arts colleges is located in a small town, more than half the faculty live in the neighboring metropolis, which offers more opportunities for spousal employment, greater selection in schools for children, and a wider variety of cultural events. Some faculty still invite students to their home for the occasional gathering, but this tradition seems headed for extinction. Beyond office hours and departmental events, contact with students is sometimes minimal. Meanwhile, the business of our students' personal development is managed by a plethora of offices organized under the dean of students: residential life, the chaplain's office, student health and counseling, academic support, and more. Relatively few faculty members regret this increased specialization; there is little nostalgia for a remote golden age when faculty lived cheek by jowl with the students they taught. Although the various offices associated with residential life are charged with a certain amount of damage control (i.e., limiting the intake of drugs and alcohol, educating students about sexual harassment, providing safe outlets for youthful energy), they also develop important programming designed to foster personal growth. These educational programs can be highly effective, even though they are usually not articulated in concert with the academic side of the student experience. Consequently, and despite some efforts to the contrary, we tend to reinforce or at least perpetuate the relative autonomy on our campuses between academic learning and personal growth.

These observations are not a complaint. Many factors have converged to produce this situation, not least of which are very real concerns about liability or the increasing need for specialized disability and counseling services.

Moreover, few would deny that personal growth occurs on college campuses, and students often forge important relationships that last a lifetime. On many campuses the student body is increasingly diverse in terms of socioeconomic status, race, ethnicity, religion, nationality, and more, and this diversity makes it at least possible for students to create social bonds across many boundaries.[9]

And yet, how well do we achieve the goals of truly integrative education on campus? Typical freshmen or sophomores sign up for four courses per semester, each one in a different department and probably in different academic divisions (arts, humanities, sciences, social sciences, etc.). They may add a couple of additional credits, perhaps in the form of music lessons or a physical education class, and they may participate in such nonacademic activities as student clubs, campus jobs, or community service.

On the face of it, this kind of schedule seems to exemplify the liberal arts ideal. Students enjoy a wide range of courses, a rich extracurricular experience, and opportunities for personal growth. However, how integrative is this learning? Although the courses are in different disciplines, the connections among them are generally weak and serendipitous. With rare exception, professors have no idea what other courses their students are taking, and they seldom seek to establish specific links with other courses that are not closely connected to their discipline. Students may make such connections on their own, and they often do, but they may be left without the opportunity to develop them. The liberal arts curriculum makes connected learning *possible*, but it does little to make it *probable*.

Meanwhile, because the extracurricular activities that promote personal growth have been subcontracted to residential life, we also miss opportunities to integrate the academic and the personal.

These comments are not meant to diminish the on-campus curriculum. It would be ludicrous to suggest that the experience at the home institution is not successful, and the fact is that many students do make important connections across disciplines and between academics and their personal life. Many campuses employ various connecting strategies, such as linked courses, guest lectures, interdisciplinary programs, and living-learning communities.[10]

However, the complaint among professors that students fail to transfer learning from one course to another is frequent enough that we should do everything in our power to address it. Certainly some skills cross over fairly easily. For instance, students who improve their writing tend to carry it over from one discipline to another, just as a well-honed ability in math will help students in quantitative work in other areas. But theoretical tools and conceptual frameworks tend to travel less well. Ideally, we would find ways to facilitate these transitions. In fact we already have: The device colleges and universities rely on increasingly to strengthen these connections goes by the name of *off-campus study*.

Integrative Education Off Campus

> *Bangladesh with its dense population and large active microfinance institutions was the perfect place to do a field study of microeconomic development. . . . [A key experience was] meeting the poor women who borrowed from microfinance institutions. Actually going out into the countryside and meeting the very poor gave all of the reading I have done about poverty a much more visceral and human connection. It's one thing to read about the lives of the very poor and another thing entirely to actually see them.*
>
> —History major, program in Bangladesh

Why is off-campus study potentially more adept than on-campus work at promoting the integrative learning we aim for? To answer that question, we need to consider the possible differences between our students' experience at home and their experience away. Unlike curricula at American colleges and universities, which tend to be structured in similar ways on different campuses despite local variations in calendars and general education requirements, off-campus study programs come in a myriad of formats with fundamentally different strengths and weaknesses, all designed to accommodate different needs.

Let's take one common example: a hybrid, or peninsula, program in which American students study on a foreign campus, their courses divided between those taught by local faculty and those offered by their director. In this kind of program a student might share some courses with other participants of the same program, while other courses are taken alongside local students. The classes each student takes may well be in different disciplines, but they will likely share close connections. It's not a stretch to imagine, for example, a student in a program in South America who has classes in Spanish (advanced language), sociology (indigenous peoples), art history (pre-Columbian), and education (with a service-learning component). The possible intersections among such courses would be considerable.

Moreover, students often live with a host family, which provides an immediate point of cultural, linguistic, and personal connection. For many students, the host family will be the most important element of their term abroad, and because of the host family or other resources, the students will become involved in local leisure activities, much as they would on their home campus—except that this one requires linguistic and cultural understandings. (We deal more with cultural learning in chapter 5.)

Such an experience abroad shares superficial similarities with a semester back home, where students have a similar number of classes and a full slate of activities. But off-campus study programs can offer important differences in the structure of the classes, leading to a more unified experience. Each class makes implicit or explicit use of the specific site abroad, which helps students connect theory to practice, motivating them by dint of the immediate relevance of all they learn. Most obviously, perhaps, the language class prepares students for operating in the local language every day, and their daily interactions with their host families, professors, and friends provide fodder for the next day's class. The art history course may help students understand current art, architecture, and design while also providing them with a historical background that feeds into their course on indigenous peoples, which, incidentally, fuels discussion about the equitable distribution of resources (including education) in the education class, where the service-learning component provides students with a hands-on experience that tests and reinforces all they have learned.

Connections among the subject areas are facilitated by the fact that many of the U.S. students are taking some classes together and even living in close proximity to one another, which means they have a naturally formed learning community; in casual conversation more connections are made. Moreover, if the program director is in touch with some of the other teachers, the director understands what is happening in the other classes, and communication among professors can occasionally allow them to coordinate on a topic. Extracurricular activities (field trips, cultural events, a short study tour) are sometimes organized to underscore or deepen classroom subjects, further reinforcing connections.

This structure provides examples of the multiplier effect discussed in chapter 1: Several high-impact practices come together. Students benefit not only from an emphasis on diversity and global issues but also from the formation of learning communities and from a common intellectual experience. Moreover, they connect to the host culture through living, internships, and service-learning. These multiple impacts are often evident in students' self-reporting about their experience, as in the following comments:

> I gained so much self-confidence from my [off-campus study] experience. I found that I was quite capable of taking care of myself in entirely different cultures and relished the opportunity that I had to explore and travel. Instead of focusing solely on readings and other assignments, I started making stronger connections between what I was seeing around me to the academic work with which I was also engaged. (Sociology-anthropology major, program in China and Thailand)

> Studying off campus was freeing and helped me become an adult, whereas studying on campus now feels rather restricted and I see it actually discouraging quite a few people from truly growing up and taking responsibility for themselves. The off-campus experience forced a strong connection with the group. (Studio art major, program in New Zealand)

The multidisciplinary integration we long for on the American campus becomes possible in fuller form in well-designed off-campus study experiences, as does the integration of the academic and nonacademic components of the program. Just as important, students experience a tremendous amount of personal growth while on programs abroad—growth borne of challenges. They confront bouts of homesickness, they fret about making insufficient progress with the language, they flinch each time they commit a cultural blunder, they shrink with embarrassment when their host families know more about the United States than they do, and they feel offended by behaviors that strike them as indecent or offensive (even though they may merely be different). For many students the program abroad is their first experience as a disempowered outsider, and every day requires an act of courage. In the end, though, they are proud to have survived it, to have understood it, and often to have loved it:

> Coming from the college bubble and a very cushioned childhood, it was a vastly different experience to be thrust into the harshness of urban living. This forced me to come out of my comfort zone at many levels and was a period of massive self-discovery and growth for me. Being uncomfortable was the best thing that happened to me. (Psychology and cross-cultural studies major, program in Minneapolis–St. Paul)

> I have a much better understanding of another culture and of myself. The experience has helped me solidify what I want to do with my life as well as show me what life has to offer. (Biology major, program in Kenya)

> You always hear about how poor people are in other countries, but actually seeing these people and how they live is life-changing. Bonding with foreigners (particularly those with whom I shared no common language) was incredibly meaningful and I plan on keeping in contact with all of my families as best I can for years to come (and I would love to be able to return to visit). (Physics major, program in Madagascar)

These students know they have moved from the status of tourist to that of a temporary resident who has picked up local knowledge. When they return to the United States, they often find that their homeland changed while they were away.

These are intense and often stressful experiences, and no one is suggesting that every semester at college should try to match the constant low-grade anxiety that students experience during their cultural dislocations off campus. For one thing, no one could bear it. However, when it works right, off-campus study becomes an incubator for experiences that match the goals of liberal education, providing learning that is abstract and concrete, that forces students to make connections across disciplines, that insists on clarity of analysis and expression, and that integrates all these academic goals into the kind of personal growth that turns students into engaged citizens and skilled professionals.

For all its successes, off-campus study is no more insulated from failure than on-campus experiences. Not all students have such powerful or positive experiences, and not all off-campus study programs willfully design integrative experiences and learning. As Passarelli and Kolb (2012) explain:

> Programs that do not adopt a holistic approach to student learning can become little more than a glorified vacation. At best, students report having fun or being "satisfied" with the experience, and return home unchanged.

They engage in the experience at a surface level, maintaining distance from the physical, social, or intellectual tensions of the learning endeavor. (p. 137)[11]

Unfortunately, many programs do not embrace a holistic approach. Consistent with what Haynes (2011) has called *study abroad hype*, some institutions have mandated numerical targets for sending students off campus, leaving harried professionals to cobble together short-term island programs that may leave little room for important experiential and especially intercultural learning.

The responsibility for failed experiences is often shared. Everyone knows of students who don't take off-campus study seriously or who find themselves so caught up in the extracurricular experience that academics run a distant second or third in the competition for their attention. But even in these cases off-campus study may have lasting effects. An example of this was provided by a student who participated in a program in France, and who wrote to his program director 12 years after his time abroad:

> I thought I'd write to apologize for my behavior on that trip. Whether or not you remember, I was not well behaved and likely caused you several headaches you didn't need. I'm sorry. For what it's worth, the trip was very meaningful to me and is one of the things I think about most frequently when reminiscing about college. (Psychology major, program in France)

This commentary reveals a student, who by his own admission, gave academics short shrift. Still, over time he came to understand the value of his experience, which he claimed had "forced a period of rapid growth and expansion." When pressed for details, he wrote of the lessons he learned outside the classroom:

> If one is likely to spend their days reading and studying, then they will learn more about French culture by reading and studying surrounded by French people and culture. If one is likely to drink alcohol and smoke cigarettes, they will learn about French culture by drinking and smoking cigarettes (a habit I've since given up) with French people. The latter was the approach I took. I didn't learn to drink alcohol in Paris, but I did learn about Parisian cafe and nightclub culture and a lot about wine. I learned how the French interact with servers and wait staff, how they order, what they eat, how they eat and what they discuss. None of that is the same as we do it here. I didn't start drinking coffee in Paris, but I did learn how to get along standing at a table having an espresso with locals next to Gare du Nord, where I lived.

I learned about economics and politics too. I was in a park when an anti-American demonstration erupted seemingly out of nowhere. I saw a Parisian friend quit his job on a whim, because he could survive on the social safety net. I had to go to the doctor and saw the high quality of care for little out-of-pocket cost.

My regret is that I didn't fully engage with the program, but I did still take much away from it. (Psychology major, program in France)

It's too bad that this student needed a dozen years to draw these conclusions; however, would that all our failures might be so successful!

The Long Game

This discussion leads to a paradoxical conclusion: The most integrative learning experience our students will ever have may well occur when they leave our campus.

Some of us might find such an assertion disturbing, even depressing. After all, why bother keeping students on campus at all if the real learning happens when they leave? However, the success of off-campus experiences depends deeply on the home campus for at least two reasons. First, the home institution reviews, approves, and sometimes even designs the *synchronic integration*—that is, the cohesion of elements during the program—of a well-designed off-campus experience.

Second, the home institution is entirely responsible for the *diachronic integration* of these experiences—that is, the integration over time. Off-campus study has the greatest impact when we prepare students for it during the semesters preceding departure, and when it feeds back into work they can do upon their return to the home campus. We're not referring here to simple predeparture meetings or reentry debriefings, which can undoubtedly be helpful; we mean instead a deep entanglement of off-campus study throughout the entire undergraduate experience. How to do this well, and in a scalable way, is a wickedly complex problem—and one that we tackle in the next two chapters.

Notes

1. DeWinter and Rumbley (2010) describe the evolution of study abroad programs from 1960 to 2005. In general, although foreign language remains a component of many programs, the focus has shifted toward more disciplinary content: "That proficiency in foreign language is no longer the major consideration in choos-

ing a program abroad that it was in the 1960s and earlier is succinctly illustrated by a notice on the Council on International Educational Exchange's website indicating that '54 out of 97 study abroad programs don't have a language pre-requisite'" (DeWinter & Rumbley, 2010, p. 63).

2. Although structured differently from exchanges with American institutions, the Erasmus Programme has provided more than 3 million European students with the opportunity to study abroad at a higher education institution or train in a company. With a budget of more than €580 million in 2013–2014 alone, the highest annual amount of the seven-year period, 272,000 students and more than 57,000 staff spent time abroad (European Commission, 2015).

3. The image is borrowed from de Certeau (1984), who refers to this practice by the slang term *la perruque*: "The worker who indulges in *la perruque* actually diverts time" to work on personal projects. The practice "differs from pilfering in that nothing of material value is stolen" (p. 25).

4. However, the rate of growth had slowed. The increase was about 46% in the past 10 years, from about 223,534 students in 2005–2006, and only 19% over the past 5 years, from 273,996 in 2010–2011 (IIE, 2017e).

5. There are no data about participation rates comparable to those provided by IIE; however, casual polling among partners in the field suggests that participation rates in domestic study away is now declining after a period of modest growth.

6. The six national goals for off-campus study are to "1) Create a more globally informed American citizenry; 2) Increase participation in quality study abroad programs; 3) Encourage diversity in student participation in study abroad; 4) Diversify locations of study abroad, particularly in developing countries; 5) Create an innovative partnership with higher education to open more doors for study abroad; 6) Internationalize U.S. higher education by making study abroad a cornerstone of undergraduate education" (NAFSA, n.d.-b, para. 3).

7. This is not the place for a full-fledged explanation of systems thinking, but its use in educational discussions is increasing. For a good introduction, see Hora, Benbow, and Oleson (2016), especially pp. 133–139.

8. It's true that the liberal arts are a European invention, springing from the late medieval traditions of the *trivium* and *quadrivium*—the seven subjects ranging from rhetoric to arithmetic that constituted what was known in Latin as the *artes liberales*. But our modern conception bears little resemblance to this aged model, and the birthplace of a term doesn't guarantee the perpetuity of the associated practice. In fact, most European universities now emphasize narrow specializations that allow precious little crossover from other disciplines. Such vertically structured programs are also dominant in Asia and Latin America, and they are at best unaccommodating of (and at worst openly hostile to) students with a liberal arts background. The American system is certainly the odd one out, although some institutions abroad have begun to experiment with pieces of our model. For years, for instance, French university administrators have spoken of the need to Americanize their campuses. A

new call for such an effort was made by the French government in 2011, although often with a caricatured notion of what this would mean.

9. Even then the connections are not automatic. As we know, it is entirely possible (and perhaps probable) that different groups will remain quite separate unless deliberate steps are taken to lower social barriers.

10. Living-learning communities (also known as *intentional learning communities*) are environments in which students who share learning goals and interests reinforce their learning by sharing residential space. They illustrate a compelling on-campus model for bridging the divide between academics and residential life. See Stassen (2003).

11. This essay further describes the specific dynamics of the experiential learning cycle, looping through concrete experience to reflective observation, abstract conceptualization, and active experimentation (Passarelli & Kolb, 2012).

3

THE LONG RUNWAY

Going abroad definitely allowed me to learn in a more comprehensive way. I took a political science class on the issues that I studied in Vietnam two years before studying them [on site]. I never fully understood the impact of water issues in Southeast Asia, even after reading articles and viewing news reports. After spending three weeks in Vietnam, I understood more than I ever could in three terms [on campus] about the issues.

—Political science major, program in Vietnam

In the previous chapter we argued that integrative learning lies at the core of higher education and that off-campus study, when well conducted, is an example of and a catalyst for such learning. Because off-campus programs are typically concentrated in students' sophomore and junior years, they occupy a central position in the undergraduate experience, often occurring about the time students make decisions regarding majors and minors. In this way, off-campus study may feel like a culmination (the end of the general education sequence) as well as a new beginning (in the major). Moreover, student expectations for such programs are high: the hype, reinforced by program brochures, former participants, and program representatives, promises to deliver a transformative experience as reliably as packages from Amazon.

The pivotal timing of the off-campus experience, along with these heightened expectations, makes it all the more important to get things right. We need to make sure students are equipped to fully benefit from their time away, and for this, preparation is crucial.

There are many well-rehearsed strategies for preparing students for health and safety challenges or for cultural transitions. We also know how to train them to manage their goals and expectations while studying off campus. Indeed, sessions focusing on these topics are part of the standard arsenal of predeparture activities. The challenge at most institutions is what might be called the *pre*-predeparture activities—those that take place on the very long runway before departure, during the months or even years of a student's academic work leading toward the experience away. Exactly how to handle this preparation is far from obvious, and for a variety of reasons. For instance:

1. When students arrive on campus their first year, they typically have few specific aspirations for off-campus study.
2. Even if they do have ideas about where or what or how they might want to study off campus, faculty or off-campus study advisers are often unaware of these ideas.
3. By the time students make choices about programs (and make us aware of these choices), there may no longer be time for appropriate curricular preparation.
4. Even if there was time, no suitable preparatory courses may exist in the curriculum.
5. Even if such courses did exist, it may be difficult to require them of our students in an already full curriculum.
6. If such courses do not yet exist, the institution may not have the money, expertise, will, or lead time to create them.

Most of us understand the importance of preparing students for whatever difficult work will take place in our on-campus curriculum. We design those curricular steps carefully through first-year seminars, introductory courses, carefully threaded majors, and capstone experiences. We do this because we know how important it is for students to develop certain skills before they tackle others. We want them to stretch themselves, but we also know how unlikely they are to succeed if they leap, say, from Calculus I to Calculus III, or if they skip from first-semester Spanish to the fourth-semester course.

Given that we stage student work so carefully on campus, why would we allow these same students to dedicate a crucial block of their undergraduate career to an activity we haven't prepared them for? Some off-campus study programs (language-based ones in particular) have clear prerequisites, but many other programs are more casual in their preparatory steps. This means that students can find themselves parachuted into a different community (whether Moscow or the South Side of Chicago) largely unaware of what awaits them, a situation that is of dubious merit and ethically problematic. (See chapters 5 and 8 for more on the ethical stakes of sending students to off-campus study sites.)

In chapter 1 we characterized the experience of off-campus study as a kind of dislocation, a significant shift occurring in one's academic, cultural, and private life. Success in an off-campus program depends largely on the student's ability to straddle a rift. As in any academic enterprise, the purpose of predeparture preparation is not to eliminate the experience of dislocation (as if such a thing were possible), but to reduce the gap to the optimum distance, leaving the chasm broad enough that students need to leap, but narrow enough that they don't tumble into the abyss. The goal is to find a Goldilocks zone of difference—a notion akin to Sanford's (1996) theory of challenge and support.

Finding the right balance is a challenge even on an institution's own faculty-led programs, and it's considerably more difficult when the institution doesn't control the program it is sending students to. Despite careful program vetting by committees, study abroad offices, and relevant academic departments, off-campus study can still become a leap into the unknown for our students. Leaving for off-campus study is similar to a transfer from one institution to another (even when dealing with in-house faculty-led programs), which means our attention to scaffolding such experiences needs to be intense.

In a sense, our opportunities for preparation precede a student's matriculation at our institution. During recruitment and admission, a college or university employee may first plant a seed in the mind of student applicants. When admissions materials emphasize off-campus study, and when faculty or student panels champion the importance of such work in front of applicants and their parents, an expectation is created. Applicants then understand that students at this institution consider off-campus study a real possibility, and when they learn about the rewards derived from the experience, they are all the more enthusiastic. When off-campus study receives the same attention as other features of the institution, and when it is institutional leaders who are doing the highlighting, new students pick out this message through the din of information. By the time they arrive on campus for their first year, the academic possibility they learned about as applicants may already have blossomed into a specific aspiration.

What next? Earlier we likened off-campus study to field trips—those excursions away from campus (usually embedded in term-length courses) that are designed to deepen, test, and complicate lessons learned in the classroom. Teachers design field trips with great care because it's important for such experiences to occur at the most propitious moment—after all the groundwork has been laid. Upon return to the classroom, the experience will become material for further analysis and reflection.

Preparation for field trips usually occurs during the first weeks of the semester; this leaves time both for the experience and for the follow-up. For the somewhat larger field trip that is off-campus study, the logic is the same, but the arc is longer. Preparation needs to be threaded throughout earlier stages of the curriculum.

How might this work? A simple example comes from Carleton College, where an opportunity arose several years ago to fund two-week off-campus experiences during the winter break—a form that is analogous to what other schools run during January terms or Maymesters. At Carleton the idea of such an abridged program clashed with existing models, and many faculty chafed at the idea of what they considered a featherweight experience, concerned that it would be little more than academic tourism. However, a few professors experimented with this format despite its limitations, and they hit on an intriguing idea: This two-week trip could be embedded in a larger course of study. In this model, a group of students takes an entire course together during the fall term. Their coursework prepares them for the two-week trip, where they continue their learning (usually including personal projects) at a remote location. Then, upon return they enroll in a second course during which they complete their projects and follow up on other work undertaken on site.[1] The model has served many different disciplines, as these examples suggest:

- *Agricultural Sustainability in the United States and China.* Students take a fall-term course on comparative agroecology during which they visit local U.S. farms. For two and a half weeks during winter break, they tour farms in China, comparing fertilizer use, pest control, and weed control. During the following term they analyze comparative data to draw conclusions about sustainability practices.
- *Studio Art in New York City.* During the fall term students enroll in an intermediate-level drawing course focusing on perception and reflection. Then, for two weeks, the group goes to New York, visiting museums and interacting with artists while continuing their own work. On returning to campus they synthesize their work and prepare an exhibit.
- *Society, History, and Popular Culture in Senegal.* Students who are already proficient in French begin with a full-credit course titled France in the African Imagination. A two-week trip to Dakar brings them in contact with representatives of artistic, financial, and religious institutions that play a prominent role in West Africa. When they return, the participants complete research projects undertaken during the trip.

Interestingly, student reports about these off-campus study experiences demonstrate the same level of satisfaction as much longer programs, including even the traditional claims about life-changing experiences. In their descriptions, students often emphasize the importance of the preparatory course and the way it connected to the experience away:

The class leading up to the trip was hugely relevant, especially the models of population growth and the discussion of microfinance. Bangladesh with its dense population and large active microfinance institutions was the perfect place to do a field study of microeconomic development. Microfinance in particular is virtually non-existent in the U.S., so being able to interact with every level of the institutions—from the directors at the top, to the local agents assigning loans to the borrowers themselves—was an experience we really could not have gotten anywhere else. (History major, microfinance in Bangladesh program)

The structure of the winter/spring break programs is very effective, having classes before and after the travel got me prepared for the trip and gave me a space to reflect upon the trip as well. I think that this structure would also be useful for international off-campus programs, but may be more difficult to coordinate. (Political science major, wilderness studies at the Grand Canyon)

Coursework prepared us to make useful observations in the field. For example, papers on the colonization of boulder corals and the impact of rising surface temperature on sea grass growth were helpful in contextualizing what we saw in the field. (Geology major, geology in Belize)

Moreover, respondents to our survey expressed how much they appreciated the opportunity to follow up on the off-campus experience after their return. The following comments are typical:

Because I participated in a winter break trip this winter break, I am currently quite engaged with my OCS [off-campus study program] material because I am enrolled in the 6-credit follow-up course. To me, this seems like such a crucial aspect of the experience for me because I collected so much data and learned so many things, but I am still wrapping my head around it all. Working on a documentary and library exhibition with my classmates is helping me to really get the most academically and personally out of the information I gathered. . . . It was absolutely life-changing. (History major, Afro-Arab women's history program in Dubai)

My Urban Studies semester left me more interested in cooperative housing and I joined the Wellstone House of Organizing and Activism; eventually becoming the house manager for Res Life. I also chose an Education Studies minor after the educational leadership seminar I took while off campus. (Math and education studies major, urban studies program in Chicago)

Despite its successes, there's no doubt that this winter break model will not suit all needs. For one thing, these programs are extreme cases of island programs, which have definite limitations in the area of cultural connection;

also, their brevity renders many kinds of work impossible. Moreover, the highly organized nature of these programs leaves little opportunity for students to wander, get lost literally or metaphorically, and to struggle, which are experiences many students find formative, albeit difficult, on longer programs. Nevertheless, the general structure of these shorter programs is of keen interest: It shows how focused and dedicated preparation can provide thrust on the runway toward the off-campus experience, helping students take best advantage of their time. Moreover, it shows how rewarding follow-up work can be, especially when students are aware of the opportunity for it ahead of time. In fact, alerting students to *postprogram* opportunities is a crucial component of *preprogram* preparation.

When students participate in short-term, embedded programs early in their college years, the experience often serves as a springboard for more extensive study abroad explorations later. For faculty, as for students, the shorter-term commitment required by an embedded program is often more manageable, personally and professionally. At the same time, it develops the skills and capacity that might later allow one to participate successfully in a term-length study abroad experience. Short-term programs can also broaden the population of students who participate in off-campus study. For example, at Carleton more science majors choose winter break field trips than other off-campus study opportunities, an opportunity that is more easily accommodated by their linear curricula. Thus, even though science majors are the largest underrepresented study abroad group at Carleton, 43% of them participated in winter break field trips between 2001 and 2011, whereas only 26% of science majors participated in other study abroad opportunities during the same time period.

Institutions that sponsor their own faculty-led programs often require two or three predeparture meetings where faculty and students gather to discuss site-specific academic, cultural, and logistical considerations. Because it's not always practical to devote an entire term-long course to predeparture work, this kind of less formal preparation functions as a light version of the embedded winter break model described earlier. Another interesting strategy is to offer a program prereading course. These are typically low-credit reading courses, graded pass or fail, that students complete on their own time before the program starts. They are either tested or asked to write an essay on their readings when they arrive on site.[2]

Something similar can be accomplished in virtual form. For example, some programs provide one-on-one online predeparture consultations regarding research projects or internship placements that will take place during the program. (This is done by Higher Education Consortium for Urban Affairs [HECUA], the Institute for Field Education [IFE], and the

Carleton Global Engagement Programs, to name a few.) Another strategy used by some programs with a field research component, such as the School for International Training, consists of asking students in one of their application essays to describe the project they hope to complete during the program. This practice is helpful not only for the faculty director who will supervise students in the field but also for the students, who are encouraged to consult with on-campus advisers about their plans. The goal is to prompt students to think about their plans and goals in a deeper way than they might if not explicitly pressed to do so.

Although these micro-strategies are clearly helpful in preparing students academically for the upcoming off-campus experience, they fall short of intentional and integrated curricular scaffolding. At most institutions it is not possible to envision a rigidly structured curriculum that marches students through multiple preparations for off-campus study. Nevertheless, it's possible to go beyond the limited predeparture activities described previously. Whatever tools we devise will have to be scalable (and thus able to accommodate significant numbers of students), flexible (not limited to just one program), and effective. In what follows, we outline certain options for a multipronged approach, which could and should be adapted for individual institutional cultures.

Student Advising and Faculty Education

Nearly all institutions rely on faculty and staff advisers to guide students through the curriculum, and for many students, their academic adviser is the campus professional with whom they have the longest sustained contact. The challenges of the job of advising are multiple. At many colleges this work is an unevaluated and unremunerated part of an instructor's job; in larger institutions professional staff advisers may be burdened with so many advisees that they barely know the students. In either of these situations, students and advisers may both tend to focus on short-term checklists. However, a rapidly expanding literature reflects a growing awareness of the importance of academic advising (e.g., Drake, Jordan, & Miller, 2013; Folsom, Yoder, & Joslin, 2015; Grites, Miller, & Voler, 2016). During advising sessions students are often focused exclusively on enrollment for the upcoming term, but advisers have the opportunity and the responsibility to nudge them to think further ahead. In particular, it is never too early to ask about interests and intentions regarding off-campus study, to urge students to consult with relevant off-campus study advisers, and to discuss the kinds of courses that might best prepare them for their experience away. While it's rarely possible to point the student toward a course tailored to a specific program (as in the winter break model described earlier), the adviser helps the student chart a personalized pathway through existing offerings to achieve something similar.

This model, although elegant in its simplicity, can be devilishly difficult to realize, and for a variety of reasons. Academic advisers don't always provide the kind of continuity we hope for. For example, students may be shifted from one adviser to another when faculty or staff go on leave or when advising loads are rebalanced. An even more common problem stems from the awkward handoff between general advising and major advising. Most students change advisers sometime around their second year when majors are declared, which may coincide with their decisions about off-campus study. Moreover, because off-campus study commitments are often required two or even three terms in advance, general education advisers are often guiding student decisions about programs meant to mesh with a major that may not yet even be selected. This is especially problematic when we want students to project how they might further their off-campus work after their return to campus—a task that may be beyond the reach and the ken of the general adviser.

Finally, many professors are ill equipped to discuss off-campus study, much less encourage or implement it. Indeed, Michael Stohl (2007), a professor of political science and communication, made this point in his bluntly titled essay, "We Have Met the Enemy and He Is Us: The Role of the Faculty in the Internationalization of Higher Education in the Coming Decade." Stohl's premise is simply that most faculty, and by extension, most campus administrators, have too little knowledge of off-campus study to be useful advocates for it. This is not surprising: Perhaps only 10% of American professors have personal experience of study abroad, and given the relatively recent development of domestic study away, the numbers are presumably even more dire in that category.[3]

Given the crucial role faculty play in advising students and, more particularly, in modeling different forms of learning, the entire enterprise of off-campus study risks grinding to a halt without considerable faculty participation. Although Stohl's (2007) language focuses on international experience, his argument could be broadened to include all forms of off-campus study:

> If we want to internationalize the university, we have to internationalize the faculty. We have to move them in the necessary directions. We thus need to consider not only how to do what needs to be done but also how what needs to be done affects the faculty and how we can mobilize their power over the process. (p. 367)

The question is, how does one accomplish this? How do you convince faculty and academic staff of the benefits of something they have never encountered? If they had no off-campus study experience during their own undergraduate career, how well can we expect them to advise students on the matter?

The solutions to these obstacles will almost certainly be specific to each institution, but explicit training for advisers about off-campus study is a first step, and there may well be ways to improve the handoff between general education advisers and their counterparts in the majors.

Moreover, collaboration between the off-campus study office, faculty, and academic departments is crucial. Thoughtfully constituted off-campus study advisory committees can help, and faculty can often be recruited to help vet programs, sometimes with the reward of a site visit. This helps faculty understand which programs are to be recommended and why, and then advise students about their choices.

In our experience, the most effective step may consist of finding ways to provide faculty and staff advisers with firsthand experience of off-campus programs. At Carleton College, for example, a number of faculty travel seminars have been conducted. These are miniature off-campus study programs lasting anywhere from one to five weeks, bringing together faculty in a variety of disciplines. Expeditions of this sort have taken faculty groups to Japan and China, Vietnam and Sri Lanka, and to many locations in Europe. One such trip was taken to DIS Study Abroad in Scandinavia, where faculty had a specific mission to consider how to improve the curricular flow of students as they move back and forth across the Atlantic. Many of these faculty members had little experience with study abroad or study away, but even this six-day experience had lasting impacts. For many Carleton faculty, such trips have been among the most formative experiences of their time at the institution. The following excerpts from their postprogram reports make this clear:

> The trip to Copenhagen was useful in a number of ways. First (and perhaps most eccentrically) I never did study abroad as an undergraduate, and so having a sense of what students do on that program gave me at least some idea of the experience. The homestay was particularly helpful for that, but so was the brief go at negotiating my way around a new city, and the field trip to Malmö, and sitting in on the classes, and the student panel. I have a much clearer idea now not only of DIS [Study Abroad in Scandinavia], but by extrapolation of a number of other study abroad opportunities. Second, it was really interesting to meet and talk to the DIS faculty; the brainstorming we did about better integration of our students' experiences there with

their post-OCS [off-campus study] academic career here was very interesting to me, and I hope that we will have made a start at seeing what our options are. Third, the opportunity for extended discussions with my . . . colleagues was extremely helpful; we paradoxically get much less time for this kind of interaction when we're all together [on the home campus]. (Professor of classics)

[I appreciated] the opportunity to focus directly on the question of if and how students might better fit their study abroad experience into their major experience on campus. For our department's program, based in Cambridge [UK], there has been a tendency to think of it as a stand-alone experience, a bit like one of our elective courses. While that may be fine (and 20 plus years of previous participants seem to have been happy enough with the experience), that does not mean we couldn't make their experience more meaningful, both personally and academically. Conversations with DIS faculty and students and Carleton colleagues have encouraged me to think about how to better integrate the off and on campus experience. (Professor of economics)

Being exposed to experiential learning/teaching in disciplines *other than my own* was a highlight. I already know I can learn things from . . . my direct departmental colleagues—but those lessons would in some ways be incremental; what we do is too similar at its base, our training too similar, our sense of what our pedagogic goals should be too similar, etc. But being exposed to entirely different modes of teaching, that come from other disciplines with other priorities and ways of thinking (and of course in another country with different underlying educational, political, social, and other philosophies) was eye-opening, edifying, and even inspiring. (Professor of English; emphasis in original)

Providing professors with exposure to the kinds of programs our students participate in deepens their willingness to integrate off-campus academic experience into the on-campus curriculum. Of course providing these opportunities for professors and academic staff requires considerable resources. However, if institutions are serious about raising the participation rates and improving the experience of off-campus study, it's hard to imagine a more effective method than hands-on training for those who engage in the formal and informal advising of students.

Another idea is to develop a pathways approach to advising, which highlights the relationships among different curricular, cocurricular, and extracurricular opportunities, connecting them to postgraduate careers (e.g., Carleton College Pathways, apps.carleton.edu/pathways). Alternatively, one can integrate advising interventions directly into the study abroad program application process. For example, the Beloit College study abroad application includes an essay assignment that prompts students to discuss their program goals, encouraging them to articulate connections to on-campus study, to demonstrate country-specific and intercultural knowledge, and to discuss nonacademic challenges (Brewer, Cannon, Kaufman, & Nixon, 2012). The essays are scored according to rubrics aligned with the college's general study abroad learning goals, and they are followed up by in-person interviews. Moreover, after returning from an off-campus experience, students are given the opportunity to reflect on and evaluate their application essays.

Several different versions of the advising strategies mentioned here are possible. In short, if off-campus study is to be the most significant part of a student's undergraduate degree, it merits an extraordinary commitment to advising and planning.

Courses

In a pathways approach to advising, one of the jobs of advisers would be to help students reflect on the courses they need to prepare for off-campus study. But where are these courses, and what do they look like? As mentioned at the beginning of this chapter, a significant challenge to robust preparation for off-campus experiences is precisely the scarcity of such courses. Even if they do exist, we and our students don't always know how to identify them.

Most programs do not and cannot offer a semester-long course to be used as a runway leading to off-campus study; however, many programs include prerequisites that may be structured to accomplish a similar form of preparation. Programs where instruction is conducted in a foreign language, for instance, typically set a minimum skill level; discipline-specific programs (e.g., an in-house political science program in Washington DC, or the Budapest Semester in Mathematics) may also have explicit expectations for previous experience in the discipline. However, many programs have no formal prerequisites. This may be because they draw students from many disciplines, requiring such programs to keep their course offerings general in order to accommodate many student profiles. Alternatively, a program may be so large that it offers courses in many disciplines, rendering it impossible to devise a single prerequisite that might cover all student participants.

However, whether or not a program has strict prerequisites, it could be helpful for institutions and third-party providers to identify recommended courses for programs. For example, HECUA programs Race in America, Art for Social Change, and Inequality in America have no formal prerequisites; however, it would be a simple matter for the sending institutions, or the receiving institution, to identify courses that might be especially helpful for students before departure. Listing these courses in appropriate places would help students and advisers contemplate the best routes to the off-campus study experience.

There are also more general ways that courses might prepare students for off-campus study. Many institutions offer first-year seminars—another AAC&U high-impact practice (Kuh, 2008, p. 9)—that serve as initiations to college-level study, including such things as library instruction and practice in writing and presenting evidence. Administrators of an institution wishing to encourage early reflection about off-campus study could include a relevant unit or activity for the benefit of these captive audiences. Alternatively, certain first-year seminars might be designed to appeal to students naturally inclined to consider off-campus study. At Carleton College, for instance, sections of the course titled Growing Up Cross-Culturally are offered each fall term. The course examines life cycles in different cultures and attracts a blend of domestic and international students, nearly all of whom end up studying off campus.

There are other ways to thread preparation for off-campus study through the curriculum. Because these preparation-for-departure activities are so crucial, many of us are learning to do them well. To assist us in this work, a vast literature exists to outline principles and theories and to provide nuts-and-bolts examples (see Brewer & Solberg, 2009; Savicki, 2008; Vande Berg, 2007). Brewer and Cunningham (2009b) take a practical, hands-on approach to curriculum integration by focusing on specific course and classroom strategies, from geography and anthropology to language study, biology, and economics. Their book describes predeparture courses that are specifically designed to integrate cultural research and country-specific knowledge; they also promote experiential learning and the application of ethnographic study methods. Even when such courses are not required, making them visible in the online course catalog via course tags, keywords, and other descriptors can help students and advisers identify useful paths.

Another common form of preparation for off-campus study is language instruction. Although this is addressed in depth in the next chapter, it's worth pointing out here that the current trend is to stretch the notion of language well beyond verbal proficiency. The Modern Language Association (2007) has stressed a change of emphasis. Although continuing to promote the study of foreign languages in the United States, where second language ability lags far behind the levels found in other industrialized nations, the Modern Language Association urges a shift from a narrow focus on language excellence and literary study toward more general translingual and transcultural competence. Moreover, it advocates for the establishment of stronger language requirements for students in all disciplines, urging us to work "with colleagues in the social sciences and in policy-oriented departments to strengthen language requirements in the design of their majors and graduate programs and encourage these colleagues to recognize the limits monolingualism imposes on research" (p. 8). Not surprisingly, the report calls for institutions to augment study abroad and not just for language majors; it should apply to students in every discipline as well as to faculty. The curricular implications of such a change (discussed further in chapters 4 and 5) concern not only internal modifications of language sequences (e.g., more cultural proficiencies) but also the extension of language into other disciplines through initiatives like foreign language across the curriculum.

Some might object that these efforts are too intrusive, that we risk guiding students too much, and that we are depriving them of the opportunity to sort such things out for themselves. However, overpreparation doesn't appear to be a legitimate risk. Few program directors we know of complain that their students suffer from an excess of knowledge about the world. At DIS Study Abroad in Scandinavia, for instance, an alarming number of students arrive in Copenhagen without being entirely sure where Denmark is located on the map. In this context, the account by Green (2005) of how a young student awakened to her own ignorance is instructive:

> My roommate last year introduced herself and her name was Marissa. She told me what country she was from and I was like, "Where in Africa is that?" and she was like, "The South American part." I was like, "Maybe I should work on that." (p. 8)

Statistics support these anecdotal impressions. The National Assessment of Educational Progress found that only about one-fourth of American students are proficient in geography, and their skills have worsened since 1994 (National Center for Education Statistics, 2011). In a poll by National Geographic-Roper Public Affairs (2006), 50% of young Americans (18- to 24-year-olds) felt it was not necessary to know where countries in the news were located on a map; only 14% could locate Israel, Saudi Arabia, Iran, and Iraq; 57% failed to locate the state of Ohio; and a third couldn't read basic compass directions. Recent polls show alarming ignorance about world history: 22% of millennials apparently have never heard of the Holocaust, and two-thirds of them don't know what Auschwitz was (Zauzmer, 2018).

When many students can't even picture the world beyond their immediate horizon, it's difficult to assert they're in danger of being overprepared. Our goals are modest yet important: We seek to move students first to a point where they might imagine themselves participating in off-campus study and, second, to a point where they are adequately prepared to benefit from it.

Channels of Communication

All the efforts described in this chapter have to do with blurring boundaries between on-campus and off-campus experiences. In some sense the off-campus experience begins well before departure, and we've shown how academic and personal preparation positions students to take better advantage of the experience itself. Eventually, they depart.

As they disappear from the previous term's class rosters, they also vanish from the consciousness of their on-campus professors. As if by mutual consent, students and their professors and advisers go incommunicado. Interactions with the home institution dwindle to a trickle of communiqués about registration or lingering library fines.

This is not altogether a bad thing. Students who report substantial personal growth during their time away benefit from (and often relish) their newly found, or newly imposed, independence. Too much contact with home can become a crutch. (See our discussion of social media in chapter 8.) It's good for students to make do with local resources and to make up their own minds. After all, there are already plenty of helicopter parents, and we don't need to add a fleet of helicopter professors to the scenario, distracting students from the cultural integration that is so crucial to many programs.

That said, it may be useful for institutions or individual departments to consider whether some checkpoint communication might be valuable. If we cease thinking of off-campus study simply as a student hiatus that we tolerate, or as an experience of primarily personal growth, we might consider it also as an academic step that will be channeled back into on-campus work. Too often students return to campus excited by a project undertaken while away only to discover to their dismay that the home institution can't support continued work in that area. How much better would it be if students and perhaps the off-campus faculty engaged in occasional consultations during the program to allow the possibility of coordination? Such an intervention won't be needed or wanted in all situations, but in certain kinds of programs, especially those involving research projects that students may wish to pursue after their return, some limited interactions between home and away could be envisioned.

The articulation of an on-campus curriculum already requires regular and disciplined communication among many bodies—at the very least, members of the academic department, the administration, a curriculum committee, and the student. But the integration of off-campus study in this larger on-campus experience would require an additional interface with one or more outside groups, such as the institution running the off-campus program, the professors teaching the classes, and possibly the support staff. To make matters more complex, because most American campuses allow students to choose from among a range of program types, there is no uniform model for interaction with the off-campus entities. Any given institution may be sending students to 30 or 50 or 200 different organizations, each with their own modus operandi. Although the multiplicity of models offers a rich opportunity for students, this same diversity presents a challenge for the reintegration of the student's off-campus experience into the domestic curriculum.

Regular communication between the home institution and its off-campus partners is rarely possible, except in cases where historic connections have been developed over years or even decades. Often, whatever communication does take place is dominated by emergency issues; understandably, the urgency of health and safety trumps communication about curricular and cocurricular goals.

However, opportunities for meaningful exchange exist. Some program providers offer program familiarization visits, whereas others send out inquiries and surveys regarding new courses and curricular changes. When directors from third-party providers visit our campuses, this creates a further opportunity for conversation. It is natural for study abroad professionals to be engaged in these collaboration efforts, but the engagement of faculty in such activities is worthy of special consideration—even if it requires incentives. Although faculty participation in such conversations is not historically part of their campus responsibilities, this interaction with third-party providers can assist in the preparation and handoff of students when they leave campus; it will also educate faculty about what they can expect when students return.

Carleton College has also experimented with an additional model for keeping students better connected with on-campus faculty while studying away. The off-campus studies office selects one or two faculty fellows each year. These specially trained advisers help students connect their off-campus learning to on-campus resources. The initiative focuses on students whose off-campus programs involve an independent research component. The fellows meet with students before departure to discuss issues of field research abroad, initiating a reflection about how their projects might later flow into advanced work (courses, fellowships, senior theses) available on campus. The fellows also make themselves available for consultations with students while they are away, and they gather the students for discussions and presentations after their return. This opportunity is clearly not for everyone, but it has the advantage of forming an on-campus learning community for students who are mostly headed for very different destinations. Although the program at Carleton is still too young to fully evaluate, it shows clear benefits for some students. We know they are eager to make these connections. In an unpublished internal survey, Carleton College (Kaufman, Nixon, & Tan, 2010) found that fully 74% of students who conducted independent research while studying off campus used this work in subsequent research, independent studies, or senior theses.

With high-quality preparation, students stand a much better chance of benefiting from their off-campus experience and, crucially, of deepening this work once they return. This opportunity for deepening is the subject for the next chapter.

Notes

1. Similar structures are embedded in many off-campus study programs. For instance, Carleton's Paris program (focused on hybrid culture) continues this work during a week-long study tour in Morocco. From their home bases in Copenhagen and Stockholm, DIS Study Abroad Scandinavia organizes several week-long study tours connected with classes, following the same field trip formula.

2. Some examples of prereading courses from Carleton College include Socio-Cultural Field Research in Guatemala, a directed reading course completed before the program in which students read selected works chosen to provide background on Guatemalan history, Mayan culture, and contemporary social issues in preparation for the field seminar. They write an integrative essay on this material and participate in discussions covering the readings during the first week of the program. Readings in New Media Studies in Europe focus on cultural and technological perspectives on place and location and facilitate student understanding of key issues and ideas central to the program.

3. We are unaware of any statistics about faculty experience in study abroad and study away. However, given that only 1 in 10 American undergraduate students currently study off campus (IIE, 2017a), a figure that was lower in the past when the current professorate was in training, it is perhaps not unreasonable to estimate a similar participation rate among faculty members.

4

BRINGING IT BACK

*If nothing else, it is likely that my [senior project] will be inspired by this trip—
be it in a project on Fouquet, Poussin, or David. I am much more devoted to
French [activities] and want to practice my language skills all the time. I also
fell in love with writing while I was in France and hope to take classes to better
my craft. . . . I know what I want to get from the rest of my experience.*

—Art history major, program in France

We began with the premise that integrative learning is the corner-stone of American higher education: Students do their best when their studies reinforce one another. Moreover, off-campus study allows for an enriching confluence of the curricular, the cocurricular, and even the extracurricular, where personal growth connects usefully to academic experience.

The principle of holistic education doesn't mean that everything happens simultaneously. Indeed, learning often requires a temporary focus on a small part of a larger whole, the way a pianist may rework a difficult passage time after time before reintegrating it into the flow of a piece. For the sake of clarity, a teacher might belabor the composition of a mitochondrion or the concept of standard deviation or the conjugation of a verb before returning these parts to the larger system to which they belong: the cell, a study of probability, a meaningful sentence. Often learning depends on a constant oscillation between parts and wholes, which helps one to synthesize understanding.

In well-designed off-campus study the oscillation between part and whole, as well as between experience and knowledge, tends to occur with heightened frequency. Students of foreign language or culture reinforce their classroom learning in everyday interactions with host families and shopkeepers—experiences they bring back to the classroom for analysis. Architecture students happen upon new forms every time they turn a corner. Students of political science find their coursework complicated (or confounded) by the political arguments they overhear in local cafés. Time and again we hear from students how lived experience animates their intellectual curiosity. For instance, here's how an English major described this convergence during her program in Moscow:

> Victory Day festivities in early May were especially memorable. It's Russia's main patriotic holiday (perhaps similar to the Fourth of July in the U.S.) but it specifically celebrates Nazi Germany's surrender to the Soviet Union. Several other students and I attended the huge military parade in central Moscow, and then went to Victory Park, where the main festivities were held. Witnessing these festivities was astonishing because the entire city nearly shut down in order to celebrate Russia's "victory" in "The Great Patriotic War" (that's the name for WWII from the Russian perspective). From my point of view as an American born in the early 1990s, WWII feels like a distant historical event, but in Moscow it almost feels as if the war happened yesterday. Statistically speaking, American casualties in the war are infinitesimal compared to Russian casualties. Roughly half of all deaths in the entire war were Russian. Still today, many Muscovites have personal connections to the war—for example, my host's father and grandfather both fought and were killed, and as a child she and the rest of her family were forced to leave their homeland of Belarus. And judging by the massive crowds at the parade and at Victory Park, thousands of other Muscovites like my host have personal connections to the war and treat Victory Day as an incredibly powerful holiday to honor their nation's history. Everyone on the street wore symbolic ribbons, and many carried red carnations to give to the few surviving veterans attending the festivities, or to lie [*sic*] on monuments at Victory Park. Some of the most poignant images I remember from the program are of the veterans—incredibly old men with decaying skeletons, wearing their old uniforms decked with dozens of metals, with overflowing armfuls of red carnations. (English major, program in Russia)

What made this moment so meaningful for the student was the sudden integration of what might be called the brain and the heart, an example of the synthesis of textbook learning with lived experience. Revelations of this sort shape us, excite us, and move us to action.

We focused on this kind of synchronic integration in chapter 2. In chapter 3 we demonstrated how it can be enhanced by careful preparation during the semesters or even years preceding the off-campus study program.

But what happens after this experience? We know how often students speak of transformative moments and life-changing encounters during their time off campus. Yet we also hear about how they shelve this experience when they return to their home institution. Despite our best efforts to offer welcome-back receptions and poster sessions, students often feel the curriculum offers little space for the personal and academic work they accomplished during their program. They aren't sure how to fit this part into the whole of their undergraduate studies. Faced with apparent indifference when they return from their adventure, many students struggle to readjust to the college environment they'd left behind for a month or a semester or a year. They may have experienced a cultural or personal reset during their time abroad, only to discover that their friends and professors expect them to be the same person they were before departure. This can leave them feeling personally and academically out of sync with the home campus, which all too often leaves their time away feeling like a wondrous detour—or even a glorious but inconvenient dead-end. Yes, we seem to tell them, you had that life-changing experience in Peru, Botswana, China, or Louisiana, but that doesn't particularly interest us. Now you're back home in the world of majors and requirements, and you need to get back to business.

Many students affirm that their time away from campus had a positive influence on their academic interests. In some cases it affects their research topics or even causes them to change majors. Still, in our surveys an alarming number of students were unenthusiastic when asked if their time away redirected their academic work on return:

> Umm . . . not really. It helped me grow as a person though. (Economics major, program in Bangladesh)

> Not really. (Physics major, program in Dubai)

> Living on my own in a foreign country really helped me gain independence. . . . It did not really effect [*sic*] my academic life at [my home institution]. My study abroad program was not related to my major or concentration. It was sort of a "term off" academically for me to try something different that I thought looked very interesting. (Philosophy major, program in Prague)

> Although my [senior project] is on Japanese, the program didn't affect [that project] at all. By the time I returned to [my home campus], it was my senior year, and most of my classes were essentially chosen for me to fulfill various requirements before I graduate. (Linguistics major, program in Japan)

> At the moment, this is hard to fully know. I just got back nine days ago, so at the moment, jet lag is the biggest lingering influence. As far as [my home campus] goes, I don't think it will change much. (Classics major, program in Istanbul)

It's important to note that these students are neither malcontents nor disenchanted souls; many of them waxed enthusiastic about their program in other parts of the survey, especially the ones dealing with personal growth.

But academically they considered the time away to be a bracketed experience, largely detached from their ongoing academic development. This is not a catastrophic outcome; after all, the experiences were thought of as worthwhile on their own. However, from the institutional perspective, we can identify a lost opportunity.

One of the most challenging aspects of education abroad is its effective reintegration into the on-campus curriculum. Although we encourage students to have such experiences, we're not always sure how they align with our institution's educational goals and mission, our assessment efforts, or the broader plan for internationalization and global engagement. In recent years, educators have made progress on curricular integration, but more can be done to improve the transition from off-campus study back to the home institution. If done right, off-campus study can truly reinforce the complex whole (e.g., the undergraduate degree) of which it is a central component.

The return to campus is the trickiest stage in off-campus study for both practical and theoretical reasons. For one thing, it's undeniable that students returning from a variety of programs can introduce major inconveniences for professors. Such students may be out of step in the course sequence of their major, and the transcript from their program may need to be evaluated for credit. Moreover, these students may put additional demands on overworked faculty members, asking to do an independent study inspired by their time away—topics like the role of songbirds in the history of Chinese music, the economics of organic wines in France, or some other wonderfully obscure topic their professors know nothing about. It's understandably tempting to escort these students back to their place on the conveyor belt of their major. But doing so often sacrifices the energy, understanding, and motivation they developed while away.

But what are the options? If predeparture training channels students toward their off-campus experience, reentry is more like a gate releasing them into a garden of forking paths. Before their departure, students heading for many different destinations have somewhat similar needs and may be brought together for some steps of predeparture training—such as issues like travel arrangements, health and safety, visas, and insurance. It's possible to provide them some generic advice about dealing with different cultures, and the entire group will benefit from reminders about campus requirements pertaining to their absence. In short, with respect to some parts of their training, predeparture students are a bit of a flock, susceptible to a certain degree of shepherding. Conversely, at the time of their return—especially when students have participated in programs run by third-party providers or have directly enrolled in a foreign university—the flock has disbanded, and students now have highly idiosyncratic needs. Moreover, before their off-campus study experience, which typically occurs in their second or third year, students have typically spent the bulk of their time in general education. During those early semesters, the institution can reach them through first-year seminars, premajor advisers, and general education requirements. After their time away, most students are increasingly absorbed into majors and minors, where institution-wide initiatives have less reach. This splintering of student experience after the return to campus makes the process of reintegration especially challenging.

Because the institution has fewer ways to connect with students after their return, it's all the more crucial for postprogram reintegration to begin before departure through various forms of advising. Indeed, if we leave reintegration until students return to campus, we have already lost many opportunities. In the on-campus curriculum, no professor would plan a field trip without considering how to use that experience afterward; according to the same logic, we need to consider in advance the opportunities and expectations that will await students when they return to the home campus. When students know that we expect their experience to feed into future on-campus work, they have an incentive to prepare themselves to meet that expectation.

This is not to say that students should commit themselves to a particular course of study after returning; the results of off-campus study are unpredictable enough to make that a fruitless enterprise. However, there should be some expectation that reentry will be less a *moment* than a *process*. The institution needs to provide relevant opportunities for students (on some campuses these may even be obligations) upon their return. If these opportunities are well articulated and if predeparture students see them as part of their possible future, they will provide further motivation for students to consider studying off campus in the first place.

The first step is for institutional leaders to determine what goals they are trying to achieve through off-campus study. The University of Minnesota Curriculum Integration Conference in 2004 (and the subsequent publication of articles and papers) contributed greatly to understanding the challenges facing institutions that see study abroad as an integral part of their educational mission (University of Minnesota Learning Abroad Center, 2018). The Minnesota model of study abroad curriculum integration, adapted since then by many institutions, stressed the necessity of building partnerships across college structures, departments, and offices. It also proposed learning outcomes for study abroad, showing how administrators can advance departmental and university-wide learning goals. Finally, the Minnesota model sought to develop a holistic undergraduate curriculum including study abroad coursework in electives and majors (University of Minnesota Learning Abroad Center, 2018). Once these goals are articulated at an institution, it becomes possible to envision how off-campus study can flow back into the on-campus curriculum and to consider which tools will be necessary to accomplish it.

Appropriate postprogram opportunities will thus depend on particular students, programs, and institutional priorities. There are three different, albeit overlapping, categories of knowledge that institutions might wish to tap and develop: personal growth, disciplinary skills and knowledge, and cross-disciplinary skills and knowledge. In the next section, we describe a few possibilities for doing this work, provisionally ignoring important practical objections like resources (to be addressed later).

Personal Growth

By *personal growth* we mean a particular basket of nonacademic skills and qualities students often develop during their off-campus experience, including independence, humility, a clearer sense of one's self and abilities, pluck, resourcefulness, resiliency, confidence, and an ability to grapple with difficulty (see McGourty, 2014, on study abroad and personal growth). An important component of personal growth is also intercultural competence, discussed in depth in chapters 5 and 7.

Some educators may wish to set aside personal growth as something that falls outside the purview of the institutional mission. They concede that such growth occurs, but it's not part of their academic work. That is to say that personal growth is not a credit-bearing part of the academic enterprise. This disregard for the nonacademic generally prevails on campuses today, but it doesn't need to be that way. Indeed, if one of the goals of higher education is to integrate lived experience with academics, we should consider taking into account very different types of curricula, including in-class and out-of-class learning. If we do so, the return to campus after a program can provide an especially fruitful opportunity. We can encourage the examination of life as it has been lived—otherwise known today as building reflection into experiential learning (e.g., Haynes, 2011; Kolb, 1984; Mezirow, 1991). A student's return to campus is an opportune moment for undertaking that work, although it may be initiated even sooner. As we discuss in chapter 7, opportunities for self-reflection before the end of an off-campus program can usefully blur the lines between assessment and continued learning.

Because personal growth is a significant outcome of so many off-campus experiences, and because it is not specific to a particular discipline, the work of engaging students in reflection about such growth need not be tied to a student's major department. Indeed, it might best be handled by way of electives, or else threaded through many different courses or even activities that are not credit bearing.

In its simplest form, reflection work often begins with social events organized by off-campus study offices or other bodies. The opportunity to share stories with others who have undergone similar experiences is always welcome: it helps students cast their experience in a coherent narrative and express it in a way that can be meaningful to others. Other kinds of informal activities, such as photo or travel writing contests, encourage students to curate their experiences and express them in ways that may receive institutional recognition, whether in the form of prizes, visibility, or inclusion in a publication or exhibit. Steps such as these are low-hanging fruit; they are relatively easy to organize and fund, and they can affect large numbers of students.

Many students, however, will want more. This is especially true of students who have grappled with difficult realities during their time away—such as situations fraught with poverty, violence, discrimination, and more. Many of these students will have had their worldviews challenged, and under the strain of cognitive dissonance, they've been forced to reassess their reality. These students may be shaken in ways that, although ultimately enlightening, are difficult for them to navigate. They may need more extensive structures to allow them to probe their experiences and come to terms with them.

Many off-campus programs have personal growth reflection built into end-of-program activities; however, as we've suggested, reentry is best considered a process rather than a moment. It takes time for students to digest their experiences and make sense of them. Often this means providing a forum for such work on campus.

One way to do this is to offer courses or workshops that allow students to analyze the experience they've just had. As mentioned in chapter 3, Beloit College has experimented with postprogram reflection activities that revisit students' essays about their preprogram aspirations (Brewer et al., 2012). Other institutions offer more theoretical options. Carleton College, for example, offers a course in which students examine theories of intercultural contact and test their usefulness by applying them to world literature, nonfiction, and the visual arts; students in this class also employ their own intercultural experiences as evidence.[1] Somewhat similar approaches have been taken with partial credit reentry courses offered at other institutions. Marquette University's Office of International Education (2019) offers such a seminar under the title Bridging the Local and Global: Unpacking Your Study Abroad Experience. Purdue University's College of Liberal Arts (2018) does something similar with its Study Abroad Reentry Seminar. These courses are intended to help students reflect on their learning and growth.

In some cases, more disciplinary-anchored courses have been envisioned. For example, at Connecticut College the anthropology department requires students to take a predeparture and a reentry course (both partial credit), described thus:

> Collaboratively designed by all of the anthropology faculty, the course brings together students who are preparing to travel with those who are currently abroad and those who have just returned. Our readings, discussions, and assignments are meant to better equip participants with the concepts and tools needed to apply an anthropological lens to living and traveling outside of the U.S. At the same time, we seek to provide recent travelers with opportunities to discuss, process, and reflect on a semester's worth of experiences gained while abroad. (Graesch, Benoit, Steiner, Bennett, & Black, 2017, para. 1)

Storytelling is another useful tool. A creative travel writing class, for example, allows students to distill their experiences into a narrative, requiring them to focus on what was the most meaningful during their program. The process encourages them to reflect on an experience, make sense of it, and ultimately communicate it effectively to others. The task is challenging. After all, part of the exhilaration of off-campus study comes from the onslaught of new experiences, which typically arrive faster than one can record or process them. A creative writing class focusing on recent experiences impels students to organize their jumble of memories into more coherent narratives, variously documented by notes, photos, music, e-mails, blogs, and videos. Some programs explicitly encourage archiving such resources during the program as preparation for the reflective work that will follow. Moreover, techniques in multimedia storytelling are moving into the mainstream, becoming topics at professional conferences and workshops, especially in the field of off-campus study.

Although the concept of storytelling may sound soft to the ears of scientists or social scientists, crafting experience into a narrative can be a crucial step for students struggling to distill what their off-campus experience meant to them. It helps them relate their experience and its lessons to peers, professors, and even potential employers in a concise and digestible form. Indeed, anecdotes are often the most meaningful mechanism for the transmission of knowledge—a fact we exemplify throughout this book through the inclusion of student and faculty stories. Typically such anecdotes include implicit or explicit reflection. For instance, one of our students wrote of her squeamishness in a women's bathhouse in Istanbul, where patrons are nude. She said she "went native" during this experience, forcing herself beyond her own norms and comfort zone. Although she described the scene tastefully and with humor, it clearly shook her, and she concluded with the following:

> As I sipped my tea, I reflected on the day. I was proud of us being able to face our fears and what now seemed like our conservative U.S. culture. But then I thought once again about that last part. Americans were surely no more conservative than traditional Turkish Muslims that have enjoyed these bathhouses since Ottoman times. Or were they? Do these two cultures have very different definitions of what it means to be conservative?
>
> Was it possible that there was another dimension to this Turkish experience that I had been missing all along? Although these women didn't flaunt their bodies in the streets, they were not uncomfortable being fully themselves with their friends and family of the bathhouse. Perhaps they respected their bodies. Perhaps, they weren't ashamed of their bodies. In any case, I was glad that I could face my fears and somehow experience this bathing process rooted in their culture alongside them. (Major in business, study tour in Turkey)

The visit to the bathhouse challenged this student's notions about privacy and the body, as well as her assumptions about Turkish conservatism and exotic practices. Because readers of her story follow her through the experience, they gain many of the benefits vicariously.

This young woman is far from alone. Although many of our students feel their off-campus program has been transformative, they often struggle to express exactly what that means or how it happened. Storytelling and other reflective exercises can help them extract academic lessons from the personal growth that is so key to the experience.

Storytelling can be effectively incorporated into another reflection-based tool gaining acceptance on U.S. campuses: ePortfolios, also known as electronic portfolios or online portfolios. These ePortfolios provide students with a mechanism for assembling evidence from disparate parts of their off-campus experience. Because they are curated by the student, the process encourages reflection about connections that may not be obvious to the casual observer. And because they draw from many aspects of the students' time away (not only courses but also personal encounters, activities, sights, impressions, etc.), they can be better suited to capturing the holistic nature of that experience.

Moreover, ePortfolios reflect student development over time. They typically begin before departure and continue throughout the off-campus study experience and, in some cases, throughout the student's entire college career and beyond (see Batson et al., 2017). With careful guidance and advising, ePortfolios can support students in collecting evidence and articulating global learning goals and accomplishments off and on campus. They serve as digital archives of student work and reflections focused on global experience. In addition to being an asset for anyone contemplating a career that values intercultural and linguistic competency, ePortfolios can help students do many things—from integrating curricular, cocurricular, and extracurricular programming to providing a bridge to postgraduation careers. They also provide a means for collecting multimedia evidence of global learning during a program, allowing one to use that evidence as a basis for reflection and presentation. Moreover, they help students develop digital presentation skills. Finally, an ePortfolio can provide opportunities for assessment by converting the lived history of a study experience into a medium that can be evaluated, thereby helping institutional leaders measure the impact of off-campus study when allocating resources and making curricular decisions.[2]

It is not necessary for an ePortfolio to end in the reentry phase, focusing exclusively on the off-campus experience; it can continue to document global learning far into the student's future.[3] The usual challenges, such as the resources in time and money, continue to apply. However, compared to many other options (e.g., dedicated courses serving relatively small numbers of students), ePortfolios hold the promise of being scalable to large numbers of students, who can each flex the format of the portfolio to suit their particular needs. For a further discussion on ePortfolios and integrative assessment tools, see chapter 7.

Disciplinary Skills and Knowledge

By and large, students seek personal growth during off-campus study, whereas departmental faculty want academic development. Language department instructors expect students to return with enhanced skills in Cantonese or Mandarin, Spanish, and German; anthropology instructors hope for keen ethnographic skills; and those in math need students to be ready for vector calculus or set theory. Most departments hope their returnees will have climbed a rung or two on the ladder of their major. For students returning from programs not related to their majors, department faculty may merely hope they haven't lost too much ground.

In any case, the way department members make use of their returning students' skills will vary according to discipline and departmental culture. Certain strategies or tools might help students apply their learning within their ongoing studies, even as they become increasingly specialized in their major.

Some skills, such as language proficiency, have a clear and direct application in courses, but many others are harder to identify. According to the principle evoked in the previous chapter—namely, that postprogram reintegration is partly a predeparture concern—some of the work may have been done in advance. At a minimum, students will know how the courses they took while away will or will not apply to the major. Moreover, in cases where communication with students during the program away is possible, the research projects students undertook while off-campus may dovetail with opportunities in the home department to be developed further—for example, as a senior project.

Faculty might accommodate their returning students' new interests and skills in other ways, some of which are low-overhead endeavors involving minor tweaks to existing courses. Hackles will likely rise among professors when customization manifests itself in its most extreme form—the much-dreaded independent study, a personalized course for which the instructor receives little or no credit, and that the instructor may never have the opportunity to repeat. Happily, there are other versions of such tailoring, and they are far easier to sustain. Typically this involves professors adapting an assignment in an existing course to allow students to pursue work started while they studied off campus. In some courses students might be encouraged to use resources in languages they have studied, do further work on a research project they conducted while away, or engage in a comparative study that relates to the region or culture where their program took place. In some cases, if there are sufficient numbers of students with similar or complementary experiences, group projects in a class may even be adapted.

This kind of accommodation-by-adaptation is a low-intensity way of folding off-campus work into the on-campus curriculum. It is even possible when the student's off-campus program was not directly related to the discipline of the upper-division course. For instance, when a biology major returns from an art program in Australia, the student may be especially motivated if the project on evolution is allowed to deal with Oceania. It's important to note that a small degree of personalization can have a large impact. Toral (2009) describes senior thesis projects that blend off-campus experience with carefully selected on-campus coursework, resulting in an academic and experiential synthesis.

In short, this technique of accommodation seeks to channel the energy and learning of the off-campus experience into existing structures. However, it doesn't happen automatically; professors need to think about which forms of accommodation are suitable for their courses and what modifications might be needed. For instance, if students are allowed to conduct some of their reading in a foreign language, they will not be able to read as much as they could if the texts were in English. Departments also need to advertise to students that such adaptations are possible; ideally, examples of work successfully accomplished by previous students could be provided. Announcing opportunities for drawing on one's off-campus experience, making it explicit in course syllabi or on departmental websites, serves to encourage it among students who have recently returned. Moreover, such announcements can also inspire students who have not yet studied away, showing them how off-campus study is part of an arc: If they choose to participate in off-campus studies, their experiences can feed back into their major.

Cross-Disciplinary Skills and Knowledge

Making an accommodation for the off-campus study experience in a major requires particular techniques and intentional participation from faculty in each department. Of course, not every department or faculty member will find time for this kind of work; moreover, the kind of accommodations we describe may be harder to implement in certain majors. Although it may at first seem counterintuitive to suggest that astronomy or computer science professors might adapt their assignments to profit from off-campus studies, it's far from impossible. A Carleton math professor noticed the following changes in students who participated in a math program in Budapest:

> Our students can take a full slate of mathematics courses and get a real feel for what graduate school in mathematics is like. Also, the Hungarians are known for their unique mathematical teaching style, which is a problems-based approach where the mathematics is taught by solving a sequence of problems, each building on the mathematical expertise gained from the previous. Students return to our classes with the mastery of much more mathematics, a new technique to approach writing proofs, and the understanding of what it means to be a mathematician. (D. Haunsperger, personal communication, January 29, 2018)

When the benefits are this substantial, it becomes attractive for professors to keep these benefits in mind as they design and teach courses. Moreover, students themselves acknowledge the cultural impact of their experience, even if their program purports not to include an explicit cultural component. According to one biology major who attended a program in Australia and New Zealand, "The immersion in the study of marine biology that this seminar provided gave me insight into the depth and interrelationships not only of ecosystems but also of people, organizations, neighbors, neighborhoods, institutions, municipalities, businesses."

Luckily, many students continue to take a large number of courses outside their major during the last year or two of their studies. At that point, institutional priorities may have lost ground to disciplinary ones (beginning with a student's transition from a general education adviser to a major one), but there are still many opportunities for curricular integration of off-campus study, especially for returning students.

In short, it's possible for the home institution to take a page from the book of off-campus study itself. As we argue in chapter 2, when they are well-designed, off-campus programs are far more integrated and integrative learning experiences than one typically finds on the home campus, and it's possible to begin replicating that integration at our institutions. A promising trend in the synthesis of off-campus and on-campus curricula is part of many institutions' internationalization efforts. Leask (2015) focuses on how one might find "a point of connection between broader institutional strategies and the student experience" (p. i).[4]

Courses like the creative writing class described earlier in this chapter seek to bridge the divide between the experiential and the academic. Other techniques exist, too, for weaving particular skills throughout the curriculum in ways that mirror the tight integration of the off-campus study experience itself. One widely recognized model for this kind of work is foreign languages across the curriculum (FLAC). Many institutions have found ways to broaden foreign language study beyond its traditional departments, embedding it in programs as diverse as history and physics.[5] FLAC thrives in a variety of forms, ranging from full-fledged subject courses (e.g., political science or philosophy) taught in a foreign language to so-called trailer sections serving as complementary labs for subject courses. Even more modest efforts can have an effect, too. For example, professors can dedicate a small amount of class time to discussing language issues in English, addressing such topics as the resonances that are lost when key terms are translated. Students who have studied in non-English environments are already used to the omnipresence and pervasiveness of language, and FLAC gives them an opportunity to further their understanding of it.

Beyond language, however, FLAC is of special interest as a model for other ways of integrating work across the curriculum. As we show in chapter 5, language and culture are different expressions of the same thing. In many institutions, FLAC has been replaced by CLAC (cultures and languages across the curriculum); CLAC recognizes the importance of the teaching of culture even when foreign language is not included.

The point here is not, however, merely to promote the study of language and culture. Instead we mean to demonstrate the interconnectedness among disciplines as well as to show how problems are embedded in physical and cultural environments. FLAC and CLAC show how language skills and cultural study may be threaded through disciplines beyond their traditional language department venues.

Threading suggests a thin strand of study that links courses over time, but it's not the only option for the inclusion of off-campus experience in advanced work. More intensive models also exist. An alternative to the metaphor of a thread is the *knot*: One can form clusters of several students with very different off-campus study experiences, helping them focus on one particular transregional issue.

Let us explain this idea further. We mention in chapter 1 that one of the goals of higher education must surely be to prepare students to deal with the enormously complex issues we find in the world today, such as infectious disease, scarcity of water, food security, immigration, human rights, or climate change. These topics are not the purview of any single discipline, and in traditional departmental categories it's hard to see where any of them might be discussed in a holistic way. It might be assumed at the outset that subjects like climate change or infectious disease are scientific problems relegated to the STEM departments, or that others, like terrorism, must be dealt with in political science. However, the reality is much more complex. If we take the single example of the spread of HIV/AIDS around the world, along with the problem of its treatment, it becomes apparent that no single field has a monopoly on the relevant knowledge. To understand and address such a topic, input is required from a variety of fields including, at the very least, the following:

- Biology, to understand the spread of the disease and the technical challenges to the development of effective treatments and protections
- Economics, to analyze the hurdles that stand in the way of the widespread distribution of these treatments, such as wages, transportation, or the availability of refrigeration
- Religion, to elucidate the cultural requirements and interdictions governing sexual practices
- Psychology, to understand the psychological effects of the disease or the effects of losing parents or loved ones to it
- Language, to allow one to communicate with the afflicted parties and with policymakers, as well as to read or listen to significant documents that may not be available in English
- Political science, to determine the will and wherewithal of governing bodies or nongovernmental organizations to meet the needs of the people

This list is incomplete, and in the case of other topics it might be rewritten completely. The point is merely that the study of global problems will require interdisciplinary understanding that includes intensely local knowledge across national and even regional boundaries. No single discipline will suffice. Coming to terms with such issues typically requires a deep understanding of regional languages, cultures, and various forms of knowledge, in addition to expertise in particular scientific, humanistic, and socioscientific fields.

No one class can bring together all these elements. No single student could master them. No professor exists who could teach them. Topics such as these truly global topics require rethinking our understanding of disciplines and interdisciplinarity. The time-honored model of disciplinary study, in which the student disciple marches ever deeper into a community of specialists, is no longer appropriate for certain kinds of study. However, the popular model of interdisciplinarity—in which a student straddles two or even three disciplines—sacrifices depth for breadth, which is also a cost we cannot always afford. The trick is to maintain depth and breadth at the same time.

There is in fact a way to square this circle. Following a method used widely in certain organizations, although too rarely in our institutions of higher learning, we can promote the effectiveness of cross-disciplinary teams. In this model, interdisciplinarity is not the responsibility of the individual; it is incarnated by the group. A course could be devised around a global theme that draws advanced student specialists from many fields. The idea would not be to dilute the specificity of the major but rather to incite students to greater depth *while communicating their work to specialists in other fields.* Incidentally they would learn more about the connections among disciplines, as well as about each discipline's blind spots. By bringing together advanced specialists in various fields, especially when some members have extensive knowledge of local conditions, we would create an environment where general knowledge also has sufficient depth to render complex problems tractable.

A number of institutions are now offering courses in global issues that require the participation of students and professors from multiple disciplines. The Mount Holyoke McCulloch Center for Global Initiatives (n.d.-b) sponsors team-taught courses on global topics that seek to "promote cross-disciplinary teaching with a focus on comparative perspectives"; it also sponsors a biennial multiday conference on global challenges. Middlebury College's (n.d.) Rohatyn Center for Global Affairs sponsors a similar course and conference; it also includes cocurricular activities, such as its International and Global Studies Colloquium (discussed further in chapter 9).

The advantages of efforts such as these are enormous. They allow students with local or regional knowledge of domestic and international sites to come together around a common topic; this alone helps to underscore the interconnections of the local and the global. Because the students hail from many different disciplines, they learn to communicate specialized knowledge across disciplinary boundaries, translating their own discipline into an academic lingua franca. Moreover, this kind of class replicates the multiplier effect of multiple high-impact practices that we discussed in chapter 2—namely, common intellectual experiences, learning communities, undergraduate research, and, potentially, collaborative assignments, often in a context that focuses on diversity and global learning.

Courses of this sort replicate many of the advantages of first-year seminars, but they do so much later in the curriculum—after students have been immersed in their disciplines. They thus blend general education with deep knowledge in disciplines.

The number of topics that lend themselves to such an approach is large. For instance, a comparative course focusing on immigration (at the time of this writing) could easily draw on situations in the United States, the Middle East, Europe, and Asia. The disciplinary knowledge one could bring to bear on the topic might include economics, political science, religion, statistics, and climate science, not to mention knowledge of local languages and cultures. One might imagine a course on the loss of cultural artifacts (from the looting after the fall of the Hussein regime in Iraq), or a class focusing on the destruction of archeological sites perpetrated by the Islamic State, or even a seminar on terrorism. Models for such courses are plentiful, and the results are promising; they help students recognize the value of the knowledge and skills obtained while off campus, and they provide opportunities for further development.

Glimpsing Beyond the Four-Year Horizon

Finally, just as predeparture students benefit from understanding how their off-campus experience can be integrated into their curricular work upon return, they will also profit from understanding how their experience might connect to future careers. As administrators of institutions of higher education think more about the college-to-career pipeline, they are increasingly highlighting pathways, which illustrate how various experiences, curricular and cocurricular, lead to certain kinds of positions. (For more on pathways, see chapter 3; the discussion is continued in chapter 6 in the context of engaged citizenship.) In addition to the statistical representations in such projects, students benefit from specific examples, especially narratives from alumni about how their off-campus experiences helped them find their career.

These tools are powerful. Here, for example, is one alumna's description of how her series of study away and study abroad experiences influenced her evolving career opportunities:

I participated in the program in Peru in spring of 2013, received a Service Internship in International Development to stay and work in Peru teaching English during the following summer of 2013, participated in a winter break program called Comparative Agroecology in the U.S. and China in the Fall/Winter of 2013, and finally I took part in the Border Studies Program in Tucson, Arizona, and Mexico in the fall of 2014. In sum, I studied off-campus for a total of 36 weeks, with 28 of those weeks counting for credit and 8 of those weeks on an internship. Although all of these experiences were vastly different, the one thing that ties them all together is that each of my study abroad opportunities had a service-learning or community engagement component. In Peru, I volunteered weekly for an organization working on college access for youth in very poverty-stricken neighborhoods of Lima, that following summer I lived in a *pueblo joven* or shantytown outside of Lima teaching English to kids and adults and leading their community garden program, through the Agroecology program I got to visit and learn from farmers in both Minnesota and China and exchange knowledge about sustainable farming practices, and finally, through the Border Studies program I was able to work alongside immigrant rights activists to improve the circumstances for undocumented immigrants in the U.S. and hear about immigrants' experiences on every leg of the journey including in detention centers, migrant shelters, and after being deported. Through these experiences, I have seen social justice work in many different contexts, which has made me a better community organizer here in the Midwest. With these experiences in tow, I am excited to head to Lincoln, Nebraska this fall to start my career in social justice and community organizing as an Economic Justice Fellow at the Appleseed Center for Law in the Public Interest. (American studies major, program in Peru)

Narratives such as this should not only appear on career center websites but also be heralded by departments as major success stories. Even better, career sessions on campus (often cosponsored with departments) can bring students face-to-face with visiting alumni who have benefited specifically from their off-campus work. In this way, the integration of off-campus study in the undergraduate experience is not merely an arc traversing the student's four-year degree; it extends deep into the future.

Notes

1. In this course, Professor Éva Posfay combines the study of intercultural concepts and frameworks with a great diversity of texts that range from readings in social psychology, postcolonial theory, world literature, film, and world music.

2. Exactly what students derive from study abroad is hard to say. See comments on the gaps between aspiration and performance in Green (2005).

3. A similar idea of documenting development of plurilingualism and intercultural awareness and competence informed the European Language Portfolio initiative developed by the Language Policy Unit of the Council of Europe (2018).

4. Leask's (2015) differentiation among formal, informal, and hidden curricula is especially helpful when imagining curriculum integration of study abroad because it parallels the heterogeneity of the study abroad experience itself. The *formal curriculum*, which is defined by Leask as courses, syllabi, and requirements on campus, corresponds to the academic and experiential learning in a study abroad program. The *informal curriculum*, such as social activities, support services, and academic and nonacademic peer interactions, aligns with the living experiences in a host country, such as homestays, daily routines, and interactions with host nationals. Finally, the *hidden curriculum*, which is implicit messages in the formal and informal curricula on campus through textbook selection, various student orientations, and academic rules and policies, is reminiscent of the iceberg analogy of culture that refers to underlying contexts, as well as collective and individual assumptions, that define the study of and in another culture. The tip of the iceberg symbolizes the observable behaviors in a culture but signals underlying cultural foundations that have a deeper meaning. The integration of the study abroad experience still seems complex but may be easier to achieve when we think of the curriculum along the lines that Leask describes. It simply provides more points of entry through which integration into the curriculum (and the campus culture) can occur: academics, student life, student activities, and so on.

5. Strategies for offering FLAC, sometimes known as LAC, or conflated with CLAC, are widespread. For an international perspective, see Grenfell (2002). A good introduction to the practice in the United States is Suderman and Cisar (1992).

5

A WORLD OF DIFFERENCE

The Culture Question

*I think I grew most in that I was able to look at the U.S. from an outsider's perspective,
which is a very hard opportunity to come by while in the U.S. Most, if not all, countries
look to the U.S. to make global decisions and intervene in international issues. The
U.S. is then either labeled as rash for making the decision or not strong enough for not
attacking the issue. Denmark on the other hand is able to just follow other countries'
decisions without a real leadership role. This power the U.S. possesses is both good and
bad. I had never had that realization before and it was pretty strange to think about.*

—Biochemistry major, program in Denmark

The previous chapters focus on the integration of off-campus programs
in the curriculum. But what about the integration of these programs
within the communities and cultures where they take place? To what
extent is such an integration possible or desirable? What purpose might it
serve? To what extent would students benefit from interaction with the local
culture, and why? Certainly there are formal and professionalized ways to
engage with these communities (as we will discuss in chapter 6), but in this
chapter we focus on broader questions of cultural practice.

Many professors are familiar with student ignorance about the world.
It's no secret that most Americans have a poor sense of world geography, politics, economy, and religion. (For more on American students' lack of proficiency in geography, see chapter 3.) Indeed, it is hard to discuss the value
of off-campus study without addressing the blindness that in part results
from growing up inside a world superpower. Young Americans often fail to
see outward through the glare of the global spotlights, real or imagined, that
are focused on the United States. Consequently, these students don't always
know very much about what lies outside U.S. borders—or even within them.

Moreover, students are like most of us; they are blind to their own blindness, and they experience the discovery of their ignorance as an epiphany.

Their limited vision is partly a result of American media, which are often focused inward, showing little about international concerns or even about domestic minority cultures. But it's also part and parcel of being human; people have a hard time seeing anything that doesn't mesh with their preexisting worldview. Psychology refers to this tendency as *naïve realism*, and it goes hand in hand with *confirmation bias*, that is, the tendency to see new evidence as confirmation of one's existing beliefs—and to fail to see anything that challenges those beliefs (see Kolbert, 2017). A simple version of this tendency was popularized by the invisible gorilla experiment, where fully half of those who view a videotaped basketball game fail to notice the presence of a man in a gorilla suit who strolls through the middle of the court (Chabris & Simons, 1999). According to the researchers, the experiment demonstrated two things: "that we are missing a lot of what goes on around us, and that we have no idea that we are missing so much" (para. 3). In this case, the appearance of a gorilla is so incongruous with what we expect for the setting that we miss it entirely—despite its obviousness.

Changing how someone views the world, to actually see something radically new, is not just hard, it's potentially frightening. Perhaps that's why naïve realism plays such a large role in hair-raising books and movies. For example, an episode of the classic television program *The Twilight Zone*, titled "A World of Difference," illustrates this well (Matheson & Post, 1960). The story begins with businessman Arthur Curtis entering his office one morning, greeting his secretary and starting his work of the day, paging through contracts and checking his vacation plans. All goes smoothly until he attempts to place a phone call, only to find there's no dial tone. He taps the switch hook and tries again to dial, giving the receiver a puzzled stare before returning it to its cradle. Something is not right. Then a voice from off-camera cries *Cut!* and when Curtis wheels around, he discovers that his office is open on one side: a wall is missing. He blinks into bright lights, making out the shape of cameras, then the silhouettes of a film crew. A script girl strides by. It turns out that Arthur Curtis is on a movie set, and he is learning this at the same time we do. It turns out he is not the person he thought he was; instead of being an individual starring in his own life, Curtis is merely an actor with a bit part in a much larger show. An entirely new world, the existence of which he had never suspected, lies on the other side of the floodlights.

The rest of the episode follows Curtis as he charges home to find his wife, hoping to reconfirm his beliefs—evidence that will shore up his initial understanding of a simpler universe. His efforts are to no avail; by the end he has come to the painful conclusion that there is, in fact, a world of difference, one that *resembles* his world but is in fact far vaster and more complex.[1]

We are not suggesting that off-campus study rubs elbows with the super-natural, or that it pits an artificial world against a real one, or even that it contains and domesticates a simpler existence in which students are trapped. But as a partial parallel this tale is revealing. What's notable is the way a pow-erfully dislocating experience can lead to a more profound understanding of an initial reality (also known as *home*). In fact, study after study identifies such confrontations with difference as the key to transformative learning.[2] When they cross into a new context, learners find themselves disoriented, confronted with dissonance. Many of the rules they had assumed to be natu-ral and universal turn out to be local and constructed, which implies they could also be constructed in different ways. The discovery of different (and yet legitimate and functioning) cultural logics can be profoundly dislocat-ing, disturbing, and revelatory. One of the challenges in advising students for off-campus studies consists of identifying programs that will provide the right level of dislocation for a particular student's makeup and experience, that is neither too much nor too little—the so-called Goldilocks zone, where students will be challenged but can still succeed.

A natural human reaction to dissonance is denial and resistance. We dis-count difference as merely weird, viewing it as unenlightened and primitive, or conversely as mysterious and exotic. However, after these initial impres-sions, and in the best cases, a transition occurs. We begin to detect the pres-ence of patterns, leading to some understanding of the new cultural grammar surrounding us. The system may be different from the one we grew up in, but it's not automatically worse or better. As in *The Twilight Zone*, we pick up a phone (which is always a terrifying device for travelers in foreign lands), only to find that normal modes of communication don't work; we need to interact differently. We undergo many of stages of culture shock, especially frustration, adaptation, and eventually (although sadly in Arthur Curtis's case) a certain degree of acceptance.

Despite these parallels, Arthur Curtis differs from our students in one crucial regard: He experienced his revelations against his will, whereas our students volunteer for it.

Not all programs consider cultural integration important or even desir-able. The director of a program in geology, for instance, might only be inter-ested in rocks, or the participants in an art history program might spend all their time in museums. Moreover, the professors leading such programs may have little knowledge of the cultures in which they find themselves, leaving them unprepared to facilitate any cultural integration or reflection. In such cases, interactions with human beings, beyond the requisite guides, hoteliers, drivers, and waiters, might be perceived as slowing things down or getting in the way.

This kind of mentality is especially prevalent on short-term island programs—those two- to four-week faculty-led programs where students participate in all their classes and activities as a block. Although some short-term programs are excellent (see chapter 3), limitations in time, money, and opportunity multiply the challenges of developing high-quality ones. On some campuses, administrators have mandated lofty targets for participation rates in study away and study abroad, but without giving much thought to the academic and institutional goals and without supporting these targets with increases in staff or budgets. This leaves harried professionals striving to crank students through an off-campus study mill, which risks producing little in the way of significant results. It's already challenging to handle the recruitment, organization, logistics, finances, health, safety, and curriculum for such programs; the idea of adding thoughtful cultural integration into this mix without commensurate increases in resources make any study abroad professional weak in the knees.

Moreover, the structure of many programs can render meaningful cultural integration difficult. Powerful centripetal forces bind students together when they participate in the same program. Indeed, this bond can contribute to many of the high-impact practices we seek to promote: learning communities, common intellectual experiences, and collaborative assignments.

Nevertheless, we feel strongly that the radical dislocation that lies at the heart of successful off-campus study experiences demands at least some cultural integration. Failure to recognize this will turn an off-campus program into little more than a colonial expedition, like Napoleon's campaign in Egypt in 1798. (The scientists on that journey were famously keen on artifacts but wished there weren't so many Egyptians getting in the way.) There are, of course, serious ethical considerations to such an enterprise (discussed in chapters 6 and 8), and they are matched by pedagogical ones. Any off-campus program that fails to engage meaningfully with the host population will have forfeited important tools for learning.

Interactions with other people allow us to acquire important lessons of difference and tolerance. In what follows, we make the case for various forms of cultural interaction, and in chapter 8 we will discuss the tools for measuring their outcomes.

Language as Culture

First of all, what do we mean by *difference*, and what is it good for? To take an easy point of departure, difference is simply the opposite of sameness, the comfortable and routine logic of everyday life, the myriad details and habits and beliefs and perspectives we take for granted. There's no guarantee that travel away from the home campus will challenge these patterns. Indeed, some people shy away from any such disruption. This is the situation Anne Tyler (1985) lampoons in her novel *The Accidental Tourist*. Her main character specializes in guidebooks for Americans who hate to travel and therefore seek hotels and restaurants recreating the cocoon of home, catering to all their culinary, customary, and linguistic habits. For them the ideal voyage consists of finding everything the same.

This gravitation toward comfort is not limited to fiction. For instance, we sometimes speak of the Club Med mentality, a reference to the French tour operator that specializes in posh tourist communities set in exotic locales, allowing what it calls its *villagers* to remain in established social circles while enjoying flourishes of local color. Day excursions are made to neighboring sights and markets, but by night the visitors return to the compound. It's not so very different from the situation described in the satirical newspaper *The Onion*, which once mocked study abroad as "dick-around abroad programs that give students the chance to hang out and do jack shit in another country" ("Report: More Colleges Offering Dick-Around Abroad Programs," 2010, para. 1).

Unfortunately, even if we dial down the caricature, some students manage to turn even well-designed off-campus experiences into moveable expat feasts. They resist the dislocation that lies at the heart of meaningful study, turning the new location into decor, a mere backdrop of difference in front of which they continue to "perform sameness." Rather than engaging with the culture, they watch things "from the veranda," viewing the foreign culture through what Ogden (2007) has called "the colonial student gaze" (pp. 39–40).

That said, students aren't the only ones to gaze colonially. Our institutions have the responsibility to structure, vet, and assess the programs they organize or sponsor, making sure that learning objectives, including those that may be part of the "hidden curriculum" (Leask, 2015, p. 8), are achieved. If our programs don't provide opportunities and incentives for students to move beyond their comfort zone, we can hardly fault these students for failing to make serious cultural connections. A particularly problematic example might be the now-defunct Scholar Ship (2017) program that ran in 2007 and 2008, placing some 200 students aboard a modified Royal Caribbean Cruise ship for semester-length educational cruises ("Scholar Ship," 2017). Hard-core advocates of cultural integration are already skeptical enough of so-called island programs; one can only imagine the number of eye rolls over a cruise ship program that made brief stops at various ports of call.[3]

Quality programs are an institutional decision. Luckily, most educators want their students to go far beyond superficial and distanced interactions.

But how do we achieve that goal? What sort of difference do we want our students to encounter, and afterward, what do we want them to do with it?

Let's begin with an extreme and obvious case of cultural learning, long associated with off-campus study: foreign language. This is not just a throwback to the origins of study abroad; it remains vital and important to today's students (see chapter 1 for a brief history of the connections between study abroad and foreign language departments). The 2008 StudentPoll showed that more than 70% of college-bound students "either plan to learn and speak the language [of the country where they will study abroad] fluently or at least expect to learn enough of the language to converse comfortably with others" (American Council on Education, Art & Science Group, & College Board, 2008, p. 4). Moreover, their interest corresponds to real needs in the workplace. The Bureau of Labor Statistics (2018) predicted that the job market for translators and interpreters will expand by 18%, a rate identified as "much faster than the average" (para. 5) from 2016 to 2026.

Like most subjects, foreign language can to some extent be taught in a classroom. We know how to convey the rudiments of French or Russian or Japanese on a campus in Seattle or Austin or Miami. However, advanced mastery of a language is much harder to achieve without an immersion experience, a fact that helps justify many study abroad programs. A stay in the country where a foreign language is spoken provides crucial opportunities. First, it places students in situations where language use is intensive and real, where everyday life provides hours of informal language instruction, and where learning the vocabulary and grammar can have immediate consequences. Second, it embeds language within the much broader culture of which it is a part, activating the language in a new way and providing a privileged connection to other cultural practices.

Foreign language acquisition provides a general model for understanding our interactions with cultural difference. Monolingual students typically take their native tongue for granted. Words tumble from their lips or stream from their pens or keyboards without triggering any reflection on the operation of language itself. Speakers wield their native language unconsciously, just as they move their hand or arm without deliberate thought. For example, English may seem so ingrained in our students that they have a hard time believing any other language could play the same role. The fact that in 2015 only 7% of American college students enrolled in a foreign language class nationwide simply underscores this reliance on English (Friedman, 2015).

Learning a foreign language forces students to think about language explicitly, turning the transparency of their native tongue murky. It not only provides an entry point for contact with a foreign population but also introduces students to a significantly different lexicon and grammar. One of the fringe benefits of this exercise is a growing awareness of the structures and strictures of one's own language, to which one becomes increasingly sensitive. When studying a foreign language, students regularly comment that they learn as much about their native tongue as they do about French or Hindi or Japanese.

This is the key point: The difference we champion in off-campus study is not just outward-looking, focused on an encounter with what is new. It also consists of turning a fresh eye toward one's point of departure, viewing the familiar from a different angle and realizing that it, too, is a little bit foreign.

Learning a new language may even introduce new ways of thinking. In the 1930s a theory, which is often and somewhat hastily associated with Benjamin Lee Whorf and Edward Sapir, arose over linguistic relativity. The basic idea was that the language you speak determines to a large extent what you can say or even think. It was an attractive theory and thus readily adopted by many thinkers despite the lack of examples or evidence. Since then supporters of this hypothesis and its detractors have waged their battles, leading eventually to a state of compromise. Many linguists now acknowledge that some aspects of thought truly are influenced by the specific language one speaks, whereas other characteristics appear to be more or less universal.[4]

A simple example of how language can shape thought appears in the use of gender. Most people know that many tongues attribute gender to common nouns; it's one of those linguistic tics that seem to have been invented to puzzle and frustrate nonnative speakers. After all, why should a shoe or automobile be feminine? Is there something fundamentally masculine about a soccer ball? Why is it wrong to say *un fleur* in French or *die Boot* in German? Moreover, what does it matter? What purpose does linguistic gender serve, aside from keeping an army of language teachers employed, armed with red pens?

It turns out that it does make a difference. Deutscher (2010a) looked at the associations native speakers make based on gender. For instance, the word for *bridge* is masculine in French (*le pont*) and Spanish (*el puente*), but feminine in German (*die Brücke*). Researchers found that French and Spanish speakers tended to describe these products of engineering by so-called masculine adjectives—words like *strong* and *sturdy*—whereas Germans more readily portrayed them as *slender* or *elegant*. The same held for a slew of other gendered nouns, even when speakers were trained in a fabricated, artificial language and control groups were used (see Deutscher, 2010b).

This is not to imply that vocabulary or syntax will reveal everything about a culture's worldview. However, recent research in the area of neuroplasticity shows that the brains of speakers of different languages are wired differently and that this wiring can still change quite late in life (Ge et al., 2015).[5] Taken together, these ideas lend some credence to the sensation commonly expressed by bilingual speakers that the language they speak influences how and what they think. The fact that Danish distinguishes between maternal grandparents (*mormor* and *morfar*) and their paternal counterparts (*farmor* and *farfar*) certainly says something (although it's hard to specify exactly what) about family relationships. Similarly, some Australian aboriginal languages have no words for relative directions (right, left, etc.) and use only cardinal directions (north, south, etc.); in this way language reflects cultural conditions (Haviland, 1998). However, grammar and vocabulary are far less revelatory than particular usages that are tied to cultural practice. Students are traditionally stymied, for example, by the way different cultures draw lines between formal and informal uses (often in forms of address, such as the famous *tu* and *vous* distinction in French). Grappling with such a problem is not merely a linguistic endeavor; it's a terribly complicated lesson in the definition of the function of formality in a culture—a lesson that often leaves even native speakers struggling.

Nonverbal aspects of communication, which according to many scholars represent the bulk of our expression (Thompson, 2011), are more deeply cultural. These can include semilinguistic behaviors, such as accent and tone. For example, in English a statement like, "We're going to the store again" can be converted into a question tinged with frustration by adding a rising intonation and stressing the word *again*, a practice not followed in all languages. Facial expressions account for a healthy fraction of communication, and although they are somewhat more universal, they are also subject to regional inflections. Body language is even more culturally determined, including the appropriate distance to maintain between speakers, or the gestures used to indicate surprise or an insult. For example, in the United States, the signal that a person headed toward you should stop is to hold up your hands with palms facing outward, fingers splayed. In Japan you hold your forearms crossed in an X. Americans nod their head to indicate yes and shake it to mean no. In Bulgaria that practice is reversed.

All of this is to say that the border between language and culture is blurred. Programs conducted at English-speaking sites typically have the potential to explore nonlinguistic or semilinguistic cultural differences. Similarly, in sites where a foreign language is spoken but where the program itself includes no language component, considerable cultural engagement is still possible. Indeed, current thinking on foreign language instruction, drawing on the notion of multiliteracies, often emphasizes the importance of nonverbal elements of communication, including social practices, images, and expectations, all of which contribute to a student's literacy in a culture (Kumagai,

López-Sánchez, & Wu, 2016). As Nussbaum (1997) has advocated, it's important for students "to understand what it is like to see the world through the perspective of another language, an experience that quickly shows that human complexity and rationality are not the monopoly of a single linguistic community" (p. 62). It's crucial for our students to step outside the illusion of the obviousness or naturalness (and thus the superiority) of their linguistic and cultural standpoints. It's not an easy process because these assumptions have become hardwired in the brain. As Doidge (2007) put it,

> Cultural differences are so persistent because when our native culture is learned and wired into our brains, it becomes "second nature," seemingly as "natural" as many of the instincts we were born with. The tastes our culture creates—in foods, in type of family, in love, in music—often seem "natural," even though they may be acquired tastes. The ways we conduct nonverbal communication—how close we stand to other people, the rhythms and volume of our speech, how long we wait before interrupting a conversation—all seem "natural" to us, because they are so deeply wired in our brains. When we change cultures, we are shocked to learn that these customs are not natural at all. Indeed, even when we make a modest change, such as moving to a new house, we discover that something as basic as our sense of space, which seems so natural to us, and numerous routines we were not even aware we had, must slowly be altered while the brain rewrites itself. (p. 299)

In part, it is the job of off-campus study to encourage this rewriting.

This thinking points in two complementary directions. On the one hand, programs that do not explicitly privilege or require a foreign language are not magically relieved of the responsibility to engage with cultural literacy. Cultural difference is multimodal, and students can and should engage with it in whatever ways are possible, seeking to learn cultural discourses, that is, "ways of behaving, interacting, valuing, thinking, believing" (Gee, 1990, p. 143). Not to do so merely encourages the colonial student gaze.

The other hand concerns programs that already do aim to engage deeply with foreign language and culture. As we improve our understanding of how deeply the construction of meaning is embedded in social practices (extending well beyond the problems of grammar and syntax), we see what a rich ecosystem off-campus study provides for this kind of work. Only during off-campus study do students enjoy the opportunity to work with language in its multimodal forms, embedded in "the visual, the audio, the spatial, the behavioural, and so on" (Cope & Kalantzis, 2000, p. 5).

Where does language end and culture take over? At what point does grammar stop referring only to verbal behaviors and start to apply to body language and cultural habits? At some point, language acquisition blends with culture acquisition, which means that students can learn to *speak* a culture and make mistakes in it. Such was the case for a Chinese major whose knowledge of language and culture was double-edged, making an impressive interaction possible that ultimately left him humbled by his own cultural misunderstanding. Here's the rather long but touching story in the student's own words:

> The most important cultural connection I had was actually after the program. I stayed in China for about another two weeks. One day in Beijing I was talking to a man who sold bananas on the side of the road, right out of a large cart that he pulled himself. When I expressed interest initially, he assumed I didn't speak any Chinese and showed me a price on a calculator.
>
> When I began speaking in Chinese, he engaged me in a conversation about what the U.S. was like, if it was prosperous or not, what kinds of things people owned, and the influence of the U.S. on China. I asked him about where he lived in Beijing. As I suspected, his answer was that he lived along something called a hutong, which is basically a remnant of old Beijing style streets (narrow, serpentine roads with small houses very close together). The hutong that remain are preserved for historical purposes (but people still are allowed to live there) and not many remain.
>
> He also wanted a photograph with me. Now, many Chinese people want to take [a] photograph with foreigners but this man had no camera of his own. He wanted someone else to take a picture of *me* with *him*, presumably so I could have it. I didn't ask him why he wanted this picture but it was not a picture he could ever have. He wanted me to have a picture of us.
>
> After purchasing some bananas and discussing China and the U.S., the man offered me a cigarette. I have never smoked in my life and have no intention to start; however, after talking with this man about his life and my life and his country and my country, after talking to this man whose life could not really be any more different than mine, I almost regret it. (He probably was alive in October 1949 when Mao Zedong announced the People's Republic of China to the world. He probably has no computer, no Internet access, no microwave. He has probably never been to another country. If he went to school, it was probably sporadically so he could help his family on the farm.)
>
> Honestly, to my everlasting shame, I turned him down. I don't remember if I told him that I didn't smoke or if I just didn't want the cigarette but either way, the banana seller was sad. He was not disappointed or slightly let down. He was sad that this foreigner who had just engaged in a (surprisingly, to me anyway) deep conversation about our lives had turned him down. This foreigner had turned down a *cigarette*. The importance of the cigarette and its function within business and social interactions (particularly between men) in China cannot be overstated.

After all that, I had insulted this man.

I will always remember that banana seller. I don't know what I would say to him if I saw him again. But I will always both value and regret the interaction. I value our conversation and our connection. And I will regret turning down the banana seller's cigarette. (Chinese major, program in Beijing)

The bittersweet lesson derives from the student's realization of his own limitations: He speaks both the language and the cultural grammar of the banana seller, but he does so imperfectly. He misread the offer of the cigarette, seeing it originally in the way such a gesture might be interpreted among Americans—that is, as a small token of exchange, easily refused in a culture where most students don't smoke. In China, however, the cigarette is laden with meaning, and in this situation its refusal is a rebuff. Only by committing this cultural gaffe does the student come to understand the importance of this simple practice and in the process realize the gulf between the social logics of the United States and China. Error is once again shown to be the royal road to learning.

As we see, the seam between language and culture is smooth and almost imperceptible, a fact that has been reinforced by the Modern Language Association and the American Council on the Teaching of Foreign Languages (Modern Language Association Ad Hoc Committee on Foreign Languages, 2007). Starting with issues of grammar and syntax, we quickly find ourselves considering questions of formality or politeness; soon we are in the arena of shrugs, waves, and nods, which even students without language training can recognize and master. It's just a small step to see other habits and practices as part of the same cultural network: ways of walking, dressing, driving, eating, believing, and more. These are the multimodal aspects of culture.

The benefits of language study are relatively easy to identify. First and foremost, it helps students interact with the host community on its terms rather than theirs. It also provides a privileged access to different ways of thinking, gliding almost imperceptibly into other aspects of what might be considered the cultural universe. But foreign language is hardly a universal component of off-campus programs. For one thing, most domestic study away programs have no need (or opportunity) for foreign language use. Moreover, programs abound in English-speaking countries like the United Kingdom and Australia. Furthermore, many students lack the time or the aptitude to achieve a useful level of fluency in a foreign language, especially when those languages are among the most difficult. Does this mean that an English-only program in China or Senegal or Denmark is doomed to fail them?

Culture as Language

In fact, the same benefits hold (in somewhat different ways) for programs that lack a foreign language component but do include other forms of cultural engagement. Anthropologists have long recognized the existence of *cultural grammars*, which is to say the systems of behavior, practices, and expressions of different groups (whether in inner-city Detroit or central Beijing).[6] There may not be a textbook or a language lab for cultural grammars, but they do conform to logics that can be learned.

A cultural apprenticeship does not need to pass through language; for instance, here is a report from a geology major who had no knowledge of the indigenous tongue and whose program took place in New Zealand:

> In New Zealand . . . the culture is pretty similar to the U.S. . . . and English is the national language. . . . One connection or memory that stands out . . . was getting to visit and spend a night in a traditional *marae*. These are meeting houses for the . . . Māori people, and are located throughout New Zealand on traditionally native lands. We had this opportunity to visit with one of our Māori New Zealand professors, and visited his *marae*. When we arrived, there was a strict, traditional greeting. We walked in women first, men second, and the whole greeting was in the Māori language. It also included singing a song in Māori, and having one returned, and then performing the traditional welcome by touching faces with the Māori caretakers of the *marae*. It was a special night, and opened my eyes to the past conflicts between native people and outside invaders, much like some of the U.S. history. The other cultural connections that stand out to me took place after the program when I worked on a rural farm, and lived and worked with native New Zealanders for a week. Becoming part of their family, and learning more about the country and people. The decision to work on a farm during my last week was the best decision I made in New Zealand, and made me appreciate the culture more—a great end to the study/trip. (Geology major, program in New Zealand)

Gradually we see how one can apply the same logic to culture that we previously applied to language: learning a foreign culture opens connections to other peoples and mind-sets. Moreover, the dislocation produced by straddling cultures encourages us to reflect on our own native way of life. This means that once we have learned to inhabit a new point of view, we have a standpoint for examining our point of departure. In the terms of the Arthur Curtis episode of *The Twilight Zone* (Matheson & Post, 1960), we can experience a world of difference, which is what a linguistics major reported about her experience in Mali:

> In Mali . . . I stuck out like a sore thumb, and nothing I did, whether
> it was adopt local dress, hair, or language, could change that. I got used
> to be[ing] stared at in the streets, being singled out in the market, being
> charged double the prices—solely because I was a white foreigner. It's
> something I've never even thought about in the States—I've never been
> on the receiving end of that kind of attention. It was eye-opening, in more
> ways than one. It made me realize what some minorities go through in the
> U.S. every day. . . . While the situations certainly weren't identical (in Mali,
> people routinely called me "white person" or "white woman" in the streets,
> and had no qualms talking about skin color; in the U.S., subjects like that
> are overtly taboo), it was enough to make me realize this was a side of life
> I had never experienced before. (Linguistics major, program in Mali)

To avoid the Club Med experience, off-campus study needs considerable
cultural contact, which in many cases might include language. In others it
may focus on practices, habits, traditions, and customs, each of which has
its own forms of vocabulary and syntax. This is not the place to rehearse the
specific pedagogies for accomplishing meaningful cultural integration (the
resources for this are plentiful),[7] but it's important to acknowledge that experiences of this sort are just as crucial for science or business students as they
are for anthropology and religion majors (see Goldoni, 2015; Kelly, 2009a,
2009b). Although it's possible for certain disciplines to ignore the local culture (the way a biology program might focus only on flora), students yearn
for the personal interactions that justify their presence in a new location.
The cultural connections are crucial for the experience to resonate and be
meaningful, and their absence results in disappointment, as a math major
discovered and recounts in the following:

> I actually found that my program did not really promote a significant cul-
> tural connection, which I found rather disappointing. We stayed in dorms
> and had classes with only the other American students on my trip. Many
> of the people staying in [our location] over the summer were in fact tourists
> themselves, so it was difficult to build a real social, cultural connection in
> that sense. (Math major, program in Great Britain)

It's not surprising that this disappointing experience took place in Great
Britain. Too often we assume that intentional cultural integration isn't needed
for English-speaking locations because there's no language barrier. What is
ignored in these cases is the vast cultural barrier separating the students from
the communities they live in, where they may have few opportunities to make
meaningful connections. What's unfortunate about such missed opportunities is how easily a cultural connection could be introduced.

One instructive example of how small changes in structure can have outsize impacts comes from a Carleton program that inadvertently offered a controlled experiment. For the first half of the term, the program took place in London, where the students lived together in apartments. Although the program included many classes, it offered no facilitated engagement with the host community, for it was assumed that English-speaking students could do this on their own. The second half of the program took place in Seville, and although about half the students spoke no Spanish, this leg of the trip included a homestay and a civic engagement project with a local school. Several students noted the marked difference of the second half of the program: even if they could not speak Spanish, students found the community contact extraordinarily meaningful. In the program's next iteration, the director introduced cultural integration during the London portion of the trip as well.

This is why many program administrators work hard to integrate students into local communities. In Denmark, for example, American students studying at DIS Study Abroad in Scandinavia can opt to live with Danish students or they can choose a homestay with a Danish family. Some sending institutions rightly insist on a culturally integrated housing option, and the students who take this step, immersing themselves culturally, consistently report higher levels of satisfaction.

The lesson is that even modest levels of cultural interaction can have a large impact, and students have a right to expect some of these experiences, even in short-term programs. Moreover, it would be wise for program directors and administrators to realize that culture rarely seeps into student experience through passive osmosis, and even English-language programs based in English-speaking locations require deliberate engineering for cultural interaction to occur. In fact, English-language programs may be the most in need of specific interventions in order to defamiliarize what students at first think is cultural sameness.

It is worth mentioning that cultural learning is not alien to what we already strive for with on-campus experiences—for example, when we encourage interdisciplinarity. Interdisciplinarity requires understanding different logics and discourses, while realizing that different disciplines can view problems in wholly different ways. This isn't so different from off-campus programs, where students often take courses that are in some way interconnected, perhaps focusing on different aspects of a culture; in any case they are embedded in a material and cultural reality of extraordinary complexity that replicates a kind of interdisciplinarity. Students who are already comfortable with interdisciplinary approaches may be more receptive to different (often foreign) perspectives. Given the complexities of the issues they encounter in their host community, different modes of inquiry and different pedagogical models (e.g., field study, service-learning, internships, and other informal curricular experiences) may be harnessed to enhance learning. In this way, one of the benefits of off-campus study may be a greater receptivity to different learning models back on the home campus, including an increased ability on the part of students to sustain multidisciplinary work and wield different tools for teaching and learning. In this way, one benefit of off-campus study may be the way it subsequently alters our students' interaction with their home culture, expanding the way they can address complex issues in their future classes or careers.

In addition to our attempts to help students bridge different disciplinary cultures, most of us are engaged in urgent work to help students deal more successfully with personal and cultural differences on our campuses. We have profound and sometimes profoundly troubling discussions about campus climate in which we encourage students to speak and listen across the divides of ethnicity, gender, social class, religion, political affiliation, and more. These issues are not so different from those encountered during domestic study away or study abroad, where additional forms of difference (national, linguistic, cultural) may also have to be negotiated. In this way, the work we do in intercultural understanding on campus is an excellent preparation for off-campus study—and vice versa.

We don't mean to suggest that cultural integration needs to become the focus of every off-campus study program. Far from it. Many programs are not primarily about the local communities, and we're not suggesting that all course syllabi need to be redirected to issues of culture. Many courses can easily be tweaked to take some advantage of cultural surroundings, but the most important social connections will typically occur outside the classroom. That's where program administrators can help students develop meaningful connections through living arrangements (e.g., homestays), gatherings, service-learning projects, and so on. Students will learn the most about the linguistic and cultural grammars where they live through these kinds of extracurricular activities.

Cultural Worldviews

It's through cultural interactions that we combat the naïve realism of students, disturbing the moral codes, language, political possibilities, and social relations they had assumed to be universal. When study abroad is successful, students realize the validity of alternative models and thus the contingency of their own. Although the exercise can entail considerable discomfort, the distance provided by the dislocated position also results in the potential for great critical understanding.

Best of all, the lessons of such dislocations are generalizable. The most important experience of disruption is the first one: It triggers a kind of Copernican revolution in thinking. Students may later experience other dislocations in other cultures, which will again force them to reassess other assumptions, but in a sense all future work is made possible by that first crack in the smooth surface of their own cultural existence.

Disruption is not a be-all and end-all. The recognition of alternative worldviews does not necessarily lead to utter relativism. Not all cultural practices are equal, and students need to learn to form judgments about them. Just because students come to understand different points of view doesn't necessarily mean they will or should agree with them. The hope is that we'll provide them with the tools to evaluate these differences. A student's experience in Israel illustrates this point well:

> One key experience was visiting the head rabbi of an ultra-religious anti-Israel sect in the most religious neighborhood in Jerusalem. Experiencing this neighborhood and talking to this rabbi were once-in-a-lifetime experiences. The rabbi spoke fervently and passionately, quoting religious scripture almost every other sentence. He proudly spoke of his personal negotiations and discussions with Mahmoud Ahmadinejad and how he was opposed to a government that seemed to be supporting him and his family financially. The whole experience was fascinating and I gained a more profound understanding of the values of this particular ultra-Orthodox religious group and the way they interact with their government. The values and life style and political actions of this man and his followers challenged my understanding of Israeli politics and its relationship with the most religious members of Israeli society. (Religion major, program in Israel)

The same student reported having been profoundly altered by his experiences abroad. After his return to the host campus, he devised a research project: "[This research project] helped me engage with and process my trip. I picked up a way of viewing the world, thinking critically, and learning to understand issues of culture, identity, politics, and religion as multifaceted." Experiences like these have real and lasting effects.

Or so, at least, we like to believe. At the beginning of this chapter we discussed the illusions of naïve realism and confirmation bias, which should make us cautious about our conclusions. How do we really know that student impressions of their experiences are merited? Can one's worldview truly be altered? To what extent can we actually access the world of difference that is culture?

These questions lead to one of the trickiest problems of them all: how we know when our efforts have been successful, and how we measure that success. The next chapter delves deeper into the issue of community engagement during off-campus study, and in chapter 7 we will tackle the challenging but important task of measuring the effect of these undertakings.

Notes

1. Variations of this story include most famously *The Truman Show* (1998), in which insurance agent Truman Burbank (portrayed by Jim Carrey) discovers he has spent his life in an artificial world, filmed for the delight of viewers around the globe. Here again the dynamics are the same: A person's life appears entirely normal, unproblematic, and innocent, until some panel of this reality falls away and reveals the existence of a separate universe that conforms to a different logic and set of rules, challenging the very integrity of the world one thought one knew. A number of horror films use this conceit in other ways, such as *Invasion of the Body Snatchers* in all of its remakes (in order of release date: Wanger & Siegel, 1956; Solo & Kaufman, 1978; Solo & Ferrara, 1993; Silver, Hirschbiegel, & McTeigue, 2007).

2. See Kiely (2000) and Mezirow (1997). The application of this idea is amply discussed with respect to study abroad in Brewer and Cunningham (2009a).

3. The Scholar Ship website has been inactive for some time. Its *Wikipedia* entry reports that "On June 11, 2008, the Scholar Ship indefinitely canceled all future voyages due to difficulties in raising the necessary finances" ("Scholar Ship," 2017, "Financial difficulties"). Apparently the fund-raising isn't going well.

4. Carr (2007) gives a series of examples of how language and writing systems shape the way the brain is wired, including differences as apparently simple as whether a writing system is phonetic (e.g., the Roman alphabet) or pictographic (e.g., Chinese characters). Some of his examples are drawn from Wolf (2007).

5. The study reveals significantly different brain development in speakers of tonal (e.g., Chinese) languages versus speakers of nontonal (e.g., English) ones. Many readers will be familiar with Pinker's (2007) attack on the Whorf–Sapir hypothesis; however, later studies have called this position into question.

6. The notion that cultures behave like a grammar begins with the structuralist anthropology; Geertz (1977) adapted the concept to the notion that culture is a symbolic system. See also Chirkov (2016).

7. See, for instance, Daren Kelly's "Lessons from Geography: Mental Maps and Spatial Narratives" (2009a) and "Semiotics and the City: Putting Theories of Everyday Life, Literature, and Culture Into Practice" (2009b). Federica Goldoni (2015) discusses several approaches to cultural integration in "Preparing Students for Studying Abroad."

6

ENGAGED GLOBAL
CITIZENSHIP

We went on a number of field trips and [had] other kind[s] of in-person experiences. It
allowed me to get out of my head and out of books and see the human side of the theories
I was learning. The two I remember most vividly was a day spent going around the city
with someone who had experienced homelessness and a school inequality tour we took
with a nonprofit, going from high [school] to high school in the city and in the suburbs,
talking about the different experiences of students in different neighborhoods.

—American Studies major, program in Minneapolis–St. Paul

lready recognized as a catalyst for academic and personal growth,
off-campus study plays a crucial role in preparing students to meet
future local and global challenges, teaching them what a life of
engaged citizenship may look like. How, then, do we educate students for
this? In the preceding chapters we discuss the various ways off-campus study
can and should provide an integrated experience for students. It can weave
together different disciplines, connect curricular and cocurricular experiences, and provide a compelling thread throughout a student's undergraduate career. But what about the integration of our students into society? In
this chapter, we explore ways different educational experiences can create
bridges between the classroom and society, providing what might be called
a civic education.

Lembright (2015) describes *civic education* as "nurturing within students
a commitment to collectively engage to overcome problems, as well as instill-
ing a balance between their personal aspirations and the common good"
(p. 32). This is an ambitious goal but one that rings familiar, for we also find
it at the heart of liberal education. Cronon (1998) identifies 10 skills of a lib-
erally educated person: listening, reading, talking, writing, problem-solving,
truth seeking, understanding and appreciating difference, leading, working
in a community, and connecting (pp. 76–8). As Cronon points out, these

skills can be honed mostly through interactions with other people and with diverse communities. There are many ways such interactions can occur—through classroom teaching on campus, through travel, in a workplace, or even within a single family. Ultimately, Cronon advocates for an education that "opposes parochialism and celebrates the wider world," one that engages students in "the world's fight" and that encourages them to solve the world's problems in ways that are informed by knowledge of and respect for different ways of being (p. 78).

Off-campus study can be a powerful tool for advancing the goals of civic education and engaged citizenship because it directly addresses the "capacity for *bridging capital*, that is, the ability to effectively work across differences with people who are unlike [us]" (Lembright, 2015, p. 32).[1] Coincidentally, this type of engagement resonates with the current generation of students who, in addition to their commitment to *learning*, are increasingly interested in *doing*. They are becoming actors in communities through civic engagement opportunities, and they are learning about careers and workplaces by way of internships. Both of these activities have been identified by AAC&U as high-impact practices, which continue to find their way into college curricula, receiving administrative and financial support from home institutions, independent foundations, and the government. Academic civic engagement centers and public works initiatives have gained prominence on U.S. campuses. Every two to four years, the Carnegie Foundation selects U.S. colleges and universities for its Community Engagement Classification, which recognizes the "collaboration between institutions of higher education and their larger communities (local, regional/state, national, global) for the mutually beneficial exchange of knowledge and resources in a context of partnership and reciprocity" (Campus Compact, n.d.).

Increasingly, such opportunities also arise as embedded or connected components of off-campus study, and they are highly popular with students. For example, during a focus group conducted at a study abroad program in Denmark in December 2015, students spoke positively about the experiential learning component that was part of their program, and they felt it was important for their education to provide such real-world learning experiences. Similarly, surveys of American undergraduates show they identify themselves as entrepreneurial and interested in real-life applicability. In one survey, 42% of respondents said they expect to work for their own companies or be otherwise self-employed after graduation (Northeastern News, 2014). They desire a high degree of choice and flexibility in most matters in life, including education (Seemiller & Grace, 2014); 72% of undergraduate students want to be able to design their own major (Northeastern News, 2014).[2]

These data suggest that most students draw a clear connection between their college degree and their life beyond the college campus.

Off-campus study environments open up possibilities for a variety of self-driven, hands-on, real-world experiences. Experiential learning opportunities, including different forms of civic engagement, work best when they are properly framed and academically supported, and when they are designed to be closely connected to the classroom-based curriculum. Moreover, when taking place in a significantly different environment, such experiences reinforce student learning in language, cultural practices, and more, making it possible for participants to imagine future activities (ranging from research to careers) in different cultural contexts.

Course-Based Community Field Trips

This program's main aim was not necessarily cultural exchange or connection, but I really appreciated our experiences learning from Native people at the Native American Community Clinic in Minneapolis, and at various Native community organizations. Learning about health disparities, historical trauma, and socio-cultural determinants of health in a classroom setting is one thing, but listening to people sharing their lived experiences is much more powerful.

—Latin American Studies major, program in Minneapolis–St. Paul

Whether taught at the home campus or at off-campus sites, some courses include opportunities for students to connect with the surrounding community, often in the form of day trips. This most basic form of experiential learning allows students to connect content learning with context, providing a structured, meaningful, and useful way to learn and engage more holistically. It is one of the main reasons that going away to a different country, state, or city makes so much sense pedagogically. Whether it consists of a simple walk through a neighborhood that was evoked in a work of fiction, a visit to a local hospital or prison, or the observation of a session of the Parliament, the power of direct observation and the ability to relate to it intellectually and emotionally is unparalleled. It connects the theoretical with the practical, the descriptive with the real. Like any kind of learning, such experiences need to be guided by a skilled teacher, and they are most effective if they are truly embedded in readings, reflections, and assignments designed with specific learning outcomes in mind (see Sobania, 2015b, for examples of pedagogical approaches to experiential learning in domestic study away). For example, students in the Biology of Marine Mammals course at DIS Study Abroad in Scandinavia participate in a field visit to a local marine mammal research lab that has captive porpoises and eels. Students and research staff discuss the ethical issues about keeping species for research, comparing how this is viewed in the United States and Denmark. Students prepared for the visit by studying high-profile cases from the media. For instance, the Copenhagen Zoo faced an international media storm after euthanizing a baby giraffe and autopsying it in front of an audience of schoolchildren. This story was compared to a lawsuit in the United States against SeaWorld condemning the capture and enslavement of wild orcas.

Brief experiences of this sort are akin to an excerpt or illustration from a reading: They activate the specificity of otherwise abstract notions. Extensive use of the site (its inhabitants, its institutions, its topography, its practices) is a common feature of off-campus study, where the classroom expands beyond four walls, merging with dynamic, living spaces. Active engagement with one's surroundings, especially when those surroundings are considerably different from what students are accustomed to, can inspire one to rethink familiar issues and reevaluate assumptions. Moving from the classroom into the world, from theory to practice, results in a rich and meaningful experience.

Course-Based Civic Engagement

I surveyed pastoralists in Ethiopia with a nongovernmental organization and helped them collaborate with communities in southwest Ethiopia to increase clean water access, disease prevention, education, microenterprise, female empowerment, and child welfare. I hope to work further in East Africa and this project enabled me to start learning four local languages, cultural nuances, and to form transformative connections with dozens of Ethiopian staff and villagers.

—Economics major, program in Ethiopia

Civic engagement projects take the course-based field trip one step further, from observation to participation. Such experiences typically involve regular interactions with a community organization in which students contribute to the organization's functioning while they develop their own skills. These are far more complicated experiences to manage. As the learning opportunity expands, so do logistical, ethical, and knowledge thresholds. Careful embedding of the experience in the course of study is central. Just like the study abroad program itself, this requires pre- and postexperience framing, preparation and reflections that repeat, deepen, and grow over time. Working effectively and respectfully with a community demands time and flexibility; it can't easily be squeezed in between classes or added as a cocurricular afterthought. Those of us in the field of education abroad can learn a lot in this respect from domestic study away programs and campus civic engagement centers that have wrestled with similar issues and offer excellent examples of integrative learning pedagogy (Sobania, 2015b). In particular, many practitioners in the field are struggling to respond to a growing body of research evoking ethical issues in certain forms of community engagement (volunteering, service-learning, and civic engagement). The positions range from Illich (1990), who denounces the paternalism of international service missions, to more current discussions of ethical and legal ramifications of learning abroad in medical, public health, and health science fields (see University of Minnesota Pre-Health Student Resource Center, 2018). In particular, issues of reciprocity present unique challenges in a study abroad context. Student sensitization to issues of positionality is especially important.

Program-embedded civic engagement spans a large spectrum of activities, from short-term projects at a local school or nongovernmental organization to complex commitments developed over several years with stakeholders in the United States and abroad. Whether students are involved in direct service, such as hands-on tutoring of disadvantaged children or supporting migrant workers by working on water improvement, or indirect service, such as assisting nonprofits and nongovernmental organizations, the actual outcomes of their work are as important as the learning that takes place.

This integration of service and learning is crucial. For example, on a Carleton study abroad program in London and Seville, students provide free sports clinics at a local school, and the experience is folded into two courses: Introductory Coaching Practicum, which helps students develop coaching skills and create a philosophy of coaching in a cross-cultural setting, and Global Athletics, which examines the emergence of contemporary athletics and current issues facing participants, coaches, administrators, and spectators. International Partnerships for Service-Learning has been developing a global network of embedded civic engagement and service-learning programs for more than three decades (IPSL Institute for Global Learning, n.d.). Community needs determine student placement on these programs, but at the same time that they study language, culture, history, politics, and community organizing, students also develop a wide range of real-life skills. The Rehearsing Change program (Pachaysana Institute, 2014), based in Quito, Ecuador, administered in partnership with the Universidad San Francisco de Quito and part of the Fair Trade Learning movement, brings together local communities and international students from institutions in the United States and from the Universidad San Francisco de Quito. They "learn together, studying development, sustainability, identity and globalization, all in the context of the reality of our local community" (Pachaysana Institute, 2014, para. 1). Residents from the local community invite students to live and work with them, and the Pachsayana Institute actually selects an equal number of community members to participate in the program. Moreover, classroom study through courses offered during the semester leads to real community development projects.

Do these experiences help us educate engaged citizens? One study that surveyed 6,391 study abroad participants showed that study abroad has had an impact on 5 dimensions of global engagement: civic engagement, knowledge production, philanthropy, social entrepreneurship, and voluntary simplicity (Paige, Fry, Stallman, Josić, & Jon, 2009). We also know that it affects subsequent educational and career choices. Among 12 college experiences listed in research by Sage, the experience with the strongest impact—affecting 83.5% of participants and outperforming the effect of friendships (73.8%) and even coursework (66.2%)—was study abroad (Paige et al., 2009, p. 10).

Nevertheless, measuring the effects in any particular case is tricky. As we show in chapter 7, assessing study abroad learning is a complex problem, which holds true here as well. It was beyond the scope of the Sage study to look into program structures to determine whether embedded civic engagement programs had a stronger impact on students' subsequent social and civic engagement than programs with other features. However, embedded civic engagement does create what we have called the multiplier effect, a unique layering of broadly recognized high-impact practices that can occur during well-designed off-campus study programs (see chapters 1 and 2). Finally, teaching students that it is important to give back to the community where they live and learn may ultimately be the most powerful lesson of civic education.

This last notion—that is, the idea of reciprocity—has fueled the Fair Trade Learning movement, a global educational partnership exchange that prioritizes reciprocity in relationships through cooperative, cross-cultural participation in learning, service, and civil society efforts. It also advocates a balance between student-centered learning and community-driven outcomes and focuses on "the goals of economic equity, equal partnership, mutual learning, cooperative and positive social change, transparency, and sustainability" (Hartman, Morris Paris, & Blache-Cohen, 2014, p. 110). It should be clear from just the few examples presented in this chapter that any form of community engagement abroad needs to begin by examining ethical frameworks of international education and standards of community engagement. It also calls for us to analyze our own positionality and agency in each specific context. We need to ask ourselves how to increase the number of American undergraduates who study, work, or volunteer away from the home campus, and how to undertake these practices ethically and sustainably. The strength and usefulness of the Fair Trade Learning concept lies, among other things, in its applicability to off-campus study and to community engagement. It prioritizes reciprocity and balance between the goals and outcomes of different stakeholders, namely students, sending institutions, local partners, host families, and communities.

There is a real danger that the practice of sending students abroad to learn, to become well-rounded employees, and, most important, to develop into engaged citizens, can be tainted by consumerism and slick marketing. We need to be cautious about sweeping claims that overpromise, and we should avoid broad pronouncements that vow to *dismantle the system* or that claim each student will chart a new and important direction for the community partner. Small, localized efforts may not make for good headlines, but they can often have a better chance for success. Strategies such as the careful vetting of local partners and vendors, matching them with a program's priorities and a student's abilities, compensating partners fairly, and offering these partners their own professional development opportunities can not only boost sustainable travel goals but also prove more economical in the long run.

Staying true to the idea of exchange and reciprocity by operating in both directions provides another powerful lesson in civic education for our students. Sometimes it's possible to invite international students and faculty guests to the United States for study, conferences, or workshop opportunities. At the very least local host families or internship coordinators can be invited to provide feedback about their experience with students; when this feedback is taken into account, it demonstrates how these participants are considered full partners. Similarly, we can strengthen our local partners and communities by connecting students to local development efforts through community-based research and other projects. As educators, through our curriculum and program design, we need to commit to educating for engaged citizenship by valuing reflection, critical thinking, intercultural conversations, and global network building.

Course-Based Practicums

My practicum, along with what we have learned in class and from readings has allowed me to appreciate the importance of early childhood education and care in a child's development. Additionally, the stark difference between the maturity of these children, and the maturity of the children of a similar age I have worked with in a U.S. preschool, as well as how adults interacted with the kids, has allowed me to understand the impact that these institutions can have. Seeing how much freedom these children are given, and how rarely this freedom leads to an issue, leads me to question the way young children are approached in America. This experience also led to some personal conflict, in terms of considering a future career. Prior to this, I would have without a doubt thought I would want to work with older children or teenagers, but now, I think that I would also enjoy working with younger kids, and that the impact of working in early childhood education and care could be equally significant to teaching older students.

—Psychology major, program in Denmark

Although popular in the United States as a requirement in graduate-level professional degree programs such as counseling, social work, or education, practicum experience is relatively uncommon in undergraduate courses and even less common in study abroad. However, the emphasis that a practicum places on observation and on connecting theory with practice works well in the study abroad context. For example, students studying education might visit a local school or day care center to observe and document how working professionals perform their job; they could then relate this experience to material studied in a carefully designed parallel course. Such practices can provide a unique insight into local cultures, putting disciplinary knowledge in a rich and thought-provoking cross-cultural perspective. For example, DIS Study Abroad in Scandinavia offers practicum experiences in its core courses, which also include experiential learning opportunities during comparatively focused local and European study tours. Clinical Psychology, Children in Multicultural Context, Innovation and Entrepreneurship, and Communications are some examples of core courses that include a practicum. Students become familiar with the work of start-up companies, hospitals, urban design studios, and schools. They learn about their disciplines in a cross-cultural context, and they learn about Denmark or Sweden by interacting with locals professionally and socially. These connections provide a rare insight into workplace culture. One student described the experience in the following way:

> Today I got to the office a little on the early side. The team was sitting having their morning chat and asked if I wanted to sit in. They were going around saying what they did the day before and what their plan was for today's work. Once the last one finished (who was sitting next to me), they looked at me as if I was next. So, we all laughed a little and then I told them what my plan was for the day. It was a good way to start the day. I know that the entire company usually holds a meeting each morning to have a debrief of what is going on in the company. I have found that this is a really important ritual because it forces you to come into contact with your colleagues and to just start off the day on a general good note. (Communications major, program in Denmark)

The opportunity to study a discipline in a cross-cultural context and to see it in a professional setting can be equally rewarding, as shown in the following:

> My European clinical psychology course and practicum are really helping me ease into Danish culture and understand how their mental health system works within the welfare state. Seeing the parallels between what

I have been talking about in my classes alongside my practicum is incredible. Having this extra perspective can only benefit me in my future career in psychology. (Psychology major, program in Denmark)

As we pointed out in the case of course-based field trips, a practicum can often fit seamlessly into study abroad coursework because of the flexibility of the program structure and student schedules. Even longer academic field trips outside the primary program location, such as multiday study tours, are possible when creative program design is used. This blending of theory with practice, observation with guided analysis, and classroom work with experiential learning provides countless opportunities for meaningful reflection on how societies work and how one may become an active scholar, practitioner, and citizen.

Internships

I remember receiving an assignment during my internship where it seemed like the staff member and I just couldn't get on the same page about what needed to get done. While I had had lots of leadership and professional experience, it was my first time actually being managed and executing on the vision of someone else. It was a really great introduction, despite being frustrated, to being able to work on a team, ask good questions, and anticipate others' needs.

—Political science major, program in Washington DC

In the context of off-campus study, career exploration opportunities that involve an independent application of skills and knowledge in a workplace setting can be credit bearing (often embedded in the off-campus study program itself) or noncredit bearing. Although data about internships abroad are skimpy, student interest in such opportunities is clearly significant. In a 2008 student poll, 46% of college-bound respondents felt it was important for the college they attended to offer internships abroad, outstripping the importance of all other international experiences (American Council on Education, Art & Science Group, & College Board, 2008). Thirty-five percent of the respondents indicated they were personally interested in participating in an internship abroad.

Although these aspirations are not always realized, the demand translates into high rates of participation. The number of U.S. students participating in for-credit internships or work abroad programs was 23,719 in 2014–2015, compared to 18,982 the previous year (Farrugia & Bhandari, 2016), and the number of students participating in noncredit work, internships, or volunteering abroad was 23,125 in 2015–2016, compared to 22,431 in 2014–15 (IIE, 2017d).

Why are these experiences so popular and so important? Partly because an internship abroad offers several interconnected levels of learning. At its most basic, an internship creates an opportunity to develop professional skills and apply them in a cross-cultural context. It can also deepen a student's knowledge of local language and culture. In fact, when embedded in program coursework or framed by readings, goal-setting exercises, and reflective assignments, it creates a unique opportunity to study, analyze, and understand the workplace environment and culture. Experiencing and examining the social system of another country—for example, during an education-focused internship—provides insights that are often transferable to other aspects of that society, such as health care, welfare, and so on.[3] The internship experience is also highly motivating for students. Because learning happens in a wider real-world context, it often teaches students a broader array of skills than standard coursework, and it may connect more meaningfully to personal and career goals.

Many internship experiences abroad today are connected to classroom-based curricula, and they include guided reflections, sometimes culminating in a capstone or portfolio project. For example, part-time (embedded) internships and service-learning projects at IES Abroad include a required internship seminar that offers theoretical and methodological frameworks to guide students in their personal internship and service experiences. Special emphasis is placed on the analytical and comparative perspective between the local reality and that of the United States. Among the learning outcomes of an IES internship seminar course, IES Abroad (2018) lists the ability to learn and analyze different institutions or programs (e.g., the United Nations Development Programme) and social phenomena (e.g., government and private sector responses to poverty issues).

Carleton College, like many other institutions and providers, places students in internships in many locations, domestic and foreign. Moreover, it has also integrated internships into its off-campus study programs in several locations, notably Paris, Berlin, and Washington DC. The DC program focuses on political science, and during the term students work part time in a news media, public policy, or political office, which intersects neatly with their courses in policy and political communications. Of course, internship experiences in foreign countries are far more difficult to organize (often involving complex visa, housing, and financial issues); however, the payoff can be tremendous. Such is the case with Carleton's Paris internships, which take place after the spring term academic program. These preprofessional opportunities are curated for each student's interest, typically involving such fields as linguistics, academic research, museums, laboratory sciences, photography, and more. Having this kind of real-world experience waiting for students at the end of their academic program is profoundly motivating (and occasionally terrifying); however, because they have spent an entire term in France beforehand, honing their linguistic and cultural skills, they perform capably, often making real contributions to the organizations they work with. As one student reported,

> The workplace forced me to observe, respond, and build relationships with people different from me. I was pushed out of my comfort zone every single day. Each time I made a mistake or had to clarify something as basic as a language block, it humbled me and forced me to ask for help. I see this as stepping-stones for a future job I might have where I will need to accept help, work with others, and know the ways to push myself. (History and French major, research center internship in Paris)

Moreover, we have seen a direct connection between these internships and the advanced work students do on campus. Survey data show that when Carleton students have participated in a program that includes an internship component, 53% of them end up using their off-campus experience as a significant basis for subsequent research, independent studies, or a senior thesis (Kaufman, Nixon, & Tan, 2010).

Appropriate scaffolding of these experiences is crucial. It requires, at a minimum, helping students identify their strengths and interests and setting realizable personal and professional goals, gathering feedback from participants and their supervisors during the experience, and announcing clear goals for student reporting or reflection. According to postinternship reports at Carleton, the internships have been some of the most rewarding experiences these students have yet encountered.

It is safe to conclude that carefully designed and framed internships abroad provide a rich and complex learning opportunity for students, deepen their off-campus study experience, and encourage them to engage with social issues and institutions in more direct and actionable ways.

Students find these internship experiences enriching, but what about potential future employers? According to a British Council (2013) study, in our increasingly changing economic reality, employers look for job candidates who can understand and adapt to different cultural contexts. They want their diverse and often international teams to work efficiently and to communicate respectfully and smoothly with clients. In fact, the most highly valued skill listed in the study is "demonstrating respect for others," followed by the ability "[to work] effectively in diverse teams" (British Council, 2013, p. 9). These skills rank slightly above direct expertise and job qualifications. Employers also value intercultural skills, and although these are not formally assessed, employers consider international experiences, such as study abroad or internships abroad, as a proxy for a candidate's aptitude in this area.

This study and others (e.g., Hart Research Associates, 2015) strongly suggest that employers value broader, transferable, cross-cutting skills and that they see internships and similar workplace experiences as spaces where those skills can be honed. Beyond skills in a specific field of study, employers are looking for broad areas of expertise, which in addition to the intercultural skills mentioned earlier, reflect democratic institutions and values, civic capacity, and the liberal arts and sciences (Hart Research Associates, 2015). In this context, the internship experience clearly connects with civic education goals and helps to fulfill the ideals of a liberal education.

Some may argue that stressing career exploration and preparation for the job market in the current higher education context is merely a result of the high demand and pressure to justify liberal education in general (and study abroad in particular); they might argue that career exploration goes against the core philosophy of liberal education. The examples presented in this chapter suggest otherwise. The typical division between theoretical and applied knowledge proves not to be a particularly useful binary. Workplace or community engagement experiences are not valued exclusively for the applied skills they provide; rather, the importance of this work lies in the integration of particular skills with deep learning, as well as in the social, cultural, and civic exposure they offer to participating students.

Educating for Engaged Citizenship

As we demonstrate in this chapter, community engagement experiences in study abroad programs, from simple field trips to fully developed internships, can and do advance the goal of engaged citizenship by connecting the classroom with society. The exploration of work and community spaces equips students with a variety of skills, from effective communication to problem-solving to intercultural competence. It is important to remember, however, that the different forms of these experiences should not be lumped together, despite their similarities. Nor should we assume that there is a single, cross-cultural understanding of what it means to participate in an internship, a community engagement activity, or a practicum. These kinds of experiences, although not new to the field of study abroad, have not been widely studied or assessed; they call for further reflection as we seek to disentangle value, learning, and responsibility.

It is also important to contextualize our main goal in designing community engagement activities abroad. If we are looking for increased language fluency, cultural knowledge, or intercultural ability, these are, for the most part, achievable outcomes that we could certainly attempt to measure (see chapter 7). However, if our goal is to educate engaged citizens who can effectively build global networks and work across physical and cultural borders, we need more than a semester or even a year abroad, which returns us to the problem that lies at the core of this book: how to integrate the off-campus experience into the entire arc of undergraduate education.

The social context and the reality in which we want our students to engage are not only complex but also constantly changing. Bauman (2012) describes our time as one of liquid modernity, a kind of a constant mobility and traveling between physical spaces and cultures as well as between real and virtual borders, changing interests and jobs, and fluid and constantly expanding identities. If modernity is a search for perfection, and if stability is that perfection achieved, liquid modernity, as Bauman asserts, is a kind of permanent progress—"no longer a temporary measure, an interim matter, leading eventually . . . to a state of perfection . . . but a perpetual and perhaps never-ending challenge and necessity, the very meaning of 'staying alive and well'" (p. 134). If we are to educate engaged citizens and prepare them for the challenges of this reality of temporary commitments, we need to understand our role as educators in this process. Bauman explains how this short-term, uncertain, constantly evolving market of ideas affects our lives, from the individual choices we make to the workplaces we choose to the way we define community. In a sense, there is more of a need than ever for a holistic, innovative college curriculum and for learning experiences where students meaningfully engage with other cultures and gain more knowledge of themselves. The profound lessons of civic education can be delivered, powerfully and experientially, by international or domestic off-campus study that offers students the opportunity to live and interact with difference. It can help them achieve understanding through confrontation and debate, as well as negotiation and compromise (Bauman, 2012).

Notes

1. Civic education and civic action are strongly connected with the idea of democracy. It is not surprising that over the past decade liberal education has been gaining ground in different parts of the world from Russia and China to India and Ghana. Liberal education now exists in at least 58 countries and on every continent, constituting a small but potentially meaningful global trend (Godwin, 2015b, p. 2). As Godwin (2015a, p. 240) asserts, experimenting with liberal education in new cultural contexts cannot be embraced without a critical analysis. There is a lot of work to be done to design culturally relevant curricula, reconcile different approaches to teaching and learning, ensure equal access to this type of education, and address

issues of cultural hegemony that could be implied in an effort to export a Western educational model (Godwin, 2015b, p. 4). It is worth noting, however, that the idea of educating engaged citizens and critical thinkers (who not only become skilled professionals but also work to create better, more just societies) is gaining an ever more pressing global importance.

2. The idea of students having more flexibility and ability to design their own education interestingly corresponds well to a futuristic scenario, like Stanford2025 (Stanford University, n.d.), which proposes that future students will or should be enrolled not in majors but in missions, designing their own degree based on their chosen mission.

3. This parallels a direct enrollment experience where students who are experiencing firsthand a different educational system learn about culturally driven assumptions that underpin it. See Chisholm and Berry (2002).

7

MEASURING CHANGE

My off-campus study changed me irrevocably. It was the most difficult thing I've ever done, but also the most rewarding. I learned more about myself than I ever have during a term on-campus. I also learned an incredible amount about my classmates and Malian culture. Even though it was an incredibly challenging program with many bouts of homesickness, it was also an amazing experience with invaluable times of self-growth and discovery. I wouldn't change it for the world.

—Linguistics and cognitive science major, program in Mali

We know more or less how to assess material we teach in our classes: After our students write papers, take tests, or give presentations, we grade the work according to guidelines and goals we have set, often applying implicit or explicit rubrics. Some of these practices transfer smoothly to off-campus study, where students also take courses. There are local challenges (students may not be used to foreign teaching methods or forms of grading), but by and large the model is familiar. In a language class, for instance, we know how to recognize when a verb has gone crooked, a pronoun has stepped out of line, or an adjective disagrees with its noun. Cumulatively, a measurement of steps and missteps helps us understand what our students have learned about the language and where they still need help.

Cultural grammars, on the other hand, are harder to learn and assess. When it comes to intercultural understanding, let alone something as subjective as personal growth, most of us are out of our depth. Some helpful tools and resources are available, such as the AAC&U VALUE rubrics (AAC&U, 2009a, 2009c), which include rubrics for global and intercultural learning (discussed later in this chapter). However, the difficulty is compounded by the fact that for off-campus study contexts we are called on to assess learning that largely occurs outside the classroom—for example, through personal interactions and discoveries that are not part of any explicit curriculum and that may be specific to each student. This merging of academic learning with direct personal experience is one of the characteristics that distinguishes off-campus study from its on-campus counterpart, and it's one of the reasons off-campus study qualifies as a high-impact learning practice. However, most of us have significantly less expertise in measuring nontraditional and non–discipline-based forms of learning (e.g., cultural understanding or personal growth), even though we have identified these as key objectives for off-campus study. In fact, administrators of colleges and universities encounter similar challenges when asked to assess on-campus learning when it crosses too many boundaries. General education requirements, which may straddle several departments or divisions, are famously difficult to evaluate. Certain broad skills are even harder. For instance, assessing whether students have "acquired skills for effective citizenship and life-long learning" (University of Minnesota, 2009, para. 1) is at least as complicated as figuring out what cultural understanding they acquired while studying off campus. We are not suggesting that this type of holistic assessment is impossible to execute; we merely seek to acknowledge the difficulty of the enterprise, underscoring how different this kind of evaluation is from the assessments we administer for individual courses.

Assessment practices in the area of off-campus study remain fraught with difficulties. There is broad disagreement about what can or should be assessed, what eludes assessment, whether assessment should extend beyond the curricular to the cocurricular (or even to personal growth). The fact that the debate rages on is sufficient proof the issue is not resolved. Nevertheless, we feel confident in asserting a few basic principles:

- Although some things may well elude assessment in off-campus study, not everything does. That is, some things can be assessed, either qualitatively or quantitatively.
- If, as we maintain, off-campus study incarnates some of the most important instances of liberal education many of our students will ever experience, it's crucial for us to be able to measure some aspects of its impact.
- Because off-campus study represents a particularly intense experience of the integrative learning that lies at the heart of higher education, any tools we devise for assessing off-campus study should also be useful for liberal education writ large.

In this chapter we address the challenges and the opportunities of assessing off-campus learning, ultimately proposing an integrative approach for accomplishing it.

Why Is It Difficult to Assess Off-Campus Learning?

Literature about learning outcomes and assessment is complex, and proponents of various points of view favor different methods, ranging from surveys to tests to portfolios. The American Council on Education advocates a multiple-method approach that measures direct evidence, such as actual student coursework, as well as indirect indicators, such as student self-evaluations or admission rates in related graduate fields (Olson, Green, & Hill, 2006).[1] Professionals in the field of study abroad have tackled this topic aggressively and, in many ways, successfully. The Forum on Education Abroad's Committee on Outcomes, Research, and Assessment provides an extensive bibliography on its website, documenting hundreds of case studies (Forum on Education Abroad, 2017b). These studies focus predominantly on the impact of study abroad. They range from explorations of the development of intercultural competence and its impact on careers, to language fluency and more, such as the significance of particular program features and specific program learning outcomes. Moreover, several book-length publications discuss theories, present tools, and encourage the practice of off-campus study assessment (e.g., Deardorff, 2015; Forum on Education Abroad, 2017a; Savicki & Brewer, 2015). All these resources, however valuable, wrestle with the complexity of the endeavor. When the Forum on Education Abroad polled its members in 2016 asking how they would describe themselves in terms of experience with assessment, it found that 76% needed help and guidance in assessing off-campus learning (Forum on Education Abroad, 2017b).

One of the challenges consists of matching learning outcomes with program design. Although this practice is in some ways similar to what is done for on-campus courses, where a course is structured to help achieve particular learning objectives, an off-campus program has many more moving parts than a class, and much of the experience takes place in an environment that is far less controlled than a classroom. At a minimum, then, when articulating learning outcomes and designing assessment tools for off-campus study, one needs to consider program length, depth of cultural engagement, program features and pedagogy, as well as the culture gap between the student participants and the program host communities.[2] The assessment of a specific program also depends to some degree on the general off-campus study goals set by institutions or program providers. However, if those goals and outcomes are not part of individual course assessment efforts (which is often the case for broad mission statements about global citizenship or engagement with the world), how can one assess them in a way that is rigorous and thorough?

Another challenge is the simple fact that certain kinds of learning lend themselves to quantifiable measurement, whereas others, like off-campus study experiences, are more elusive. Although test scores may demonstrate mastery of course content, cultural (or intercultural) understanding often requires self-reporting or even anecdotes (e.g., those included throughout this book). This necessarily introduces a greater degree of subjectivity. We discuss the assessment of intercultural learning later in this chapter, but it may be helpful to have a baseline understanding of what we mean by *intercultural understanding*. Harvey (2017) proposed the following to recognize four core intercultural competencies:

1. Increasing awareness and understanding of our own characteristic ways of making meaning and acting in familiar and unfamiliar contexts
2. Increasing awareness and understanding of others' ways of making meaning and acting in familiar and unfamiliar contexts
3. Responding mindfully in contexts that disorient or challenge us
4. Bridging cultural gaps in those contexts: shifting perspective, attuning emotions, and adapting our behavior in effective and appropriate ways

These competencies can be developed and assessed only in a specific context provided by the program structure, its disciplinary focus, and specific courses offered. However, the first step toward measuring intercultural understanding is to set these competencies as explicit learning outcomes.

Our institutional missions and pedagogies aspire to offer students holistic, integrated learning that extends beyond the curriculum, and at the institutional level our assessment efforts are increasingly focused on measuring not only the parts but also the entirety of our educational offerings, including cocurricular programming.[3] Study abroad faces a similar challenge. Although students abroad learn languages and study a variety of disciplines, we need to acknowledge that important portions of the program—usually the ones where the most learning has occurred—are often extracurricular. Yet, we typically focus assessment efforts on the in-class aspects of off-campus study, and some faculty may even object to assessing anything that is not a credit-bearing component of a program.[4] However, there are powerful reasons to change this practice. Assessment of all the components of the off-campus experience can satisfy at least three important needs. First, it can help an institution's administrators determine whether their programs are successful in achieving academic and personal growth. Second, it can help measure students' skills, thereby identifying the level of academic engagement they may be ready for on their return. Third, it can help students recognize and value cultural and personal aspects of the experience—an important skill in the toolbox of interculturally competent graduates.

Assessing Language Learning

To address the challenges mentioned earlier, let's begin with a relatively simple example: assessment of language skills. Potentially, this type of assessment presents the least amount of difficulty for off-campus study programs because it lends itself to quantitative evaluation and to pre- and posttesting that measures the progress students have made during their time away. In short, we already know how to measure language competency reasonably well on campus; it shouldn't be too hard to extend that practice to off-campus experiences.

However, even this apparently simple example quickly turns complex. Although different approaches can be used in a language classroom on campus, circumstances provide what might be considered a controlled environment: For an hour a day students practice language skills they have learned together from the same book under the guidance of their instructor. Even if some version of this model takes place during an off-campus study experience, the in-class instruction is often dwarfed by extracurricular language practice. After all, we send language learners off-campus to immerse themselves in the target language and to experience it in real-life situations (e.g., at home, in the streets, at work, or in volunteer placements). The result is that what they learn depends largely on individual experiences that may vary dramatically from one student to another, even in the same program. The immersion experience is substantially different from classroom learning, and it tends to be highly idiosyncratic. Moreover, students who learn on off-campus programs often return with greatly enhanced communication skills that are still flawed with basic grammatical errors; they have achieved a high degree of proficiency without always attaining accuracy. This means that the assessment tools typically used for measuring skills on campus may no longer be as relevant for measuring the abilities of returning students. The use of external guidelines, such as the standards developed by the American Council on the Teaching of Foreign Languages (ACTFL, n.d.) or the Common European Framework of Reference for Languages (CEFR, n.d.), can be useful; however, these require individualized evaluations of each student by a trained professional, a process that is out of reach for many institutions and probably not scalable for larger ones.

Furthermore, how do we compare the language learning of students in different programs in an equitable fashion? A deep understanding of program structure becomes increasingly relevant; to know how effective the program is, we need to know how long it lasts, whether it offers structured and unstructured immersion opportunities, if it includes a language pledge, whether intensive classroom instruction complements a homestay or local dorm experience, and if there are volunteer or internship opportunities.

Do these variables matter, and how? Some best-practice resources, such as the IES Abroad MAP for Language and Cultural Communication (IES Abroad, n.d.), explore the relationship between program design and language acquisition; however, even the most carefully designed programs intersect with students who bring their individual expectations to that mix. For example, Surtees (2016) analyzes the interaction among language learning and student beliefs, motivations, perceptions, and expectations. She points to the important role that a realistic and intentional framing of the study-abroad experience plays in language learning outcomes.

In their exhaustive and still current study, DuFon and Churchill (2006) further stress the complexity of the assessment effort, reminding us that during study abroad, "linguistic development is further mediated by the complex interaction between initial abilities, individual differences, and changes in these factors that occur in the host context" (p. 27). (Their work does not explicitly address domestic study in which language learning is not typically a component.) They confirm that the study-abroad context increases language fluency in some areas, such as effectiveness, confidence, and motivation in language use, as well as pragmatics, pronunciation, and fluency.

Language learning definitely does occur abroad and it can be measured, but imperfectly. As Twombly, Salisbury, Tumanut, and Klute (2012) state, "the effects of study abroad on language acquisition are (more) nuanced but generally positive" (p. 85).

Assessing Intercultural Learning

This discussion of the supposedly simple example of language assessment underscores the daunting complexity of endeavors to assess aspects of off-campus study experiences. What happens when, in addition to language learning, we decide to assess intercultural competence, or global learning during study abroad programs?[5] A constructive argument could be made that these concepts are distinct but overlapping forms of learning. AAC&U developed two separate VALUE rubrics to address these areas. The first defines *intercultural knowledge and competence* as "a set of cognitive, affective, and behavioral skills and characteristics that support effective and appropriate interaction in a variety of cultural contexts" (AAC&U, 2009c, para. 2). In the second rubric, *global learning* is defined as "a critical analysis of and an engagement with complex, interdependent global systems and legacies (e.g., natural, physical, social, cultural, economic, and political) and their implications for people's lives and the earth's sustainability" (AAC&U, 2009a, para. 1). The global learning definition and rubric, with its emphasis on understanding global systems and global contexts, still belongs in the realm of academic disciplinary and interdisciplinary competence, if a bit tentatively. We can easily imagine courses in a single discipline or across multiple disciplines with assignments, capstone projects, and collaborating teams that advance learning and assessment of global learning on and off campus. However, the process becomes progressively more difficult when we move to intercultural competence.

Intercultural learning is the most widely recognized goal for off-campus study participation; at the same time it is one of the most difficult to define (see the discussion on intercultural competence assessment in Twombly et al., 2012). Although some agreed-on definition is necessary to assess a competence, we're often hard pressed when called on to compare vastly different student experiences and statements. For example, consider the following student accounts about some very different kinds of cultural understanding:

About halfway through our study abroad program, we all went to see the German-language musical *Elisabeth*, which was based on the life of an assassinated Austrian empress. Not only was the musical extremely entertaining (and the music extremely catchy), but it was also a great way to ga[u]ge my progress with German. It was extremely satisfying to be able to understand almost everything that was said (and sung!), and to be able to laugh along with the audience at all the jokes. I think attending the musical reinforced what I had been learning and absorbing about German through the course of the trip. (Math and statistics major, program in Austria)

One key experience that I had on this trip was the first time we went to a village to see how a village meeting works for microfinance. It was incredible what they were able to do with the loans that they received, and I just particularly remembered the hope that they had in their faces, even though their quality of life is not considered as good as ours. (Economics major, program in Bangladesh)

When I left my program I had to fly out of Ben Gurion airport. Upon learning I lived in the West Bank, the pre-security pre-check-in airport security took me aside, screened my luggage separately, strip-searched me, questioned me, gave me a rougher time, and escorted me through security. This showed just how distorted of a perspective the Israelis have about Palestine. They believe anyone associated with the country is a risk. The people who questioned me asked if I "mixed with the natives." I explained that yes, since I lived there, I did interact with people in the West Bank. The way the security people referred to Palestinians was very unpleasant. Going through checkpoints to get in and out of the West Bank (into or out of Israel) was very instructive. People are herded like cattle through metal and barbed wire gates and made to stand for hours as the IDF [Israel Defense Forces] takes their time letting them through. (Political science major, program in the West Bank)

It becomes clear when reading these comments that, as Deardorff (2015) and other researchers (e.g., Twombly et al., 2012) affirm, intercultural learning straddles several developmental domains—psychosocial, cognitive, personal, moral—to arrive at a combination of communication skills for the math major, knowledge for the political science major, sensitivity for the economics major, and cultural awareness for all of them. The group of intercultural experts who participated in Deardorff's study agree on only one aspect of the *intercultural competence* definition: "the ability to see from others' perspectives" (p. 132). While analyzing this attempt to arrive at a consensus definition, Deardorff draws three main conclusions: A variety of skills that make up intercultural competence can be identified and measured; intercultural competence is a developing, ongoing, lifelong process; and a successful intercultural learning experience requires cultural mentoring and intervention. In fact, when we measure language fluency, critical thinking skills, attitudes (e.g., respect, curiosity, or openness), and culture-specific knowledge, we are assessing, at least in part, progress toward our goal of intercultural competence. These competencies can be measured as part of the assessment in individual courses.

Some courses offered in off-campus study programs are designed to specifically address goals of intercultural communication or cultural competence.[6] However, in most cases, intercultural ability, personal growth, and even global competence are skills that are woven throughout the program in courses and extracurricular activities. It's often expected that cultural learning of this sort will find its way onto the syllabus of language classes, but the practice of cultural framing will require some intentional effort in non–culture-specific courses, such as a biology or geology class. In any case, many faculty who lead off-campus programs consider increased cultural competence not only desirable but also even crucial.

In the Carleton College Ecology in Australia program, one of the three courses offered blends the study of physical and cultural environments. In Learning Country: Culture and Environment in Australia, students learn about the natural history of the Australian landscape and the cultural history of the people who settled there. Through course readings and guest lectures, supplemented with experiential and reflective assignments, students specifically consider the role cultural context plays in the way sustainability is viewed by aboriginal, colonial, and modern Australian cultures. In the DIS Study Abroad in Scandinavia course in Sweden, Psychology of Emerging Adulthood, students prepare a cross-cultural panel discussion on the theme of psychological challenges and changes that occur over a human lifespan, with the goal of comparing the experiences of young adults in Scandinavia with those of the students' home country. Based on the outcomes of the discussion, students then write a reflective essay on how a different cultural model of emerging adulthood (i.e., Swedish or Scandinavian) compares to what they see in their home country, and how these cultural insights might be relevant to their personal understanding of the emerging adulthood concept.[7]

The different kinds of cultural mentoring that are necessary for students to meaningfully engage with local cultures have many proponents in the field of education abroad today, and research about best practices is present and growing.[8] The integration of cultural learning with disciplinary coursework can help students integrate their learning in different areas, both academic and personal; however, this kind of blending presents a special challenge for assessment, which typically works by measuring skills individually. Moreover, measurements of a student's progress toward intercultural competence will typically emphasize a formative assessment delivered at different points throughout the program rather than in a single summative one, such as a final essay or exam. Ongoing assessments are useful because of the developmental and process-oriented nature of this learning outcome, as described in a variety of models, such as Bennett's (1993) developmental model of intercultural sensitivity.[9]

Viewed this way, an assessment of intercultural learning seems less elusive, and it begins to resemble the assessment efforts found on college campuses. Still, assessing intercultural learning is difficult for reasons similar to that of assessing language competence on study abroad. The environment (i.e., an off-campus program with all its variations) cannot be controlled or regulated to the same extent as a classroom, and the students' identities and positioning (intellectual, personal, social) play much larger roles than they traditionally would on campus.[10] At least one study has successfully addressed some of these potentially confounding factors. Salisbury (2011) examined the effect of study abroad on intercultural competence by taking into account pre-college characteristics, educational aspirations, and college experiences. His findings are encouraging; his careful study demonstrates that, on average, study abroad has a positive influence on the development of intercultural competence, and this influence is not dependent on gender, race, institutional type, precollege tested academic preparation, pretest scores, or college experiences (Salisbury, 2011). However, the study also shows that although this growth in intercultural capability increases one's inclination toward contact with diverse cultures and people, it has no effect on one's comfort with diversity or relative appreciation of cultural difference (Salisbury, 2011). This finding should not be interpreted as a weakness of the off-campus study experience, but rather as a powerful push toward better integration of off-campus study with on-campus learning. In other words, we cannot and should not expect study abroad or study away to single-handedly produce interculturally capable graduates. It is the university or college's responsibility to integrate this learning goal and the steps for achieving it into the entire undergraduate curriculum.

Toward An Integrated Assessment

Where does this leave us? Throughout the preceding chapters, we have emphasized the richness and heterogeneity of the study abroad experience. While reaching outside the traditional education abroad discourse in search of models or frameworks that address this complexity, we have found that discussions about global networks can be especially helpful. For example, one could approach the assessment of off-campus study as a complex problem, one that is entangled with multiple disciplines, spread between cultures, and focused on criteria that are as elusive as they are contested. The assessors of off-campus study aspire to measure a complicated learning experience that involves disciplinary and interdisciplinary learning in the classroom and beyond; this learning intersects at the same time with each student's personal history, beliefs, and worldview; it involves a variety of stakeholders, such as students, parents, educators, administrators, and program providers; and all of this work is subject to the difficulty of operating across various geographic and cultural borders.

Knight (2007) discussed the difficulty of assessing complex (sometimes referred to as *wicked*) competencies, which are often described in higher education as soft skills. These include the ability to develop supportive relationships and emotional intelligence, to participate in group work, to listen and assimilate, to communicate orally, and so on. One response to these assessment challenges would be an *integrative assessment*, defined as "bringing the various strands of assessment together in a coherent way that addresses the desired goals" (Knight as cited in Crips, 2012, p. 36). Such an assessment would do the following:

> [integrate] the testing of knowledge, skills and personal qualities . . . using a number of criteria or outcomes concurrently . . . using evidence of student achievement from multiple sources . . . integrating the use of discipline content and work experience. (p. 36)

In addition to stressing the coherence and alignment among different learning objectives and different types of learning, Crips's (2012) approach also emphasizes the assessment of this learning. In this kind of process, students are asked to demonstrate skills that will facilitate future learning or, in other words, to show they have developed metacognitive abilities allowing them to make judgements regarding their own learning process (Crips, 2012). Such an integrated assessment practice would align especially well with the off-campus study context, matching the integrative learning we associate with our programs.

In chapter 2 we discussed the concept of *integrative learning* as defined by the AAC&U's (2009b) VALUE rubric and Palmer and Zajonc's (2010) idea of integrative education. Both stress the importance of connecting ideas and experiences across the curriculum and cocurriculum, a practice that can have a profound impact on learners. A similar working definition, crafted specifically with assessment in mind, can be found in Reynolds and Patton's (2014) book on ePortfolios. It defines *integrative learning* as "the ability to learn across context and over time and to be motivated to learn this way" (p. 26).

If integrative learning is the goal and strength of much off-campus study, why would we not measure it by way of an integrative assessment? If we were to do so, what might this assessment look like?

In addition to our existing assessments for coursework, an integrative assessment in the study abroad context would propose assignments and teaching practices that ask students to document and frame their personal growth, intercultural capability, and identity development. It would include the academic components of the program and the experiential learning that occurs outside the classroom. Learning (and then assessing) across contexts would need to stress the synthesis and integration of material from courses across the program curriculum and its cocurriculum, bringing together different types of learning—ideas, concepts, and knowledge to be sure, but also experiences, personal reactions, emotions, cultural preconceptions, identities, and languages. If we focus only on discrete aspects of this unique learning experience, and if we fail to help students make connections between formal instruction and the world beyond the classroom, off-campus study will become an expensive and unfulfilled opportunity (Trosset, 2016).

How do we help students connect the dots and reflect, encouraging them (as Reynolds and Patton, 2014, suggest) to learn in different situations, not only integrating new knowledge but also skillfully translating between different ways and kinds of knowing? What specific assignments could make an integrative assessment successful so we know we are achieving our learning goals? Cross (1999) suggests that "learning occurs, not necessarily as a result of the experience itself, but as a result of reflecting on the experience and testing it against further experience and the experience of others" (p. 22), and recognizing this allows us to design reflective assignments that connect experiences that occur in widely different contexts.

In our discussion on intercultural learning, we emphasized the importance of formative assessment—assignments that stress the developmental
nature of this type of learning and that guide students as they develop intercultural skills. These could be reflective journals, blogs, or guided activities
such as neighborhood walks or field observations that are repeated several
times throughout the program. They could include photo essays or a variety of group projects. Summative assessment assignments, such as formal
essays and presentations or digital stories, can also provide a nuanced insight
into how students apply and analyze different concepts, methodologies, and
experiences.

A few of Carleton College's programs have experimented with this kind
of integrative assessment. For example, on one off-campus study program
in India, two Carleton faculty directors assigned a comprehensive reflective
essay that prompted students to integrate academic, experiential, global, and
intercultural learning with personal growth. The autobiographical essay, as
they called it, asked students to do three things. First, they must position
themselves in the context of the off-campus study program and chart their
intellectual journey through the material. Second, they reflect on how the
activities of acknowledging, contextualizing, and historicizing have affected
their own positionality and shaped their intellectual and experiential journey
through the program. Third, they are called on to organize the essay into five
discrete sections. By asking students to take notes on their personal reactions
(emotions, thoughts, feelings, preconceptions) while engaging with a variety
of texts and experiences (e.g., published scholarly articles, films, lectures, discussions, field trips, and encounters with local people), the assignment effectively engaged the students in the construction of meaning and in a reflection
that was far-reaching and rigorous.[11]

This assignment encouraged students to build a conceptual argument
and connect it to something larger than a single experience. One student,
for instance, started from an anecdote to arrive at a cultural analysis, moving
from the specific to the abstract:

> Maria always wore a sari and gold jewelry, embodying what I interpreted
> as traditional Indian womanhood. Maria occupied the role of the emis-
> sary strategically as a means to make a sale. She would talk at great lengths
> about the opulence and marvelousness of India, lauding the nation for its
> precious resources, like textiles and metals. Maria appealed to what she
> assumed were my own exoticist perspectives about India, thus rendering
> her an Indian emissary. Maria's role as an emissary is not surprising, con-
> sidering that on the macro-scale of interactions between nations, women
> are forced to perform nationhood. Because it is on the site of women's

bodies that notions of nationhood are constructed and contested, women are expected to act as emissaries of the values represented by their nation. Therefore, I would argue that it is a result of these macro-structural forces that Maria is able to perform the position of the emissary for her Western audience. (History major and women and gender studies minor, program in India)

The same student also found opportunities for self-interrogation, recognizing even the constraints of the reflective exercise:

When we went to [the family's] apartment for tea one afternoon we sat through an indoctrination session during which [the father] presented the merits of Brahma Kumari, and tried to convince us to convert by attending one of their seven-day seminars. I was fascinated by their religion as a case study, especially because I saw many parallels between Brahma Kumari and Scientology in the U.S. Nonetheless, because I was so focused on my own emotional and intellectual reactions to the religion, I made little attempt to get to know the family outside of their religious beliefs. Positioning them as a mirror prevented me from interacting with them outside of the context of their religion. While I strongly believe in the importance of practicing self-reflexivity, when one is too focused on one's own emotional and intellectual reactions, cross-cultural connections on a human level are compromised.

Although the assignment provided vocabulary and frameworks for students to engage in the assessment of their own experiences, it also presented the faculty with rich material for assessing each student's global and cultural self-awareness, perspective, attention to cultural diversity, understanding of global systems, and more—some of which are benchmarks identified in the AAC&U (2009a) VALUE rubrics. Moreover, this assessment was skillfully embedded in the disciplinary frameworks of the history and sociology courses taught in the program. At the same time, it connected the exercise to the curriculum, encouraging the use of intentional language, and avoiding, for the most part, the easy homogenization of culture that often results from free-form reflective ruminations about homestays and interactions with local students.

Similar assignments can be designed using a medium other than writing, such as photography, film, or drawing. Guided drawing and photography assignments are especially effective in slowing down and focusing field-based activities to avoid quick and often ethnocentric judgments.[12] In the Carleton New Media program in Portugal, students were given specific directions on how to navigate the city of Lisbon and then photograph select urban neighborhoods. While visiting their designated neighborhood, in addition to specific tasks and questions, students were asked to consider some general elements of urban development, architecture, activities, levels of gentrification, and even the balance between touristic and local daily life. After a three-day photo shoot, they presented a photo essay that skillfully integrated readings, films, and lectures about urban history, along with knowledge of photography, and each student's particular point of view as a tourist, traveler, resident, or new guest in an urban environment.

The containers for these new forms of assessment are not always obvious. What should they look like? How can one provide a flexible structure that lends itself to a wide variety of experiences and forms of expression? One possibility, mentioned in chapter 4, is to expand the use of ePortfolios, one of the more comprehensive tools available for fostering integrative learning and assessment in the context of off-campus study. Although outward-facing ePortfolios are often used for digital self-presentation to an outside audience (e.g., employers), the tool can also be designed to face inward, serving as an assessment instrument in a single course or an off-campus program. In this context, an ePortfolio platform can be particularly successful in connecting different experiences, curricular and cocurricular. When students engage in creating this electronic gallery of their experience, it can help them articulate and integrate those experiences into an identified learning goal, such as global or intercultural learning. At the course level, the experiences they document in the ePortfolio could include field trips, structured explorations, intercultural interactions, and textual and visual readings. At a programmatic level, an ePortfolio could bring together multiple courses, capstone experiences, field trips, homestay interactions, internships, community engagement activities, research, and more. As with other assessment tools, the ePortfolio can be interpreted according to previously designed rubrics. When successful, this type of integrative assignment can reveal skills and competencies while reflecting the experience as it was lived by the students. Thoughtful design of the process, however, is crucial; without appropriate reflection assignments to provide the connective tissue of a portfolio, one risks producing a simple catalog rather than a coherent and integrated whole.

Finally, a low-credit ePortfolio project may ultimately be a mechanism for granting actual credit for the extensive learning that happens outside of class, especially when that learning is connected to what students have done in the classroom. The ePortfolio serves in this case as a vessel for collecting personal and academic work that might otherwise be difficult to measure. In this way, we can show students that the broader goals of their program, which are often aligned with ethereal mission statements for global understanding and personal growth, actually matter and count as part of their education.

In the end, how we assess or measure student development depends on the needs and goals of the program as identified by the institution. Only by determining the goals of a particular program, whether run by the home institution or by a third party, can we begin to measure progress toward them. There is value in making such objectives explicit—not the least of which is to make sure that all participants are working in the same direction, striving to integrate the experience abroad into the educational mission, the curriculum, and the undergraduate degree.

Notes

1. The methods described here are ostensibly for international education, but they apply as well to domestic study away programs.

2. Salisbury (2015) defines a *cultural gap* as "any way in which substantive or systemic differences between individuals or groups might hinder interaction or collaboration toward a common goal" (p. 42). He further explains that a cultural gap "does not require extensive travel; instead it is predominantly shaped by the relative cultural "location" of both participants in the interaction" (p. 42). Engle and Engle (2002, 2003) and Engle (2013) have called attention to the impact of program types and features on learning outcomes in consecutive studies.

3. The charge to assess what students learn in college, not only in their courses but also across the curriculum and cocurriculum, is also a response to articles and studies that attempt to respond directly and often critically to that question, such as Hersh (2005) or in a much more comprehensive study by Arum and Roksa (2011). It is interesting that study abroad is often put on notice in the same way all higher education regularly is. We need to prove the value of the study abroad experience. This is also the reason quantitative assessment of the study abroad experience is often preferred over qualitative.

4. Although we often recognize that the most important learning during off-campus programs occurs outside the classroom, we typically have no mechanism for rewarding this learning with credit and grades—except as it seeps indirectly into classroom work. One way around this problem may be the use of ePortfolios or similar instruments, discussed at the end of this chapter.

5. Although intercultural learning is also a major component of domestic study away programs, the overwhelming majority of resources in the literature focus on study abroad. Thus we feel that methods proposed for study abroad programs should be easily adapted to domestic programs.

6. In the University of Oregon's Italian language and culture program in Siena, students take a mandatory course titled Cross-Cultural Communications/Cross-Cultural Perspectives in Service Learning. The course is structured around two main themes: Italian life and culture as experienced by the students living and learning in the city, and the students' own cultural assumptions through which they experience and make sense of the Italian life around them (Minucci, 2010). The course

includes a service-learning component and a project designed in partnership with a local organization that encourages students to reflect on their involvement and the cross-cultural context in which they are participating. At the conclusion of the program, students present a portfolio of reflection papers, résumés, and project analysis. Another example is a Council on International Educational Exchange course, Intercultural Communication, Identity and Leadership, developed for several of the council's centers (Harvey, 2017). The course explores contemporary local cultures through the lens of intercultural studies. Students examine the complexity of cultural values, beliefs, and practices and learn to identify the cultural differences and similarities between local and U.S. cultures. They also learn about key intercultural theories, frameworks, and leadership practices to deepen their cultural self-awareness, acquire new perspectives, and effectively communicate and interact with culturally different others.

7. At Carleton College, over time, several science-focused programs developed courses that address the cultural understanding of the physical environment. One example is Ecology in Australia; another is Energy, Health, and Environment in Ethiopia and Tanzania, which had a cultural studies course added in its third iteration.

8. Anderson, Lorenz, and White (2016) build on their 2012 through 2014 research to further explore whether intentional instructor engagement with intercultural content while on site is critical in fostering student intercultural growth. Using the Intercultural Development Inventory (IDI), the study analyzes "the influence of gender, prior language study, country challenge, instructor intercultural development inventory score, and number of times the instructor has led the program to quantitatively measure students' intercultural sensitivity gains" (pp. 3–4). The key finding confirms that frequent and spontaneous facilitation by instructors has a strong impact on achieving intercultural gains in students. These instructor interventions include creating a safe space to debrief cultural challenges, supporting and guiding students through the incidents of cultural discord, and creating a healthy intragroup dynamic. See Vande Berg, Paige, and Hemming Lou (2012).

9. Bennett's (1993) model is a framework to explain how people experience and engage cultural difference. According to Deardorff (2015), "The key to this model is its developmental nature, emphasizing that the acquisition of intercultural sensitivity is a developmental process—six stages in this case. The first three stages of this model—denial, defense/polarization, and minimization of difference—are considered to be ethnocentric stages, focused on the individual's cultural lens, while the latter three stages—acceptance, adaptation, and integration of difference—are considered to be ethnorelative, moving beyond one way of seeing the world" (pp. 132–133).

10. There is a growing awareness of identity issues on our campuses. Positionality plays an important role in how different topics are approached inside and outside the classroom. Whether they are aware of it or not, students take their campus culture along with them on their programs abroad. Education abroad professionals, program leaders, and on-site staff need new strategies to support students and help

them reconcile the dissonance, difference, and discomfort that they may feel on the intragroup level as they interact with fellow Americans (from their own or other U.S. campuses), as well as with the culture outside it. In this case, as in others presented throughout this book, the feeling of dissonance is an intrinsic part of the off-campus study experience, and when properly framed it can have a positive effect on the depth of understanding of one's identity and one's self in general.

11. Reynolds and Patton (2014) identify guiding principles for reflection based on Rogers (2002). In addition to being a meaning-making process and a systematic, rigorous, disciplined way of thinking, reflection needs to happen in interaction with others and "requires attitudes that value personal and intellectual growth of oneself and of others" (Reynolds & Patton, 2014, p. 57).

12. A good example of this practice is the Gordon College drawing-based course Disegno in Orvieto, designed for art and nonart majors, that prepares students to engage deeply with their surroundings, using the visual language to help them develop a relationship with the landscape and townscape (Doll, 2017).

8

PRESSURE POINTS

The Future of Off-Campus Study

I think this worked well for me because they were summer programs. Even though it is shorter, you still can learn a lot and meet a lot of people. I was really lucky to find things like this that matched with my major so well, and that I was interested in.

—Biomedical engineering major, program in the Dominican Republic and Nicaragua

T hroughout this book we focus on the challenges and benefits of integrating off-campus study among its various components, in its ways of learning, with the home institution's curriculum, and in the local communities where the experience takes place. Our premise is that off-campus study done well can be the most powerful educational experience our students will have throughout their undergraduate studies, and it can even provide a model for work we undertake on campus.

Despite the promised benefits, however, administrators of many institutions will struggle to adjust their goals and practices regarding off-campus study. Change can be difficult and costly. No matter how large its endowment or how great its revenues, every college and university deals with limited resources, and discussions about reordering priorities are never easy. Moreover, anyone with a career in higher education knows how resistant long-standing practices are to change.

Thus, no matter how significant the educational and personal benefits of off-campus study, hurdles remain. Some are institutional (lack of stakeholder acceptance, financial concerns, etc.), whereas others have to do with growing pains in the field of study abroad itself, such as the threat that increased participation poses for program quality, or the scarcity of programs in underserved regions or for underserved majors. Still other obstacles concern societal and cultural shifts that lie largely beyond our grasp. Each of these broad categories includes a set of *pressure points*—that is, issues that elude easy resolution and call for animated discussion in the local and national contexts.

In many cases no one-size-fits-all answer may be possible, and the approach institutions take to these questions will require trade-offs tailored for local needs and aspirations.

Our goal in this chapter is thus modest. In what follows we outline significant pressure points and suggest tools for weighing institutional priorities, hoping in this way to stimulate and frame discussions. At the end of this chapter, we turn our attention beyond the institution to discuss trends in the field of education abroad, as well as wider societal shifts affecting off-campus study.

Overall, we have identified three different categories of pressure points: those that are internal to each institution (institutional hurdles), those that are currently emerging in the field of study abroad (pressures in the field), and those that might be attributable to outside forces (external pressures).

Institutional Hurdles

Like everything else we do, off-campus study costs money. Even institutions with substantial resources must come to terms with the opportunity cost—the fact that investments in off-campus study necessarily drain funds from other potential endeavors. Beyond this, there may be programmatic or institutional constraints. For example, some students, faculty or administrators may be hesitant about or even resistant to off-campus study.

Decisions about the appropriate level and form of these experiences necessarily vary by institution according to local goals and resources. However, we have identified five challenges to the integration of off-campus study at our institutions, any one of which could be sufficient to thwart successful implementation:

1. Insufficient funding
2. Faculty inexperience
3. Departmental territorialism
4. Complexity
5. Lack of support from campus leadership

This list is hardly exhaustive, and the ranking of these challenges will be different on each campus, but we will touch on each one briefly in hopes of kindling discussion.

Insufficient Funding

If faculty and administrative leaders at an institution decided to implement a tight integration of off-campus study with the on-campus curriculum, what would it take? More of everything: more preparatory workshops; more ongoing communication; more mini courses and seminars for returning students; and more opportunities and incentives for professors, upper administrators, staff, and students. In short: more money.

The conversation about securing and managing resources goes beyond the already tricky task of developing programming and services. It also concerns the actual cost of off-campus study programs themselves. The main pressure point in this context is the cost students incur for the programs they choose. Different institutions manage this differently: Students at some institutions pay the same tuition whether they stay on campus or participate in off-campus study, regardless of the actual cost. Others pay a charge only if participating in a program operated by a different institution than their own. Still others may incur fees even for in-house faculty-led programs. Some institutions cover travel costs, others do not. Some allow students to apply their financial aid to off-campus study, others do not. Some cover visa charges, others do not. Even at institutions where the majority of expenses are covered, there may still be additional handling fees that nibble away at students' ability to participate. In this area, every institution is idiosyncratic.

Campuswide discussions may be required to weigh options and manage costs. Most administrators hope to see their participation rates in off-campus study increase over time, and everyone wants the experience to be accessible to all students; however, material reality introduces constraints. Although creative solutions (e.g., raising funds for scholarships and grants) can be helpful, usually compromises will be needed. What is educationally desirable may not always be financially feasible.

The complex models for financing off-campus study should give us pause for at least one reason: At nearly every institution, our methods for funding this experience are radically different from the way we budget every other aspect of our students' education. The historical reasons for this are clear enough: off-campus study began as a desirable but nonessential supplement to liberal education, and it was not surprising to find supplemental fees attached to it. Now, however, when off-campus study lies at the center of much of what we do, and when it is arguably the densest collection of high-impact practices that our students will ever encounter, it's odd that our financial models rarely reflect this centrality.

Despite touting the importance of off-campus study by way of buzzwords like *global citizenship* and *global engagement* or other manifestations of globalness, our institutions often struggle to pair the allocation of resources and financial structures with these good intentions. As Heyl (2011) points out:

Some see study abroad as a drain on campus revenues (especially if students pay third-party providers for semester- or year-long services abroad) and, despite global rhetoric to the contrary, seek to cap the total number of students permitted to study abroad in a given year. Others see study abroad as a profit center and expect it to be managed as a business, much like executive or online education. (p. 6)

Similarly, to balance their internal budgets, many off-campus study offices are obliged to balance enrollments in high-cost programs with enrollments in the more affordable programs in their portfolio. Some institutions take it a step further and set higher grade point average requirements for some programs than what the program itself has defined as the appropriate threshold, not because the academic level of these programs requires more brain power, but simply to throttle down participation in more expensive programs.

One revolutionary way to approach the financing of off-campus study would be to stop treating it differently from all other credit-bearing activities on campus. According to Heyl (2011), "If study abroad were truly central to a campus mission—as with the philosophy or history department—its costs would be included in the tuition charged students" (p. 6). An example of this model is Soka University of America, where a semester-long study abroad experience is required of all students, and the cost is built into the tuition.

How the financial setup is conceived inevitably varies from institution to institution. We do not propose a particular model but simply underscore that the current methods for financing off-campus study are neither immutable nor especially suitable. They may seem natural and obvious in our institutional culture, but that's only because we have lived with them for so long. The financing of off-campus study was constructed in particular ways for historical reasons, but that means that it can also be deconstructed and reconstructed. Campus leadership would do well to assess whether the financial frameworks established for off-campus studies offices are aligned with the institutional vision for education and equity.

Faculty Inexperience

In chapter 3 we spoke of how few faculty members have participated in off-campus study during their own undergraduate years: roughly 1 in 10 (see note 3 in chapter 3 for our calculation). However, this fact does not just affect their ability to advise students; it ripples through campuswide discussions of curriculum and priorities. Although upper administrators may manage campus discussions and hold the key to resources, faculty members are typically the linchpin in educational initiatives. To a large extent they control educational priorities on college and university campuses, and they implement these priorities in their classrooms on a daily basis. Administrative leadership is clearly necessary, but any educational policy is stillborn if faculty are not prepared to support it. Moreover, if faculty are generally inexperienced in the area of off-campus study, it is hard to see how they will promote it in the general education curricula or the major curricula for which they often serve as the gatekeepers.

We addressed some mechanisms for faculty education in chapter 3. As Stohl (2007) advocates, the first step to internationalizing the university is to internationalize the faculty by way of faculty travel seminars, sending faculty to visit existing programs where they witness the student experience firsthand, or making it possible for a faculty member to teach abroad at a partner institution.

In short, we believe off-campus study is important for our students because it gives them an unmediated connection to something radically different, and we believe this encounter will shape them personally, academically, and professionally. It should be no surprise that the same holds true for professors.

Departmental Territorialism

There are many good reasons to defend the territory of departments, including considerations of principle and matters of practicality. Either way, when professors are trying to keep their students focused on a narrow specialization, off-campus study can appear as a breach in the wall of the departmental fortress.

The protectionist impulse fears a triple loss due to off-campus study. Loss Number 1: If off-campus study is not part of a departmental program (e.g., because it is conducted during the semesters before a student has declared a major), then it is part of that great inland sea known as general education. However, because students only take a limited number of classes during their time at the institution, any classes taken off campus will necessarily reduce the number of classes taken on campus, potentially draining students from existing lower division classes—courses that feed the upper-division classes the professors most want to teach. Even if this erosion is minor, the discussion about integrating off-campus study into the on-campus curriculum may mean that faculty fear they will be forced to compromise their own goals in order to accommodate someone else's objectives.

Loss Number 2: If off-campus study *is* part of a departmental major, the situation may be even worse. The major may consist of only a dozen courses, when suddenly an off-campus program effectively outsources two or three or four of those classes to another institution. It is the same zero-sum game imagined in the previous point but with more drastic results: The department loses the student from precisely those upper-division classes it most wishes to populate.

Finally, Loss Number 3: Departments value the cohesiveness of their curriculum, and professors fear that courses taken on another campus won't meet the same standard as those taught locally. They may also worry these courses won't mesh well with the rest of the department's offerings. Indeed, some department directors might be so concerned about the cohesiveness of their curriculum that they restrict students from taking courses abroad even if those courses are well suited to the major. For example, an art history department might have a blanket policy not to accept any credits from overseas institutions, regardless of academic quality and despite the access certain programs offer to world-renowned art collections and museums. Or perhaps an economics department refuses to transfer any credits from the London School of Economics or Oxford University. The departmental curriculum is viewed as a fragile mechanism, whose hand-crafted parts cannot be swapped out for generic replacements. As a result, no programs, no matter how excellent, will ever meet the high standards of home.

To some extent these objections are legitimate concerns, and they require substantial answers. After all, one can imagine scenarios in which departments that encourage off-campus study too zealously end up whittling away at their own existence. Professors are subject to the same drive for self-preservation as other animals, and to think otherwise would be naïve.

However, there are strategies for addressing these concerns, even if they require customization for each institution. A few solutions may include a combination of the following:

- Faculty-led programs. Not all administrators of departments or institutions wish to go into the business of running their own programs, and not all faculty wish to take on the responsibility of leading one. However, in the context of the current discussion, there is a double benefit: The participating faculty members develop a deep experience with off-campus study, which helps them build bridges between that experience and on-campus work. Also, student enrollments are kept largely within the department, for some portion of the students' classes may be taught by the faculty accompanying the students abroad.
- Many institutions and departments set residency requirements, limiting the number of courses a student may apply to the major

from off-campus study. This measure has the additional benefit of encouraging students to engage in multiple disciplines while abroad.

- The enrollments question may be less of a zero-sum game for majors than it appears at first blush. In our experience, students who study off campus in their major often gain perspectives through their work abroad that spark greater curiosity; they are more likely than those who do not study away to take additional courses in their major after their return. This means that students may actually take more than the minimum number of courses required.[1]

- Similarly, students who study off campus remain interested in the subjects they studied there, especially when those subjects are connected to the culture or region where they studied. A Spanish major returning to campus is more likely than before to sign up for a Latin American history or political science class, thereby raising enrollments in such classes, even though the student may not be majoring in the subject.

- Finally, one of the results of increased off-campus study at some institutions is a gentle increase in the size of the overall student body, which is made possible by the fact that a predictable number of students are off campus at any given time. Such an increase may compensate to some degree for those students who disappear for a semester or two.

In any case, the issues warrant discussion. The impact of off-campus study on on-campus enrollment and staffing are legitimate concerns that need to be addressed.

Complexity

Even if academic departments can be brought on board, it is no simple matter to coordinate the efforts required among campus offices to support off-campus study. On many campuses the process for supporting internationalization efforts is patched together, and when the system is put under stress (e.g., because of growing numbers of students or because of emergencies that need to be managed), the seams begin to split.

All this is to say that off-campus studies can never operate as an autonomous office. It needs to have connections to the academic programs it supports, while also relying on partnerships with many other offices and stakeholders on campus. To successfully send students off-campus, these offices need to foster coordination and collaboration with a wide range of stakeholders, including student financial services, registrars, risk managers, diversity officers, and the dean of students, not to mention the connections that need to be maintained with overseas providers, insurers, troubleshooters, and more.

The level of complexity is daunting, especially when staff members in each of these institutional offices have their own work to do and may not see off-campus studies as part of their mandate or their highest priority. (See chapter 9 for more on this topic.) Strong institutional leadership is typically necessary to encourage stakeholders to align their interests.

Lack of Support From Campus Leadership

Earlier we mentioned that faculty interest is the bedrock of any educational initiative; however, even bedrock is subject to the plate tectonics of institutional support. All the efforts described here for introducing faculty to the strengths and challenges of off-campus study also pertain to upper administrators. Together, these groups can craft institutional missions and educational policies that define the role and goals of off-campus study.

However, institutional leaders typically control one other crucial component of this equation: the purse strings. Incentives for faculty and relevant staff to learn about off-campus study, experience it, forge connections with colleagues abroad, and integrate it into their work will demonstrate that these are institutional priorities. They send a signal to faculty that such work will be valued and will not, for instance, weigh against them when it's time for tenure and promotion.

At another level, leadership can facilitate the integration of off-campus study in more structural but equally important ways. The Senator Paul Simon Award for Campus Internationalization presented by NAFSA (n.d.-a) recognizes U.S. colleges and universities that are making significant progress toward comprehensive internationalization. A review of the award winners of the past five years reveals a pattern of well-applied administrative efforts and resources by

- investing in faculty development (as described earlier), setting aside at least modest funds for faculty program and site visits, participation in international conferences, scholar-in-residence programs, and grants that encourage new courses with international content;
- engaging the staff by creating collaborations among such offices as off-campus studies, the registrar, the business office, the career center, and student health and counseling;
- engaging alumni in providing stepping-stone experiences to international careers;

- building collaborative partnerships with similar institutions and organizations worldwide;
- widening the circle of international activity on campus to include cocurricular and extracurricular activities, such as internships, fellowships, student research, and community engagement; and
- investing in assessment by measuring off-campus study's impact on students and faculty to advocate for resources and the implementation of new ideas

It bears repeating that none of this can be achieved without the support and guidance of institutional leadership.

Pressures in the Field

Organizations dedicated to study abroad and study away—including program providers like CET Academic Programs, IES Abroad, the Council for International Educational Exchange (CIEE), Institute for Study Abroad-Butler, as well as organizing bodies like NAFSA and the Forum for Education Abroad—are diligent in their efforts to identify and share best practices. Nevertheless, no shortlist or handbook of such principles applies to all scenarios. The very notion of a best practice begs a question: best for achieving what? Off-campus study programs are educational tools, and different tools have different functions. Just as a short-term, domestic island program conducted in English is probably not the ideal venue for students attempting to improve their Japanese, a year-long program in France with deep cultural and linguistic immersion may fail to meet the needs of a student hoping to focus on high-level work in the sciences. Each program serves at least slightly different needs, and so-called best practices have to be adapted to the programmatic goals.

All of this is to say that there is little agreement among specialists about what constitutes the ideal program in any particular context. Debate about off-campus study programs will continue in the field. The principal pressure points in this area concern several aspects: program format, the differences between study abroad and study away, ethical considerations in off-campus study, and the perennial dominance of Europe in study abroad.

Program Format

In the opening chapters we discussed the evolution of off-campus study from the early model of year-long study abroad in foreign countries (often where foreign languages are spoken), to what has become the new normal: a world in which short-term (two- to eight-weeks) programs count for the majority of off-campus study experiences. Moreover, we have tried to illustrate how effective short-term programs can be in certain circumstances—when designed carefully.

It's important not to fool ourselves into thinking that because short-term programs *can* be the right tool, they always *are*. The temptation to do so is great, for short-term programs typically cost less money, interfere less profoundly with our students' on-campus experience, are relatively easy to either outsource or handle in house, and allow us to boost our ever more public statistics for participation in off-campus study. However, while well-designed short-term programs have some clear advantages, they also suffer from severe limitations.

On the one hand, short-term programs can serve as effective and focused complements to on-campus curricula—often as a kind of culminating experience that has been prepared in classrooms on the home campus. Ideally, the experience will also lead to follow-up work after the return. They are also a good way to initiate inexperienced students into off-campus study; from this point of view, a short-term program represents a "safe" option for some students—one requiring less dramatic cultural and personal dislocation than a more extensive and more independent program. Such programs may serve as a stepping-stone to longer and more immersive experiences later. Of course, each student is different. Some may need a culturally familiar stepping-stone (e.g., to Great Britain), whereas others, with more worldly backgrounds, might try a two-week trip to Morocco before committing to a semester in the Sultanate of Oman.

Many language professions tend to dismiss short-term programs for the purposes of language acquisition, although even here they have their place. Research has shown that short-term immersion can provide students with real growth in their language skills; perhaps just as important, the experience motivates students for continued study by showing them the value of the work they have already undertaken (Willis Allen, 2010).

Finally, short-term programs are extremely useful for students who, for reasons of academic requirements or finances or inclination, could not otherwise study off campus. In short, an experience of nearly any duration, assuming it is well crafted and executed, is better than no experience at all.

On the other hand, it's important not to overlook the limitations of short-term programs. The vast majority are island programs; at best they are peninsula programs, and even there the local connection is often a vanishingly thin isthmus. Students who are confronted with severe cultural dislocation for a short time can sometimes hunker down and survive it unaffected, rather like a person who has been plunged underwater and holds their breath. Civic engagement opportunities, along with other experiential activities (e.g., internships or homestays), are severely limited on short-term programs. On such brief experiences, the cultural integration that is key for many students is difficult to achieve in a meaningful way. Finally, certain kinds of learning simply cannot be rushed; this includes much in the category of personal growth, which requires struggling with cultural difference for an extended period of time.

In short, it would be convenient if short-term programs offered a cost-effective, universal solution for administrators who want to augment the role of off-campus study at their institutions; unfortunately, this is not the case. They do have a role, but it is limited.

Differences Between Study Abroad and Study Away

Throughout this book, we use *off-campus study* as an umbrella term for *study abroad* and *domestic study away*. There are many reasons to discuss these two initiatives together: They share several structural components and they have similar implications for the curricular, cultural, and social integration that preoccupies us in these pages.

Moreover, because the field of domestic study away is less institutionalized than that of study abroad, fewer statistics are available for it, and this further encourages a blurring of lines between the two. However, similarity is not sameness.

Domestic study away appeals to many institutions and to many students. Colleges and universities may be drawn in part by the lower cost of study away; if nothing else, it doesn't involve international plane fares or visa hassles, and this alone helps bring the experience within reach of many students. Also, because the distance of the cultural dislocation is assumed to be smaller, such programs may strike students as less risky and less uncomfortable. Who would argue that a semester-long program in California is as bold a leap as a direct matriculation experience in Chile?

However, these assumptions can be faulty. For instance, studying inequality in immigrant Somali and Latino communities in Minneapolis–St. Paul, Minnesota, may be more culturally disruptive for a student than a tranquil semester in Cambridge, England. Domestic programs may offer immersion in communities that are next door, but that doesn't mean the dislocation will be any less powerful. Also, the knowledge students on a study away program have of American social systems, practices, and policies (not to mention their mastery of English), can make it possible for them to experience a deep connection in their host community, leading to a meaningful learning or service experience that might have been out of their reach abroad. Domestic study away can also integrate most of the high-impact activities that we point to in the opening chapters: The student cohort can form a learning community undertaking a common intellectual experience, perform collaborative assignments, and be engaged in research opportunities. Moreover, such programs are often internship based, include significant community engagement components, and have a strong focus on diversity. As Sobania (2015a) put it, "It is not about the location; it's about learning" (p. 3).

Nevertheless, domestic study away is not without its own challenges and limitations. Study away programs face competition from civic engagement initiatives that seamlessly integrate experiential learning into the community with an on-campus curriculum. Moreover, few domestic programs offer experiences of true global entanglement. Even more important, they rarely provide the experience of extreme otherness that well-designed study abroad can offer. Although study away students wrestle with such issues as gender, politics, and personal identity, they rarely escape the general culture and framework of the United States. In chapter 5 we discuss how stepping out of the American mind-set has a dual benefit. First, it allows the distance necessary for perceiving the logics and structures of one's home culture. Second, it opens one's eyes to the issues, plights, fears, dilemmas, interests, and accomplishments of the other 95% of the world's occupants. Although the experience of intracultural diversity in the United States is undeniably important, we need to be careful not to conflate it with the firsthand experience of a foreign culture. Foreign exposure is perhaps especially important now, when citizens of many countries equate globalization with Americanization. Domestic students benefit from stepping away from American culture; it allows them access to alternative views of the world, and it helps them understand how others perceive America's role in the world.

Ethical Considerations in Off-Campus Study

Increasingly students, faculty, and administrators are concerned about the ethics of off-campus study. Especially in programs where relatively well-heeled students land in locations where they experience no meaningful integration with the local culture, the program can smack of a new form of colonization. One is reminded of a (we hope apocryphal) tourist complaint about a trip to Spain: "There are too many Spanish people. The receptionist speaks Spanish. The food is Spanish. Too many foreigners now live abroad" (Zoeylola, 2012). Programs that eschew meaningful connections with people, favoring instead a context-free focus on museums or rocks or institutions, run the risk of cultural insensitivity. They evoke a new form of colonization, where resources are exploited, albeit academically, without regard or respect for the people inhabiting these spaces.

In chapter 6 we discussed the ethics of community engagement, but it is becoming increasingly obvious that issues of fair trade, ethics, positionality, and reciprocity need to be integrated into most forms of off-campus study. Just how that is to be done, and to what extent, remains to be seen. The topic looms large in the field, and administrators of each institution will need to grapple with it in their own way.

Perennial Dominance of Europe in Study Abroad

The goal is clear at the national level and on university and college campuses: More students should have the opportunity to engage in off-campus study. A sign of this is the effort of IIE (2018), through its Generation Study Abroad initiative, to make study abroad more accessible and to increase the participation rate across the United States. Most of us applaud this effort. But it's worth asking what the consequences will be if it succeeds. Take the example of the region that exerts such a magnetic attraction for our students: Europe. In 2016, 54.4% of students from U.S. colleges and universities chose Europe as their study abroad destination (IIE, 2017b). If institutions suddenly multiply their study abroad numbers by three or four, certain European cities may well be inundated with American students. Indeed, this is already a complaint concerning certain destinations that we treasure for the high-quality programs they offer. European cities and our provider partners cannot absorb unlimited increases in numbers: The customized care and cultural integration we value is not infinitely scalable. To make matters worse, some of these destinations have been made especially attractive because they offer courses not found at many other study-abroad locations: math and computer science in Budapest, theater and dance in London, or STEM in Edinburgh. In short, any increases in study abroad are unlikely to be evenly distributed around the globe; this will funnel even more students to Rome and Paris and Barcelona and Berlin.

One option would be to diversify offerings, and many institutions are making conscious efforts to offer study abroad opportunities in other locations—not only other regions of the world but also smaller European cities (away from the traditional study abroad hot spots). Moreover, some students do venture off the beaten track and study abroad everywhere from Uruguay to Nepal. However, the growth of these opportunities appears to be insufficient to meet the needs of increasing participation rates. Adding new, less well-traveled destinations is certainly commendable and provides exciting new opportunities for adventurous students, but in terms of accommodating and attracting high student volume, the effect of these innovations may remain minor for many years to come.

The goal to increase the number of students studying off campus in sustainable ways will require more than scaling up our existing structures. Sutton (2013) proposes the idea of *collaborative internationalization* and suggests building international academic alliances that "employ partnerships, consortia, and other linkages that span institutions and nations as both philosophical underpinning and key methodology for institutional growth" (pp. 40–41). This idea underscores the shift from institutional internationalization to one that is multilateral and multinational in its reach. No matter what, growth will entail a multitude of initiatives: new models, new destinations, and perhaps most challenging of all, new efforts to draw students away from the powerful appeal of destinations like Barcelona, London, and Florence.

External Pressure: Technology, Cultural Friction, and Uberization

Earlier in this chapter we focused on obstacles to off-campus study that abide within our institutions. However, off-campus study also faces challenges from external trends that are even more difficult to control. Technology, cultural friction, and *uberization* (i.e., the disruption of off-campus study by new economic models and new media) pose challenges to the traditional ways study abroad has been approached.

Technology

College students today are electronically connected most of the time. They are digital natives who value getting the information they want at any place and at any time. They are impatient and will "quickly discount those who can't immediately deliver on their needs" (Merriman, 2015, p. 10). A study of American study abroad students conducted in Denmark shows, not surprisingly, that the majority of study abroad students bring two or three electronic devices with them (Hofer, Thebodo, Meredith, Kaslow, & Saunders, 2016). Many of them engage in multitasking, such as being on social media, texting, or checking a website, even during class. Fifty percent of students communicate with friends back home at least once a day; 30% do it several times each day. Almost 50% of students communicate with their parents a few times per week, and more than 20% communicate with their parents at least once a day (Hofer et al., 2016). They are e-mailing, texting, Facebooking, Skyping, blogging, and Instagramming their way through their off-campus study experience. No sooner have they lived a moment than it appears in a post on social media. Kahneman (2010) describes them as a generation that experiences the present as an anticipated memory.

The role of information technology is growing in the lives of students, and there's no doubt that the experience of being away from home today is different from what it was even 10 years ago. Students are never more than a text or Skype call away from their parents or peers, and the narrative of being far away is now different from what many of today's professors or administrators experienced during their own off-campus study. At that time, departures were often akin to miniature emigrations, where the time away was long, and communication to the homeland was both difficult and expensive. Scholars have discussed the disruption and lack of focus that mobile technologies bring about in higher education (Chromey, Duchsherer, Pruett, & Vareberg, 2016), and off-campus study is not immune to these changes. Many faculty who teach on off-campus programs lament the loss of mental presence that occurs when students can always be in touch with family and friends back home.

Some students recognize the dangers of constant connectedness. A program participant cited in Hofer and colleagues (2016) offered this advice for other students:

> Stay away from cell phones for a bit each day to practice being more fully in the present. Many students tend to focus on being on Facebook and other social media to a point where it blocks them from experiencing study abroad to the fullest extent possible. (p. 35)

Another student advised: "Enjoy the time you have traveling, and stop looking for a wifi signal every minute! Enjoy just being on your own and take time to explore some things without friends and see what happens!" (Hofer et al., 2016, p. 35).

The fact that students are only a click away from reconnecting with home poses particular challenges for off-campus study. Experiences of cultural confusion and dislocation lie at the heart of this enterprise, providing valuable, teachable moments. If students stay in a digital comfort zone, such opportunities for learning can be lost or diminished.

But what is to be done about it? Is it really preferable or even plausible to ask students to turn off their cell phone? Does engagement with the local culture require behaviors that are old-fashioned and parochial?

Rather than demonizing students' dependence on devices, it may be more productive to explore how our own pedagogies can harness the enormous energy and interest many students have in technology. After all, we already use many technologies in our teaching, from teleconferencing to course management software like Moodle, Canvas, or Blackboard. Our students relish the way technology allows and encourages social connections. It would be possible to blend these activities, academic and social, using technology not just to maintain an existing social network but to create new ones that connect students to their host community. From this point of view, technology's greatest educational potential may lie in virtual exchanges among students from different parts of the world.

It is still relatively uncommon for a study abroad or domestic program to bring U.S. and international students together intentionally to work in a sustained, meaningful way on a commonly developed project. However, successful forays into virtual exchanges between campuses do exist and could be implemented and used in a study abroad setting as well. One of the most developed program is the State University of New York's Collaborative Online International Learning (COIL) Center. It offers a model for collaborative work that involves course modules or even entire courses linking home campuses with colleges and universities abroad. Professors from different institutions work together to develop a common curriculum, and they create a framework for learning that may be synchronous or asynchronous. The former includes real-time discussions and demonstrations that stress collaborative, experiential student interactions; the latter focuses on activities that don't require the simultaneous presence of all participants—such as assignments and self-directed learning guides, lecture recordings, and reading materials. Courses supported by COIL range from an advanced writing seminar to Engineering Ethics and the Psychology of Terrorism (State University of New York COIL Center, n.d.-b).

Virtual exchanges are also not new to foreign language educators. Some professors create bilateral language learning exchanges between classrooms in two different countries, with the course alternating between English and the foreign language. In other cases, multilateral exchanges may make sense. These involve learners from multiple countries who work together using a lingua franca like English (Hauck & O'Dowd, 2016). The European Commission has supported a launch of an online platform, UNICollaboration (unicollaboration.eu), that serves as a hub where educators can find partners and resources for collaborative exchanges. Creative solutions with technologies like these can help prepare students for off-campus study, especially if the virtual encounters are a prelude to real ones.

Navigating Cultural Friction

Many students come to off-campus study carrying their regional or ethnic or religious culture with them. Their engagement with the Black Lives Matter or #MeToo movements or with lesbian, gay, bisexual, transgender, queer, asexual, and other communities have shaped their expectations that the classroom will be a safe space. They may expect trigger warnings to be issued in advance of potentially upsetting texts or topics. Today's students also experience the challenges of fraternity cultures and gender equality, often in the context of Title IX, including campus conversations about sexual consent.

The changing climate and expectations in terms of classroom culture, considerations about bias, and related issues are challenging for all professors teaching undergraduates. However, in the context of off-campus studies, and especially for international study abroad, the plot thickens. When students leave their campus environment, they bring as much baggage as they do luggage. Foreign educators who are teaching U.S. students often have a basic knowledge of the U.S. educational system, and they typically follow general debates and the political climate in the United States. But often they lack in-depth knowledge of current developments on U.S. campuses, partly because that discourse changes so rapidly (at a rate that seems to be accelerating), and partly because this discourse varies from school to school.

The struggle to strike a balance between sensitivity and academic integrity is difficult enough on a U.S. campus. But faculty abroad are often at a loss about how to meet student expectations regarding, for example, the use of gender pronouns, or the definition of the classroom as a safe space. When students see their new environment through the lens of their home campus, new teaching styles, interactions, and expectations can come as a surprise, and students may be quick to judge them. Because they don't understand to what extent racism, sexism, individualism, and political correctness are cultural constructions, defined differently in different cultures, they judge their new environment according to the standards of home. Thus, a student in France may insist on referring to a Black politician in Paris as *Africaine-Américaine*, even though this term is at best meaningless in France, and at worst offensive. When the new culture doesn't agree with their preconceived ideas, it's the foreign culture that is often accused short-sightedness. The professors on these programs—especially if they are products of the culture in question—can find themselves in a defensive posture.

This friction can produce a good deal of heat, but it can also fuel education. Instructors in off-campus study (especially in foreign locations) should not be expected to eliminate friction by reproducing the coziness of the home institution. After all, what would then be the point of studying away? However, they can often meet the students halfway, using cultural difference and cultural friction as a lever for learning. It often means dealing with the notion of cultural friction explicitly, using provocative pedagogies that put students intentionally (but not gratuitously) before difficult topics. Initiating a conversation with students at the beginning of a program to discuss local perspectives about sensitive topics will at least help students begin to do this work.

The Uberization of Study Abroad

As discussed throughout this book, different study abroad models and designs can have different aims and outcomes. Are semester-long programs better than short-term programs? Is direct enrollment preferable to provider programs? Are language programs more valuable than English-language offerings? In the field of study abroad such questions have been scrutinized and debated for decades, but this discussion of fairly subtle differences might suddenly become a moot point. Some students are drifting away from the off-campus programs we have so carefully designed for them, pursuing off-campus opportunities they have cobbled together for themselves.

This tendency is part and parcel of innovative business models spreading around the world. Taxi companies and hotels are facing a new market reality as they struggle to compete with Uber and Airbnb; the old market has been disrupted. Off-campus study could face a similar disruption—one that would turn the definitions and structures of the study abroad field upside down. In this era of heightened individualization (at least in the United States), some students chafe at being limited to an institutionally approved list of programs; they may feel they can customize their own study abroad trip faster and cheaper—while making sure it caters entirely to their own preferences.

It's easy to see how this might work. Imagine a do-it-yourself student who is determined to study at a popular destination like Barcelona, takes a leave of absence from the home institution and enrolls in an independently offered language course in Barcelona. The student secures housing through Airbnb or a housing provider specializing in student accommodations (e.g., studyabroadapartments.com). Because the student stays for fewer than 90 days, there's no need to bother with a visa. After completing the program in Barcelona, the student reenrolls at the home institution and applies to transfer the Barcelona credits. Voilà.

While our institutions work to develop off-campus study programs that are fully integrated, the new do-it-yourself movement threatens what can only be called a *disintegration*. These students bypass the home institution, its approved list of programs, and the off-campus studies office altogether, creating their own study abroad or study away experience, enabled by technology and new business models.

Will we see an uberization of off-campus study in the years to come? Probably not on a massive scale. After all, universities and colleges have ample instruments and solid arguments for keeping strict control over where and when students may study. But the specter of this possibility should sound an alarm for study abroad professionals. It reflects how some students might already view study abroad, and it shows how easily they could circumvent the system. If campus leadership signals that off-campus study is merely a pleasing supplement rather than a core experience, and if faculty fail to emphasize and illustrate the value of well-integrated experiences, students may see a do-it-yourself option as attractive, viable, and legitimate.

These pressure points are certainly just the beginning. The field of study abroad continues to evolve rapidly as it responds to the tugs of an increasingly globalized and tense world. As rates of participation increase, placing ever more strain on the organizations that support students and on the communities that host them, new challenges and solutions are bound to arise.

Note

1. Off-campus programs are also a way to recruit majors, as reflected in survey responses such as the following: "I was interested in scientific research as a possible career prior to [starting college], and this was a major factor in my choice of biology as my major. However, I was also considering medical school (and music), and so I had not made up my mind. This off-campus program cemented my interest in research. To put it another way, this experience, above all others, was the one that finally helped me to decide to go to graduate school and to pursue an academic research career" (Biology major, program in Denmark).

9

SUSTAINING INTEGRATION

In the preceding chapters we sought to demonstrate how off-campus study ranks among the most powerful experiences our students will ever have. However, the success of this endeavor is far from guaranteed, for the very features that make off-campus study promising also present opportunities for failure. After all, the operations are complex. In the best cases, off-campus study combines multiple high-impact practices, helping our students integrate work and experiences from quite different aspects of their life. Not just interdisciplinary, the experience is also holistic, thanks to its emphasis on cocurricular, intercultural, and interpersonal learning. On the face of it, these multiple entanglements can make off-campus study look like a Rube Goldberg contraption, one of those gratuitously complicated devices for accomplishing simple tasks, and subject to utter failure if any single part of it breaks down.[1] However, it need not be such a fragile apparatus.

Off-campus study can be organized in robust, nonlinear ways so that small failures do not endanger the overall success of the enterprise. When the off-campus experience is properly embedded within other aspects of undergraduate education, the multiple reinforcing elements heighten the chances for success. The challenge is whether we can design this level of integration in ways that are highly reproducible. The practical impediments are considerable, for the integrative experience we imagine for our students is not reflected in the Balkanized structures that define our campuses.

Consider the difficulty. It's already challenging for faculty in an academic department to agree on such internal matters as the required curriculum for their major—despite the fact that the professors tasked with this decision typically know each other well, share an academic field, and have years of experience measuring the needs and abilities of their students. This kind of difficulty is not particular to academic programs; similar tugs-of-war take place in the library, information technology, or any large administrative unit on campus. Then, if such entities are asked to collaborate with another office or program, the difficulties are often compounded, not because people are fundamentally recalcitrant or uncooperative but because each office's mission is different, a fact that is often reflected in reporting lines.

Devising fully integrated off-campus study opportunities for an entire campus is an ambitious project. Such experiences require coordination among a multitude of stakeholders. Minimally this would involve off-campus study offices, academic departments, and third-party providers (which may themselves be embedded in different academic and national cultures). Moreover, as off-campus experiences expand into areas like internships and civic engagement, they draw increasingly on the expertise of career center professionals, community and civic engagement offices, student financial services, language centers, international student offices, and even offices of residential life and student safety. In short, successful off-campus study requires coordinated involvement from faculty, study abroad professionals, administrators, and many others, who are usually spread across the divisions of the institution. Only when a critical number of these stakeholders collaborate efficiently can one provide the proper predeparture scaffolding, optimize curricular and cultural integration throughout a program's duration, help students build on their experience after their return, and begin the difficult task of measuring results.

Our message, in short, is that the integration of student experience requires commensurate integration of the relevant offices on campus. How this coordination will occur is far from obvious. To assume that the representatives of these offices, who often do not even know each other, will collaborate spontaneously would be naïve. Impediments to collaboration are often built into the very structure of our campuses. After all, we create separate offices for a reason: Boundaries encourage focus. We don't want our study abroad professionals running the language center or our career counselors determining the curriculum. Moreover, we staff these offices with professionals who are highly trained in their area, and we need them to be passionate about their area of expertise. Specialization is often a strength, but single-mindedness presents challenges. Tensions may rise when we ask these specialists to share time, resources, and expertise with others who are equally committed to a different area.

One might add to this complexity the arborescence of administrative flowcharts. Different stakeholders in the off-campus study universe often have different reporting lines, leading into academic or nonacademic branches of the institution. Finally, these differences may be compounded by geography, as the relevant offices are often located in different buildings in remote locations on campus.

One might rightfully assert that collaboration remains possible even if the material conditions are not ideal; the proof of this is that many institutions living with structural challenges have nevertheless offered highly satisfactory off-campus study opportunities to their students. However, the fact that success remains possible in the face of serious obstacles is hardly an argument in favor of keeping impediments. In such situations, even when collaboration is not curtailed, it remains hampered. Eliminating impediments and facilitating collaboration may demand modest reorganization, but it can be worth the effort. The trick lies in finding the right balance—where each entity retains the autonomy it needs to accomplish its fundamental mission, while simultaneously yielding slightly in favor of certain shared goals or projects.

As Carpenter and Lanoux (2016) have shown, poor coordination can lead to duplication of efforts, missed opportunities, and internal competition for resources. How, then, might one imagine a model for achieving and sustaining integration?

One answer might be to consider how we approach this issue on other parts of our campuses. After all, academic departments, even when they contain subdisciplines, typically occupy the same space, budget, and facilities. Often we see the wisdom of clustering departments we consider to be similar—such as all the foreign languages or multiple social sciences. In these cases we recognize that bringing together faculty and students who have similar missions in mind can be fruitful.

A particularly good example at many institutions involves the integration of the sciences. Because many STEM fields rely on collaborative work, our institutions recognize the importance of shared collaborative spaces, usually represented on campus by science complexes that unite chemists and biologists or physicists and astronomers. It's increasingly common to find integrated science complexes on college and university campuses, such as Boston College's (2018) Schiller Center for Integrated Science and Society, Amherst College's (n.d.) Science Center (which advertises interdisciplinary spaces), or entities like the Science Learning Center at the University of Michigan (2018), which is designed to "support teaching and learning in the natural sciences" (para. 1). The interconnection of science programs is also reflected in the sources that fund undergraduate student research, such as the National Science Foundation and the Howard Hughes Medical Institute. Even undergraduate curricula reflect entanglements among the sciences. A major in physics often includes requirements or prerequisites in math; biology requires work in chemistry, biology, and math; and chemistry requires math and physics.

In addition to being open to multidisciplinarity, the sciences typically require collaboration with staff in the form of lab technicians or instrumentation specialists. Moreover, science courses often involve students in experiences outside the classroom, in the form of labs, field trips, and even research—all those extracurricular activities that have been as central to science education as off-campus study has traditionally been to the culture-focused majors. Because colleagues in the sciences have long recognized the need for such experiences, and because so much external funding is available to support them, they have devised organizational structures to help with this work. Many institutions have devised formal or informal boards or centers to encourage and administer this work, and at large universities such centers may even become separate colleges of instruction.

Lest administrative readers shudder at these comparisons, we hasten to clarify that we're not suggesting that the construction of expensive new buildings is necessary. As a thought experiment, however, the STEM example shows the kind of action we take on our campuses when we're serious about integrating apparently disparate practices. Such an endeavor requires change, typically in resource allocation, habits, and institutional culture.

Change is a problematic concept on many college campuses. Bolstered by long years of tradition (both institutional and disciplinary), we tend to be averse to evolution—at least until we're sure that new trends are not flash-in-the-pan fads and that they offer substantive and worthwhile benefits. Moreover, it's often important for us to customize our involvement with new practices, adapting them to the idiosyncrasies of our institution.

Given our collective cautiousness regarding change, we should address several questions before making major new commitments. In particular:

- What is it that we're trying to change and why?
- Who is responsible for designing and implementing this change?
- How—that is, by way of what structures—do we intend to accomplish and sustain the proposed changes?

The what, who, and how are interrelated: *What* we're trying to accomplish will help define *who* is responsible for the task, as well as *how* we intend to achieve it.

What We Are Trying to Change and Why

The goal of the preceding chapters has been to describe models for what might change in our thinking about study abroad and study away. Rather than considering off-campus study as a remarkable one-off experience (which, depending on your point of view, contributes to or interferes with your students' on-campus work), it would behoove us to consider multiple ways of integrating off-campus study into the four-year experience of our students. Moreover, given the increased relevance of internships and other forms of professional and cultural training (discussed especially in chapter 6), these experiences also lead beyond the four-year degree to careers and work our students will undertake after they leave our institutions. (Regarding the growing body of research about the connection between off-campus study and careers, see, in particular, British Council, 2013; Hart Research Associates, 2015; National Association of Colleges and Employers, 2015; Trooboff, Vande Berg, & Rayman, 2007.)

However, the specific change required at any given institution to achieve these outcomes reaches well beyond what this book can tackle. Accomplishing the kind of integration we recommend requires a considerable number of steps, and these need to mesh with the priorities, structures, and resources of each institution. Although we have attempted to lay out general principles and talking points in this book, no simple checklist exists for integrating off-campus study at a given institution.

Therefore, most campuses need a mechanism for devising their own checklist and thereafter for mapping the steps by which the recommended changes will be implemented. New channels and forums will be needed for discussing off-campus study, assessing it, allocating necessary resources for it, and for making decisions about its function and integration. The current practice on many of our campuses is based largely on magical thinking—a simple hope that disconnected structures will spontaneously result in well-connected experiences. Sadly, that is unlikely to occur. The solution to this problem is to create a structure that encourages the relevant stakeholders to collaborate. More on this later.

Who Is Responsible for Designing and Implementing Change?

Who should be in charge of this discussion? Given the great number of stakeholders (not only academic departments but also study abroad offices, career centers, civic engagement professionals, and student advisers), it's hard to imagine a decision-making process that proceeds uncontested. Moreover, even universally supported recommendations will languish if the necessary resources are not allocated to them. Therefore, regardless of who else is involved, the participation of those empowered to make decisions and loosen purse strings (typically associate deans, deans, provosts) is crucial. This is even more important when collaboration among significantly different reporting lines—such as academic and nonacademic offices—is hoped for.

There are three principal models for effecting change on our campuses, each with its advantages and disadvantages. The first corresponds to a top-down model in which upper-level administrators (e.g., senior international officers) make decisions and allocate resources. Often the resources for new initiatives include institutional grant applications, which can only be advanced by deans, provosts, or presidents; in other cases, institutional resources may be available. In any case, the obvious advantage to the top-down model is that administrators are actually empowered to authorize change on campuses; things can happen in ways that are aligned with strategic priorities, and they can be funded. This augments the chances that the resulting changes will be institutionalized and sustained. However, there are also drawbacks to this model. Initiatives championed only by administrators can evoke reactions of skepticism among faculty, especially when "new opportunities" sounds like a euphemism for greater efficiency or cost cutting. In cases where soft money in the form of grants supports new projects, faculty may hesitate to commit time to the effort for fear that the sponsored initiative will wither once funding dries up. Moreover, because grants often place tight restrictions on how funds can be spent or on who is eligible to receive them, certain stakeholders (especially those who hold what might be considered nonacademic positions) may be excluded from participation. In these cases, it's crucial for institutional resources to be made available to compensate for gaps in funding.

The second model for institutional change is the bottom-up alternative—a grassroots project by faculty to advance certain principles and practices. There is no doubt that faculty engagement is necessary for any effort to overcome institutional inertia in the area of academics. After all, faculty are the main gatekeepers and practitioners of the academic mission. However, because of the separation of powers at our institutions, faculty typically have limited access to resources. Although professors are adept at smaller, tactical solutions in the fiefdom of their courses or departments, broad institutional change is typically beyond their reach. Trying to recruit other faculty to participate in projects that don't enjoy administrative support is often a losing proposition. As Carpenter and Lanoux (2016) put it:

> Many seasoned faculty members suffer from "pilot fatigue," having thrown their energies into too many campus initiatives funded by external sources that tend to disappear along with the grant funding. When new programs are haunted by the ghosts of previously expired initiatives, faculty grow wary. Until we can demonstrate a proven recipe for lasting institutional change, many faculty will continue to protect their time from efforts that, though promising, risk petering out after support is depleted. (p. 28)

Given these obstacles, it seems unlikely that faculty can institute lasting change on their own. A bottom-up approach can only be successful if it meets with support at the administrative level of the institution.

The third model swaps the vertical descriptors of top-down or bottom-up for something more horizontal, which has to do with the lateral collaboration required across different offices, each of which operates at roughly the same level of the institutional hierarchy, albeit in different branches. For the kind of integration we advocate, thoughtful discussion across offices is the only path to success. At this level compromises and innovations can be envisioned and implemented. For instance, at Carleton College, when internship opportunities were added to select off-campus study programs, it required close collaboration (even entanglement) among the off-campus studies office, the career center, the language center, relevant academic departments, and student financial services. The participation of each of these players was necessary, and the absence of any one of the parties at the table would have doomed the project to failure.

Which of these three models should one pursue? The answer, of course, is all of them. As Carpenter and Lanoux (2016) put it in the context of campus internationalization, a "three-pronged approach" (p. 28) is the most promising. In this way, senior administrators can provide support and resources in a way that meshes with the solutions that faculty and other campus partners devise. When necessary, these senior administrators can work with their counterparts in parallel reporting lines to negotiate authorizations or encouragements that will then trickle down to the relevant offices or departments, thereby facilitating collaboration among offices. Moreover, senior administrators are in a position to watch for inequities and to act to rectify them. As Carpenter and Lanoux (2016) wrote,

> Although doling out carrots can help . . . counteract institutional inertia and fulfill the goals of a grant by incentivizing colleagues to try new things, offices and staff excluded from such incentives are less motivated to try new ideas, since each such trial comes at an uncompensated cost. Even worse, resentments may arise when a temporary money pot is distributed selectively to a small number of experimenters, further impeding institutional change on a broad scale. Some collaborative leadership and supplemental funding (often less restricted than grant funding) can help to ease the way forward. (pp. 28–29)

Certainly the most difficult role in these discussions is that of senior administrators, who must walk the line between overinvolvement (sometimes the same as micromanaging) and underinvolvement (which sometimes means watching a worthwhile initiative flounder). In many cases, their role may also be to enable conversation without too actively directing it by intervening at crucial moments to remind participants of available resources and strategic institutional priorities. Faculty and the nonacademic directors of the relevant offices need to have primary ownership of the work, but they also need to know they have institutional support.

Finally, regardless of the model employed, there is the question of how discussions about change are managed on campus. Detweiler (2018) describes the kinds of interactions we engage in when attempting to institute change. The first of these is the imperial model—orders given from on high, simply to be carried out. While such imperatives may occasionally be necessary, they rarely contribute to an ongoing collaborative atmosphere. The second is the transactional approach—a tit-for-tat where participation is secured by way of incentives. These interactions are also often necessary, but the relationships they build tend to last precisely as long as the incentives. The gold standard is the "relational approach" (p. 5)—built up over time, based on shared goals and successes. The relational approach is the one that can be truly transformational.

How Do We Accomplish and Sustain Change?

There are nearly 3,000 institutions of higher education in the United States, and each has its own practices, culture, opportunities, constraints, and mission. Administrators at each will need to consider how best to embed off-campus study into their local curriculum. We hope to have provided a framework that allows various stakeholders to come together and elaborate steps that are suitable for their institution. However, off-campus study is also like existing curricula in another way: It is subject to change and cannot be accomplished once and for all. This means that the three-pronged approach mentioned earlier needs to exist as something other than an ad hoc committee, dissolved once its work is complete.

As chapter 8 shows, there are significant pressure points in the areas of study abroad and domestic study away, and most of these are unlikely to be fully resolved any time soon. New pressure points will emerge, as will new program models and best practices. Like any other component of undergraduate education—be it curricular or cocurricular—off-campus study will require ongoing discussion and adaptation. The challenge is that most campuses have no natural locus for such discussions, which makes off-campus study different from many other components of general education, such as first-year seminars or language and writing requirements, which are typically administered by academic offices or standing committees. It is also different from the advanced coursework students do in particular disciplines, which remains largely the purview of the individual department.

Conversely, despite the fact that off-campus study's effects permeate the undergraduate experience, it is often handled in a piecemeal way. Study abroad offices might be presumed by many to be the headquarters for this work, but that is rarely the case. The professionals in such offices are experts in the often overwhelming operational aspects of off-campus study, such as advising students, assessing programs, managing predeparture training, securing insurance, managing medical forms, and more, but they are rarely charged with the responsibility of the broad integration of the experience in the curriculum and cocurriculum. That work requires, at a minimum, the input of faculty and upper-level administrators, in consultation with professionals in other offices. Moreover, on most campuses there is a dearth of conversation between study abroad professionals and the faculty or campus administrators. These groups rarely meet on campus—and even more rarely attend the same conferences. They operate in parallel universes, seldom intersecting.

Given the need for these disparate offices to coordinate their work on an ongoing basis, many colleges and universities are investigating structures that will help them institutionalize the resources and planning needed to integrate their students' global experience. Over the past decade global centers of one sort or another have sprouted on a number of college campuses, including such institutions as Middlebury, Bates, Carleton, Mount Holyoke, Wesleyan, Franklin and Marshall, Grinnell, Macalester, and Connecticut College, to name a few. At universities the trend holds, too, with centers like Wesleyan University's Fries Center, the University of Wisconsin's International Division (including the Institute for International and Regional Studies), Yale's Whitney and Betty MacMillan Center for International and Area Studies, Northwestern's Buffett Institute for Global Studies, the University of Florida's International Center, or Princeton's Institute for International and Regional Studies.

Although many might shrink from the idea of creating yet another body on our already overcrowded campuses, the formation of some kind of entity to organize aspects of global education strikes us as essential.

Global Centers

What does a center for global affairs (or one of the other common avatars: global engagement, global issues, or global studies) actually mean, and what does it do? Different campuses have defined entities of this sort in a variety of ways. Often the center is connected to a specific academic program or collection of programs—most commonly political science or area studies.

Sometimes it is run by a faculty director; alternatively, it may be the purview of an associate dean or provost. Many campuses have a senior international officer charged with the responsibility of overseeing broad efforts at internationalization, including off-campus study. To train these people, organizations like AIEA offer boot camps, where instruction is offered on such important topics as communication, planning, strategic alliances, and faculty engagement. Moreover, AIEA (2016) provides important and achievable guidelines that will prove useful for all those engaged in campus internationalization efforts. This set of 22 standards fall into four key categories: internationalization expertise, advocacy, leadership and management, and personal effectiveness (AIEA, 2016). The standards outline the knowledge, experience, and ethical qualities that are crucial for this work.

As its name implies, AIEA focuses on internationalization, which only partly overlaps with the way many administrators of institutions envision their engagement with the global. For one thing, many institutions are increasingly interested in community outreach and service-learning, especially in areas where the local intersects with the global, as in issues of immigration, economic disparity, climate change, or public health. These topics may well involve off-campus study, but they also connect to the community in ways that are increasingly important to many on-campus projects.

Venues for shaping and developing the cross-institutional principles of global education (however it is defined) are multiple but often limited in scope. Entities such as the Forum for Education Abroad, NAFSA, CIEE, AIEA, and others offer regular conferences on international or global topics. However, many of these focus on a particular aspect or on particular groups of stakeholders. However, smaller conferences sometimes occur, bringing together faculty, administrators, and cocurricular staff (especially from study abroad offices) to build connections across traditional organizational barriers. The Global Liberal Arts conferences were started in 2015, first at Connecticut College, and then hosted at Hamilton College in 2016, Carleton College in 2017, and Colby College in 2018. A 2018 conference at Soka University of America broadened the reach further, emphasizing the role of institutional leaders in the promotion of integrated global education. These and other groups seek to address issues not fully explored in the more traditional venues.

Many of the institutions participating in these efforts have also begun the process of creating structures on campuses to help with the integration they seek to achieve. Traditional study abroad offices certainly play a crucial role, but they are newly invigorated by robust connections to the curriculum through interaction with career centers, community engagement offices, fellowship advisers, and more.

Just as each institution needs to customize its approach to the integration of study abroad, any center or organizing office will need to mesh with institutional culture, needs, idiosyncrasies, and resources. A global center will likely draw on existing models on campus—those other clusters of activity that require the participation of multiple departments and offices. On some campuses this may translate into a building that serves as a hub for multiple activities, whereas in others it may take the form of a simple committee comprising the representatives of stakeholder entities.

The work of such centers is only now becoming clear. Although regular panels at AAC&U address issues of global education (e.g., Penprase, Jensen, Boyle, Mayer, & Carpenter, 2018), other conferences have sprung up to advance discussions on the topic. Conferences on the global liberal arts (or even the globalizing of the liberal arts) have multiplied (e.g., Yale University, 2015). Whatever the particular form these centers take on a given campus, their work can generally be summarized in three verbs: coordinate, distribute, advocate.

Coordinate

Because the activities on any campus that brush against global issues are numerous, it's useful to have an entity responsible for centralizing their organization and advertising, and perhaps even their funding. On some campuses (e.g., Middlebury College and Mount Holyoke College), it has been possible to organize annual themes that touch many courses and events. Some institutions sponsor on-campus conferences highlighting global topics as wide ranging as water scarcity, human liberty, immigration, public health, resource allocation, and more. On other campuses, the work of coordination includes tracking student participation in these activities, leading to a transcript notation.

However, even without such high-profile programs, a global center can help coordinate many portions of a student's experience. Such centers bridge the divide between academic departments and off-campus studies offices, career centers, and more, offering advising and guidance. They may sponsor speakers and other events, providing a coherent program that connects explicitly with existing courses. Moreover, a center can bring together faculty from disparate programs, helping them discover areas of common interest, through reading groups or workshops, which may in turn result in team-taught courses, FLAC opportunities, or other collaborative ventures. Finally, such centers might help member programs come together to plan for upcoming faculty hires, proposing position descriptions that reach beyond the confines of a single discipline. The result may be a description that is

more compelling in the eyes of administrators who face increasingly strait-
ened budgets—especially in the area studies and foreign language or culture
programs.

Distribute

A center with a budget has the means to make good on its aspirations.
Programs that are the most involved in global issues, such as area studies,
are often small, and they struggle to present a profile that can compete with
other entities on campus. However, when a center brings together many
small programs, there is strength in numbers. Multiple small budgets can be
shared for a larger impact, and a center with its own resources can dangle the
carrot of financial assistance to encourage collaboration.

Ideally, the available resources would go beyond what is needed for
events. A center could usefully deploy course development funds for faculty,
research fellowships for students, and, perhaps most important, privileged
access to funding for team-taught courses or guest instructors.

Advocate

A center needs to be the voice of the programs it represents. By maintaining
visibility and serving as a clearinghouse for events and information, a global
center can make sure its member programs receive the attention they deserve.

Models

At smaller institutions, global centers tend to have a campuswide reach,
striving to affect the experience of all or most students. In the majority
of cases, such as Mount Holyoke College's McCulloch Center for Global
Initiatives or Wesleyan University's Fries Center for Global Studies, the new
entity reorganizes several existing offices. The most important of these is
often study abroad, but entities like language centers, international internships, and even civic engagement may come under their purview. At Bates
College, the Center for Global Education was introduced in an effort to
boost global engagement, both on campus and off. The center brought
together off-campus study and international student programs in a shared
space, collaborating on programming designed to enhance and enliven the
Bates (n.d.) experience.

One might be tempted to dismiss these organizational changes as a mere
rearrangement of chess pieces. After all, it's not immediately clear what is
new about an entity composed almost entirely of preexisting parts. However,
even if these centers did not attract additional resources and responsibilities, the simple fact of joining the offices speaks volumes. For one thing, it

facilitates the kind of integration we promote in this book. A language center, for instance, is no longer conceived of as an island of resources for beginning language classes, but is reimagined as a hub of activities that connect to off-campus study, international internships, and even community engagement.

Moreover, because certain cocurricular entities may now come under the umbrella of an academic center, their important contributions to undergraduate experience and learning are highlighted. The academic aspect of the enterprise is further emphasized by additional programming. At Connecticut College the Walter Commons for Global Study and Engagement also administers the Center for the Study of Race and Ethnicity. Middlebury's Rohatyn Center for Global Affairs sponsors an annual academic colloquium, as well as a student-designed international conference. Through features like these, along with occasional sponsored courses that are often interdisciplinary, global centers reinforce their academic rigor. Because they naturally connect to student experiences in off-campus study, internships, civic engagement, and more, they incarnate and illustrate the kind of integration that used to be found primarily in the off-campus programs themselves.

Although global centers at smaller institutions tend to have many responsibilities, there is one thing most of them are not: academic majors. Although intimately connected to the educational mission of their institution, they typically operate in the interstices of existing majors and minors. Many institutions have global studies programs associated with political science, but separate from global centers. The center's job, then, is to link the many courses, majors, minors, events, speakers, off-campus study experiences, and internships that constitute the global experience at an institution. In this way, the center draws together disparate experiences, helping students chart pathways through them. In particular, these entities are well placed to help students link curricular and cocurricular learning—the same high-impact combination that characterizes successful off-campus study.

The kind of integrative work we have described is easier to envision at colleges of 2,000 students than in universities with 10,000 or 20,000 undergraduates. In particular, off-campus studies offices at large universities already perform phenomenally complex work, often dealing with thousands of graduate and undergraduate students in 150 or more departments.

Not surprisingly, large university centers tend to be less comprehensive. Nevertheless, the principle of integration persists. The University of Wisconsin's International Division houses study abroad and international internships, while maintaining a partnership with the Institute for Regional and International Studies. Yale's Whitney and Betty MacMillan Center for International and Area Studies clusters an array of academic programs through an aggressive program of events (lectures, conferences, workshops, roundtables, symposia, and films); however, it does not oversee off-campus study, internships, or civic engagement. Similarly, Northwestern's Buffett Institute for Global Studies fosters community-engaged scholarship, international projects and internships, and career support for students aiming for globally engaged professional lives.

In all these cases, the common theme is integration. Even at large institutions these centers are helping students connect their learning to the world beyond the borders of campus.

Recognizing Achievement

Because global centers encourage and organize curricular and cocurricular aspects of student experience, they are also well positioned to record, assess, and recognize the work students do in this area. Therefore, global centers may be an ideal site for capturing student work through tools like ePortfolios, leading to credentials or other forms of recognition of student achievement in areas of global citizenship, service-learning, intercultural competency, language proficiency, and more.

At some colleges and universities, embedding global experience into the curriculum has led to efforts to render this integration more explicit and visible, especially for students. Thus, institutions as different as Mount Holyoke College with a student body of 2,000 and Florida International University (FIU), with its student body of 50,000, have introduced ways to recognize a student's level of global or international engagement, resulting in a notation on the student's official transcript. Unlike academic majors or minors, such notations reach beyond course requirements in a given department, seeking instead to capture the far-flung experiences across and beyond the curriculum. They typically include certain courses, to be sure, but they also reflect participation in off-campus study, internships, civic engagement, and cocurricular events.[2]

At Mount Holyoke's McCulloch Center for Global Initiatives (n.d.-a), for instance, Global Competence Award winners must fulfill five different requirements that may be entirely separate from their academic major. Students must demonstrate foreign language competence, cultural immersion (through study abroad or other international experience), global perspectives (through coursework), and cross-cultural learning on campus (through cocurricular activities). Finally, they are required to integrate these experiences through a reflective essay. The awards are listed in the commencement program and noted on the transcript.

This form of recognition is scalable to larger institutions. For instance, Florida International University, which caters to a very different student body, has organized a Global Learning Medallion program to recognize student achievement (FIU Global Learning, 2018). Core courses with the global-learning designation have been identified and sometimes created in both lower- and upper-division curricula, including courses in virtually every major on campus. By requiring coursework at the lower and upper levels, FIU helps ensure that students will maintain their engagement throughout much of their undergraduate career. Furthermore, students choose from a palette of other forms of involvement, such as internships, language instruction, off-campus study—all while participating in occasional cocurricular events like talks, films, and roundtable discussions. Although relatively few students participate in formal off-campus study at Florida International University, the institution is ideally poised to connect to global communities in the rich cultural mix of Miami. The culmination of the experience is an ePortfolio that helps students draw together the connections of their global learning experience; it is also a document that can highlight their background for employers.

Final Thoughts

Ultimately, we hope we have made the case for integrating off-campus study deeply into the undergraduate education. However, we don't claim to know how that integration should be implemented on your campus. Different models achieve different ends, and these must be negotiated with the institutional mission and culture.

In short, only you can do this work. Indeed, you *must* do it, for ignoring the issue is unlikely to serve any campus well. Our students continue to study off campus in increasing numbers, and many of them will work in fields touched by global issues. The global entanglement of economics, health, climate, culture, ethics, religion, and politics demands that we adjust the education we offer to respond to changing and overlapping fields. Never before has an awareness of the global felt more crucial—not just to our understanding but to our very survival.

Early in this book (especially in chapter 2) we sought to illustrate how off-campus study realizes the highest ideals of integrative learning, and how the practices of study abroad and study away have moved from the margins of liberal education to its core. Off-campus study, in its best incarnations, is nothing short of a model for learning today.

We leave the final word to students. As illustrated in the following comments, they know far better than we the various ways the integrative experience of off-campus study can shape their lives:

One key experience was my village homestay. Initially each student lived in their own village with a host family for six days. These families had no running water or electricity, and were very poor. I thought it would be really hard for me, but found that I easily adapted to their lifestyle. In fact, I enjoyed my time so much that I returned for another three and a half weeks. I was surprised by how easily I was able to integrate into their very different lifestyle, and was also surprised by how quickly I became one of them and was no longer a spectacle, particularly to the little children in the village. (Major in physics, program in Madagascar)

We had students who were responsible for guiding us through Japan and getting us to be culturally aware and mindful throughout the program. For example, they took us on an excursion to Mt. Hiei, a very significant religious and cultural fixture in Japan, and showed us around, informing us on correct Buddhist temple etiquette and explaining things that were going on in the temple. By going with our Japanese peers, we were able to see Japan in a totally new way, which helped to integrate us better into the country. (Major in linguistics, program in Japan)

One of our courses was on environmental economics, and while we were traveling near Cusco, we were able to interview people in the communities, to see how the Interoceanica interstate (newly completed) had impacted their local community, and we also visited a gold mining site. In Lima, our other classes integrated museums and service-learning projects into the curriculum. (Major in American studies, program in Peru)

One class was an internship somewhere in DC. My internship happened to be at the national defense university on a military base. Other people interned on the Hill, others in think tanks and nonprofits. Our program was entirely designed to integrate DC into our lives. I am forever grateful. (Double major in political science and German, program in Washington DC)

Notes

1. Anyone not familiar with Rube Goldberg should see www.rubegoldberg.com.

2. These programs differ from a minor. Rather than representing a particular depth of study in a discipline, they reflect a breadth of experience, including curricular and cocurricular components. This is especially helpful for students who wish to highlight their involvement in global issues for prospective employers. When such certifications include activities like ePortfolios (see chapter 7), the reflection process also helps students in their own integration of their experience because they learn to put into a narrative what they have accomplished.

REFERENCES

American Council on Education, Art & Science Group, & College Board. (2008). *College-bound students' interests in study abroad and other international learning activities.* Retrieved from http://www.acenet.edu/news-room/Documents/2008-Student-Poll.pdf

American Council on Education, Center for Internationalization and Global Engagement. (n.d.-a). Retrieved July 15, 2018 from http://www.acenet.edu/news-room/Pages/Center-for-Internationalization-and-Global-Engagement.aspx

American Council on Education, Center for Internationalization and Global Engagement. (n.d.-b). *Internationalization Toolkit.* Retrieved July 15, 2018 from http://www.acenet.edu/news-room/Pages/Internationalization-Toolkit.aspx

American Council on the Teaching of Foreign Languages. (n.d.). *ACTL proficiency guidelines 2012.* Retrieved from https://www.actfl.org/publications/guidelines-and-manuals/actfl-proficiency-guidelines-2012

Amherst College. (n.d.). *The new Science Center.* Retrieved February 13, 2018, from https://www.amherst.edu/amherst-story/future/greenway-campus/science-center

Anderson, C. L., Lorenz, K., & White, M. (2016). Instructor influence on student intercultural gains and learning during instructor-led, short-term study abroad. *Frontiers, 28,* 1–23.

Anderson, L. C. (Ed.). (2005). *Internationalizing undergraduate education: Integrating study abroad into the curriculum.* Minneapolis, MN: University of Minnesota.

Arum, R., & Roksa, J. (2011). *Academically adrift: Limited learning on college campuses.* Chicago, IL: University of Chicago Press.

Association of American Colleges & Universities. (2002). *Greater expectations: A new vision for learning as a nation goes to college.* Washington, DC: Author.

Association of American Colleges & Universities. (2009a). *Global learning VALUE rubric.* Retrieved from https://www.aacu.org/value/rubrics/global

Association of American Colleges & Universities. (2009b). *Integrative and applied learning VALUE rubric.* Retrieved from https://www.aacu.org/value/rubrics/integrative-learning

Association of American Colleges & Universities. (2009c). *Intercultural knowledge and competence VALUE rubric.* Retrieved from https://www.aacu.org/value/rubrics/intercultural-knowledge

Association of International Education Administrators. (n.d.). *AIEA Leadership Academy for new senior international officers.* Retrieved from http://www.aieaworld.org/aiea-sio-academy-

Association of International Education Administrators. (2016). *Standards of professional practice for international education leaders and senior international officers.* Retrieved from http://www.aieaworld.org/standards-of-professional-practice

Bates (n.d.). *Center for global education.* Retrieved from http://www.bates.edu/global-education/global-education/

Batson, T., Coleman,.K. S., Chen, H. L., Watson, C. E., Rhodes, T. L., & Harver, A. (Eds.). (2017). *Field guide to ePortfolio.* Washington, DC: Association of American Colleges & Universities.

Bauman, Z. (2012). *Liquid modernity.* Cambridge, UK: Polity Press.

Bennett, M. J. (1993). Towards ethnorelativism: A developmental model of intercultural sensitivity. In R. M. Paige (Ed.), *Education for the intercultural experience* (2nd ed.), (pp. 21–71). Yarmouth, ME: Intercultural Press.

Boston College. (2018). *The Schiller Institute for Integrated Science and Society.* Retrieved from https://www.bc.edu/bc-web/schools/mcas/sites/schiller-institute.html

Bourdieu, P., & Passeron, J. C. (1990). *Reproduction in education, society and culture.* London, UK: SAGE.

Braskamp, L. (2009). Study abroad or study away: It's not merely semantics. *Peer Review, 11*(4), 23–26.

Brewer, E., Cannon, R., Kaufman, H., & Nixon, A. (2012, March). *Integrating study abroad assessment into institutional practice.* Panel presentation at the meeting of the Forum on Education Abroad Standards of Good Practice Institute: Assessment Outcomes in Education Abroad, Denver, CO.

Brewer, E., & Cunningham, K. (2009a). Capturing study abroad's transformative potential. In E. Brewer & K. Cunningham (Eds.), *Integrating study abroad into the curriculum: Theory and practice across the disciplines* (pp. 1–19). Sterling, VA: Stylus.

Brewer, E., & Cunningham K. (Eds.). (2009b). *Integrating study abroad into the curriculum: Theory and practice across the disciplines.* Sterling, VA: Stylus.

Brewer, E., & Solberg, J. (2009). Preparatory courses for students going to divergent sites. In E. Brewer & K. Cunningham (Eds.), *Integrating study abroad into the curriculum: Theory and practice across the disciplines* (pp. 41–62). Sterling, VA: Stylus.

British Council. (2013). *Culture at work: The value of intercultural skills in the workplace.* Retrieved from https://www.britishcouncil.org/sites/default/files/culture-at-work-report-v2.pdf

Brockington, J. L., & Wiedenhoeft, M. D. (2009). The liberal arts and global citizenship: Fostering intercultural engagement through integrative experiences and structured reflection. In R. Lewin (Ed.), *The handbook of practice and research in study abroad: Higher education and the quest for global citizenship* (pp. 117–132). New York, NY: Routledge.

Brownell, J. E., & Swaner, L. E. (2009). Outcomes of high-impact educational practices: A literature review. *Diversity & Democracy, 12*(2), 4–6.

Brownell, J. E., & Swaner, L. E. (2010). *Five high-impact practices: Research on learning outcomes, completion, and quality.* Washington, DC: Association of American Colleges & Universities.

Bureau of Labor Statistics. (2018). *Occupational handbook: Interpreters and translators.* Retrieved from https://www.bls.gov/ooh/media-and-communication/interpreters-and-translators.htm

Burn, B. B. (Ed.). (1991). *Integrating study abroad into the undergraduate liberal arts curriculum: Eight institutional case studies.* New York, NY: Greenwood Press.

Campus Compact. (n.d.). Carnegie Community Engagement Classification. Retrieved from https://compact.org/initiatives/carnegie-community-engagement-classification/

Carpenter, S., & Lanoux, A. (2016). On the power and limits of faculty-led internationalization. *IIE Networker, 28–29.*

Carr, N. (2007). *The shallows: What the Internet is doing to our brains.* New York, NY: Norton.

Chabris, C., & Simons, D. (1999). *The invisible gorilla.* Retrieved from http://www.theinvisiblegorilla.com/gorilla_experiment.html

Chirkov, V. (2016). *Fundamentals of research on culture and psychology: Theory and methods.* New York, NY: Routledge.

Chisholm, L. A., & Berry, H. A. (2002). *Understanding the education—and through it the culture—in education abroad.* Portland, OR: International Partnerships for Service Learning.

Chromey, K. J., Duchsherer, A., Pruett, J., & Vareberg, K. (2016). Double-edged sword: Social media use in the classroom. *Education Media International, 53*(1), 1–12.

Common European Framework of Reference for Languages: Learning, Teaching, Assessment. (n.d.). *A transparent, coherent and comprehensive reference instrument.* Retrieved from https://www.coe.int/en/web/common-european-framework-reference-languages

Cope, B., & Kalanzis, M. (2000). Multiliteracies: The beginnings of an idea. In B. Cope & M. Kalantzis (Eds.), *Multiliteracies: Literacy learning and the design of social futures* (pp. 3–8). New York, NY: Routledge.

Council of Europe. (2018). *European language portfolio (ELP).* Retrieved from https://www.coe.int/en/web/portfolio/home

Crips, G. T. (2012). Integrative assessment: Reframing assessment practice for current and future learning. *Assessment & Evaluation in Higher Education 37*(1), 33–43.

Cronon, W. (1998). "Only connect . . . " The goals of a liberal education. *The American Scholar, 67*(4), 73-80.

Cross, K. P. (1999). *Learning is about making connections* (The Cross Papers No. 3). Laguna Hills, CA: League for Innovation in the Community College; Princeton, NJ: Educational Testing Service.

De Certeau, M. (1984). *The practice of everyday life* (S. Rendall, Trans.). Berkeley, CA: University of California Press.

Deardorff, D. K. (2015). *Demystifying outcomes assessment for international educators: A practical approach.* Sterling, VA: Stylus.

Detweiler, R. (2018). *Developing global education networks: transactional and relational approaches?* Retrieved from http://sites.soka.edu/GLA/wp-content/uploads /2018/06/Detweiler-Panel-2-June-4.pdf

Deutscher, G. (2010a, August 26). Does your language shape how you think? *New York Times Magazine.* Retrieved from http://www.nytimes.com/2010/08/29/ magazine/29language-t.html?pagewanted=all&_r=0

Deutscher, G. (2010b). *Through the language glass: Why the world looks different in other languages.* New York, NY: Metropolitan Books.

DeWinter, U. J., & Rumbley, L. E. (2010). The diversification of education abroad across the curriculum. In W. W. Hoffa & S. C. DePaul (Eds.), *A history of U.S. study abroad: 1965–present* (pp. 55–111). Carlisle, PA: Frontiers.

Doidge, N. (2007). *The brain that changes itself.* New York, NY: Penguin Books.

Doll, M. (2017). *Disegno in Orvieto.* Retrieved from https://forumea.org/resources/ curriculum/curriculum-resources/curriculum-toolbox/disegno-in-orvieto

Drake, J. K., Jordan, P., & Miller, M. A. (Eds.). (2013). *Academic advising approaches: Strategies that teach students to make the most of college.* San Francisco, CA: Jossey-Bass.

DuFon, M. A., & Churchill, E. (2006). *Language learners in study abroad contexts.* Clevedon, UK: Multilingual Matters.

Engle, J., & Engle, L. (2002). Neither international nor educative: Study abroad in the time of globalization. In W. Grünzwieg & N. Rinehart (Eds.), *Rockin' in Red Square: Critical approaches to international education in the age of cyberculture* (pp. 25–39). Münster, Germany: LIT.

Engle, L. (2013). The rewards of qualitative assessment appropriate to study abroad. *Frontiers, 22,* 111–126.

Engle, L., & Engle, J. (2003). Study abroad levels: Toward a classification of program types. *Frontiers, 9,* 1–20.

European Commission. (2015). *Erasmus—facts, figures & trends: The European Union support for student and staff exchanges and university cooperation in 2013–14.* Luxembourg: Publications Office of the European Union.

Farrugia, C. A., & Bhandari, R. (2016). *Open doors 2016 report on international educational exchange.* New York, NY: Institute of International Education.

Florida International University Global Learning. (2018). *Earn a prestigious global distinction.* Retrieved from https://goglobal.fiu.edu/medallion/

Folsom, P., Yoder, F., & Joslin, J. E. (2015). *The new advisor guidebook: Mastering the art of academic advising.* San Francisco, CA: Jossey-Bass.

Forum on Education Abroad. (2017a, June 26). *OAR Committee Meeting Minutes.* Carlisle, PA: Author.

Forum on Education Abroad. (2017b). *Resources: Outcomes.* Retrieved from https:// forumea.org/resources/outcomes/

Friedman, A. (2015, May 10). America's lacking language skills. *The Atlantic.* Retrieved from https://www.theatlantic.com/education/archive/2015/05/filling- americas-language-education-potholes/392876/

Fulbright U.S. Student Program. (n.d.). *History.* Retrieved from https://us.fulbrightonline.org/about/history

Ge, J., Peng, G., Lyu, B., Wang, Y., Zhuo, Y., Niu, Z., . . . Gao, J. H. (2015, March). Cross-language differences in the brain network subserving intelligible speech. *Proceedings of the National Academy of Sciences 112*, 2972–2977.

Gee, J. P. (1990). *Social linguistics and literacies: Ideology in discourses.* London, UK: Falmer Press.

Geertz, C. (1977). *The interpretation of cultures.* New York, NY: Basic Books.

Godwin, K. A. (2015a). The counter narrative: Critical analysis of liberal education in a global context. *New Global Studies, 9*, 223–243.

Godwin, K. A. (2015b). The worldwide emergence of liberal education. *International Higher Education, 79*, 2–4.

Goldoni, F. (2015). Preparing students for studying abroad. *Journal of the Scholarship of Teaching and Learning, 15*(4), 1–20.

Graesch, A. P., Benoit, C., Steiner, C., Bennett, J., & Black, R. (2017). *Anthropologists abroad.* Retrieved from https://forumea.org/resources/curriculum/curriculum-resources/curriculum-toolbox/anthropologists-abroad/

Green, M. (2005). *Internationalization in U.S. higher education: The student perspective.* Washington DC: American Council on Education.

Grenfell, M. (Ed.) (2002). *Modern languages across the curriculum.* London, UK: Routledge.

Grites, T. J., Miller, M. A., & Voler, J. G. (Eds.). (2016). *Beyond foundations: Developing as a master academic advisor.* Hoboken, NJ: Jossey-Bass.

Hart Research Associates. (2015). *Falling short? College learning and career success.* Retrieved from https://www.aacu.org/leap/public-opinion-research/2015-survey-results

Hartman, E., Morris Paris, C., & Blache-Cohen, B. (2014). Fair trade learning: Ethical standards for community-engaged international volunteer tourism. *Tourism & Hospitality Research, 14*, 108–116.

Harvey, T. (2017, November 7). Assessing intercultural learning: Beyond assessment tools [Webinar]. Institute for Cross-Cultural Teaching and Learning.

Hauck, M., & O'Dowd, R. (2016). Telecollaboration and virtual exchange in university foreign language education. *IIE Networker, 22*–23.

Haviland, J. B. (1998). Guugu Yimithirr cardinal directions. *Ethos 26*(1), 25–47.

Haynes, C. (2011). Overcoming the study abroad hype. *Journal of the National Collegiate Honors Council 12*(1), 17–24.

Hersh, R. H. (2005, November). What does college teach? *The Atlantic.* Retrieved from https://www.theatlantic.com/magazine/archive/2005/11/what-does-college-teach/304306/

Hersh, R. H., & Schneider, C. G. (2005). Fostering personal and social responsibility on college and university campuses. *Liberal Education, 91*(3/4), 6–13.

Heyl, J. D. (2011). *Third-party program providers in education abroad: Partner or competitor?* Retrieved from http://www.aieaworld.org/occasional-papers.

Hofer, B. K., Thebodo, S. W., Meredith, K., Kaslow, Z., & Saunders, A. (2016). The long arm of the digital tether: Communication with home during study abroad. *Frontiers, 28*, 24–41.

Hoffa, W. W. (2007). *A history of US study abroad: Beginnings to 1965*. Carlisle, PA: Frontiers.

Hora, M. T., Benbow, R. J., & Oleson, A. K. (2016). *Beyond the skills gap: Preparing college students for life and work*. Cambridge, MA: Harvard Education Press.

Hovde, P. (2002). Opening doors: Alternative pedagogies for short-term programs abroad. In S. E. Spencer & K. Tuma (Eds.), *The guide to successful short-term programs abroad* (pp. 1–7). Washington, DC: NAFSA–Association of International Educators.

Hubert, D., Pickavance J., & Hyberger, A. (2015). Reflective E-portfolios: One HIP to rule them all? *Peer Review, 17*(4), 15–18.

IES Abroad. (n.d.). *Map for language and intercultural communication*. Retrieved from https://www.iesabroad.org/study-abroad/advisors-faculty/ies-abroad-map/map-for-language.

IES Abroad. (2018). *Internship and service learning seminar*. Retrieved from https://www.iesabroad.org/study-abroad/courses/santiago/fall-2017/sl-in-395

IIPSL Institute for Global Learning. (n.d.). *Make a difference with your . . . study abroad*. Retrieved from https://www.ipsl.org/

Illich, I. (1990). To hell with good intentions. In J. C. Kendall & Associates (Eds.), *Combining service and learning: A resource book for community and public service* (Vol. 1, pp. 314–320). Raleigh, NC: National Society for Internships and Experiential Education.

Institute of International Education. (2017a). *Fast facts*. Retrieved from https://www.iie.org/Research-and-Insights/Open-Doors/Fact-Sheets-and-Infographics/Fast-Facts

Institute of International Education. (2017b). *Host region*. Retrieved from https://www.iie.org/Research-and-Insights/Open-Doors/Data/US-Study-Abroad/Host-Region

Institute of International Education. (2017c). *Leading institutions*. Retrieved from https://www.iie.org/Research-and-Insights/Open-Doors/Data/US-Study-Abroad/Leading-Institutions

Institute of International Education. (2017d). *Non-credit work, internships, and volunteering abroad, 2012/13–2015/16*. Retrieved from https://www.iie.org/Research-and-Insights/Open-Doors/Data/US-Study-Abroad/Non-Credit-Work-Internships-and-Volunteering-Abroad

Institute of International Education. (2017e). *Open doors 2017 executive summary*. Retrieved from https://www.iie.org/Why-IIE/Announcements/2017-11-13-Open-Doors-2017-Executive-Summary

Institute of International Education. (2018). *Generation study abroad*. Retrieved from https://www.iie.org/en/Programs/Generation-Study-Abroad/About

Kahneman, D. (2010). The riddle of experience vs. memory [Video file]. Retrieved from https://www.ted.com/talks/daniel_kahneman_the_riddle_of_experience_vs_memory

Kaufman, H., Nixon, A., & Tan, V. (2010). [Off-Campus Studies Integration Survey]. Unpublished raw data.

Kelly, D. (2009a). Lessons from geography: Mental maps and spatial narratives. In E. Brewer & K. Cunningham (Eds.), *Integrating study abroad into the curriculum: Theory and practice across the disciplines* (pp. 21–40). Sterling, VA: Stylus.

Kelly, D. (2009b). Semiotics and the city: Putting theories of everyday life, literature, and culture into practice. In E. Brewer & K. Cunningham (Eds.), *Integrating study abroad into the curriculum: Theory and practice across the disciplines* (pp. 103–120). Sterling, VA: Stylus.

Kiely, R. (2000). What "form" transforms? A constructive-developmental approach to transformative learning. In J. Mezirow (Ed.), *Learning in transformation: Critical perspectives on a theory in progress* (pp. 35–69). San Francisco, CA: Jossey-Bass.

Knight, P. (2007). *Fostering and assessing "wicked" competences.* Retrieved from http://www.open.ac.uk/opencetl/resources/pbpl-resources/knight-2007-fostering-and-assessing-wicked-competencies.

Kolb, D. A. (1984). *Experiential learning: Experience as the source of learning and development.* Englewood Cliffs, NJ: Prentice Hall.

Kolbert, E. (2017, February 27). Why facts don't change our minds? *New Yorker.* Retrieved from https://www.newyorker.com/magazine/2017/02/27/why-facts-dont-change-our-minds

Kuh, G. D. (2008). *High-impact educational practices: What they are, who has access to them, and why they matter.* Washington, DC: Association of American Colleges & Universities.

Kuenzi, J., & Riddle, W. C. (2005). *National Security Education Program: Background and issues.* Retrieved from https://fas.org/sgp/crs/misc/RL31643.pdf

Kumagai, Y., López-Sánchez, A., & Wu, S. (Eds.). (2016). *Multiliteracies in world language education.* New York, NY: Routledge.

Landorf, H., Doscher, S., & Hardrick, J. (2018). *Making global learning universal: Promoting inclusion and success for all students.* Sterling, VA: Stylus.

Leask, B. (2015). *Internationalizing the curriculum.* New York, NY: Routledge.

Lembright, J. A. (2015, fall). Civic values and narrative imagination: The role of international higher education. *IIE Networker, 32–33.*

Lewin, R. (2009). Introduction: The quest for global citizenship through study abroad. In R. Lewin (Ed.), *The handbook of practice and research in study abroad: Higher education and the quest for global citizenship* (pp. xiii–xxii). New York, NY: Routledge.

Marquette University Office of International Education. (2019). *Re-entry programming.* Retrieved from http://www.marquette.edu/abroad/reentry-programming.shtml

Massachusetts Institute of Technology. (2017, August). *MIT Bulletin 2017–18, 153*(1).

Matheson, R. (Writer), & Post, T. (Director). (1960). A world of difference [Television series episode]. In R. Serling (Producer), *The Twilight Zone.* Culver City, CA: Columbia Broadcasting System.

McCullough, D. (2011). *The greater journey: Americans in Paris.* New York, NY: Simon & Schuster.

McGourty, R. (2014, April). Does study abroad accelerate personal growth? *Trends and Insights for International Education Leaders,* 1–5. Retrieved from http://www.nafsa.org/_/File/_/ti_growth.pdf

McKeown, J. S. (2009). *The first time effect: The impact of study abroad on college student intellectual development.* Albany, NY: SUNY Press.

Merriman, M. (2015). *The rise of Gen Z creates new challenges for retailers.* Retrieved from https://www.ey.com/Publication/vwLUAssets/EY-rise-of-gen-znew-challenge-for-retailers/%24FILE/EY-rise-of-gen-znew-challenge-for-retailers.pdf

Mezirow, J. (1991). *Transformative dimensions of adult learning.* San Francisco, CA: Jossey-Bass.

Mezirow, J. (1997). Transformative learning: Theory to practice. *New Directions for Adult and Continuing Education,* 74, 5–12.

Middlebury College. (n.d.). *Rohatyn Center.* Retrieved from http://www.middlebury.edu/international/rcga

Minucci, S. (2010). Cross-Cultural Communications/Cross-Cultural Perspectives in Service Learning [Course syllabus]. Retrieved from http://geo.uoregon.edu/sites/geo.uoregon.edu/files/siena_crosscultural_communications_crosscultural_perspectives_in_service_learning_fall_winter_spring_0.pdf

Modern Language Association Ad Hoc Committee on Foreign Languages. (2007). Foreign languages and higher education: New structures for a changed world. *Profession,* 234–245.

Mount Holyoke McCulloch Center for Global Initiatives. (n.d.-a). *Global Competence Award.* Retrieved from https://www.mtholyoke.edu/global/global-competence-award

Mount Holyoke McCulloch Center for Global Initiatives (n.d.-b). *Global curriculum.* Retrieved from https://www.mtholyoke.edu/global/curriculum

Mulholland, J. (2011). First Lady Michelle Obama says study abroad and "100,000 Strong" initiative make America stronger. Retrieved from https://www.nafsa.org/2011/01/19/first-lady-michelle-obama-says-study-abroad-and-100000-strong-initiative-make-america-stronger/

NAFSA–Association of International Educators. (n.d.-a). *Senator Paul Simon Award for Campus Internationalization.* Retrieved from http://www.nafsa.org/About_Us/About_NAFSA/Awards/Simon_Award/Senator_Paul_Simon_Award_for_Campus_Internationalization/

NAFSA–Association of International Educators. (n.d.-b). *Report of the Commission on the Abraham Lincoln Study Abroad Fellowship Program.* Retrieved from http://www.nafsa.org/Policy_and_Advocacy/Policy_Resources/Policy_Reports/Report_of_the_Commission_on_the_Abraham_Lincoln_Study_Abroad_Fellowship_Program/

NAFSA–Association of International Educators. (n.d.-c). *Trends in U.S. study abroad.* Retrieved from http://www.nafsa.org/Policy_and_Advocacy/Policy_Resources/Policy_Trends_and_Data/Trends_in_U_S__Study_Abroad/

NAFSA–Association of International Educators. (n.d.-d). *Senator Paul Simon Study Abroad Program Act*. Retrieved from https://www.nafsa.org/Policy_and_Advocacy/What_We_Stand_For/Education_Policy/Senator_Paul_Simon_Study_Abroad_Program_Act/

NAFSA–Association of International Educators. (2018). *Report of the Commission on the Abraham Lincoln Study Abroad Fellowship Program*. Retrieved from http://www.nafsa.org/Policy_and_Advocacy/Policy_Resources/Policy_Reports/Report_of_the_Commission_on_the_Abraham_Lincoln_Study_Abroad_Fellowship_Program/

National Association of Colleges and Employers. (2015). *Job outlook 2015*. Bethlehem, PA: Author.

National Center for Education Statistics. (2011). *The nation's report card: Geography 2010* (NCES 2011–467). Washington, DC: Author.

National Geographic-Roper Public Affairs. (2006). National Geographic-Roper Public Affairs *2006 geographic literacy survey: Survey highlights*. Retrieved from https://media.nationalgeographic.org/assets/file/Roper-Poll-2006-Highlights.pdf

Northeastern News. (2014, November 18). *"Generation Z" is entrepreneurial, wants to chart its own future*. Retrieved from https://news.northeastern.edu/2014/11/generation-z-survey/

Nussbaum, M. (1997). *Cultivating humanity: A classical defense of reform in liberal education*. Cambridge, MA: Harvard University Press.

Ogden, A. (2007). The view from the veranda: Understanding today's colonial student. *Frontiers, 15*, 35–56.

Olson, C. L., Green, M. F., & Hill, B. A. (2006). *A handbook for advancing comprehensive internationalization: What institutions can do and what students should learn*. Washington, DC: American Council on Education.

Pachaysana Institute. (2014). *Rehearsing Change*. Retrieved from https://www.pachaysana.org/rehearsing-change

Paige, R. M., Fry, G. W., Stallman, E. M., Josić, J., & Jon, J. E. (2009). Study abroad for global engagement: The long-term impact of mobility experiences. *Intercultural Education, 20* (Suppl., 1), S29–S44.

Palmer, P., & Zajonc, A. (2010). *The heart of higher education: A call to renewal*. San Francisco, CA: Jossey-Bass.

Passarelli, A., & Kolb, D. (2012). Using experiential learning theory to promote student learning and development in programs of education abroad. In M. Vande Berg, R. M. Paige, & K. Hemming Lou (Eds.), *Student learning abroad: What our students are learning, what they're not, and what we can do about it* (pp. 137–161). Sterling, VA: Stylus.

Parcells, C., & Woodruff G. (2016). *Curriculum integration: Best practices*. Retrieved from https://www.nafsa.org/Professional_Resources/Browse_by_Interest/Education_Abroad/Network_Resources/Education_Abroad/Curriculum_Integration__Best_Practices/

Penprase, B., Jensen, E., Boyle, N., Mayer, T, & Carpenter, S. D. (2018, January). Global citizenship in 2018—Linking experience, curriculum, and student development. Panel discussion at *Association of American Colleges & Universities Annual Meeting*, Washington DC.

Pinker, S. (2007). *The language instinct.* New York, NY: Harper Perennial.

Purdue University College of Liberal Arts. (2018). *SCLA courses.* Retrieved from https://www.cla.purdue.edu/academic/SCLAcourses/index.html

Report: More colleges offering dick-around abroad programs. (2010, September 16). *The Onion.* Retrieved from https://www.theonion.com/report-more-colleges-offering-dick-around-abroad-progr-1819571758

Reynolds, C., & Patton, J. (2014). *Leveraging the ePortfolio for integrative learning: A faculty guide to classroom practices for transforming student learning.* Sterling, VA: Stylus.

Rogers, C. (2002). Defining reflection: Another look at John Dewey and reflective thinking. *Teachers College Record, 104*(4), 842–866.

Salisbury, M. H. (2011). *The effect of study abroad on intercultural competence among undergraduate college students* [Doctoral dissertation]. Retrieved February 14, 2018, from http://ir.uiowa.edu/cgi/viewcontent.cgi?article=2458&context=etd

Salisbury, M. H. (2015). Matching program and student characteristics with learning outcomes. In N. W. Sobania (Ed.), *Putting the local in global education: Models for transformative learning through domestic off-campus programs* (pp. 36–51). Sterling, VA: Stylus.

Sanford, N. (1966). *Self and society: Social change and development.* New York, NY: Atherton Press.

Savicki, V. (2008). Experiential and affective education for international educators. In V. Savicki (Ed.), *Developing intercultural competence and transformation: Theory, research, and application in international education* (pp. 74–91). Sterling, VA: Stylus.

Savicki, V., & Brewer, E. (Eds.). (2015). *Assessing study abroad: Theory, tools, and practice.* Sterling, VA: Stylus.

Scholar Ship. (2017, April 1). In *Wikipedia.* Retrieved February 11, 2018, from https://en.wikipedia.org/wiki/The_Scholar_Ship

Seemiller, C., & Grace, M. (2016). *Generation Z goes to college.* San Francisco, CA: Jossey-Bass.

Senator Paul Simon Study Abroad Act of 2017, S. 601, 115th Cong. (2017).

Sideli, K. (2010). The professionalization of the field of education abroad. In W. W. Hoffa & S. C. DePaul (Eds.), *A history of U.S. study abroad: 1965–present* (pp. 369–417). Carlisle, PA: Frontiers.

Sobania, N. W. (2015a). Introduction: The local-global nexus. In N. W. Sobania (Ed.), *Putting the local in global education: Models for transformative learning through domestic off-campus programs* (pp. 1–13). Sterling, VA: Stylus.

Sobania, N. W. (2015b). *Putting the local in global education: Models for transformative learning through domestic off-campus programs.* Sterling, VA: Stylus.

Solo, R. H. (Producer), & Ferrara, A. (Director). (1993). *Invasion of the body snatchers.* [Motion picture]. United States: Warner Bros.

Solo, R. H. (Producer), & Kaufman, P. (Director). (1978). *Invasion of the body snatchers.* [Motion picture]. United States: Solofilm.

Silver, J. (Producer), & Hirschbiegel, O., McTeigue, J. (Director). (2007). *Invasion.* [Motion picture]. USA: Warner Bros.

Stanford University. (n.d.) *Stanford2025.* Retrieved from http://www.stanford2025.com

Stassen, M. L. A. (2003). Student outcomes: The impact of varying living-learning community models. *Research in Higher Education, 44,* 581–613.

State University of New York COIL Center. (n.d.-a). *A brief history of the SUNY COIL Center.* Retrieved February 4, 2018, from http://coil.suny.edu/page/brief-history-suny-coil-center

State University of New York COIL Center. (n.d.-b). *Examples of COIL-supported courses.* Retrieved from http://coil.suny.edu/page/examples-coil-supported-courses

Stohl, M. (2007). We have met the enemy and he is us: The role of the faculty in the internationalization of higher education in the coming decade. *Journal of Studies in International Education 11,* 359–372.

Suderman, D., & Cisar, M. (1992). Foreign language across the curriculum: A critical appraisal. *Modern Language Journal, 76,* 295–308.

Surtees, V. (2016). Beliefs about language learning in study abroad: Advocating for a language ideology approach. *Frontiers, 27,* 85–103.

Sutton, S. B. (2013). The growing world of collaborative internationalization: Taking partnership to the next level. *IIE Networker,* 40–41.

Thompson, J. (2011, September 30). Is nonverbal communication a numbers game? *Psychology Today.* Retrieved from http://www.psychologytoday.com/blog/beyond-words/201109/is-nonverbal-communication-numbers-game

Toral, P. (2009). Synthesis and career preparation: The international relations senior thesis. In E. Brewer & K. Cunningham (Eds.), *Integrating study abroad into the curriculum: Theory and practice across the disciplines* (pp. 191–208). Sterling, VA: Stylus.

Trooboff, S., Vande Berg, M., & Rayman, J. (2007). Employer attitudes toward study abroad. *Frontiers, 15,* 17–33.

Trosset, C. (2016, November). *OCS assessment: The challenges of learning from experience.* PowerPoint session presented at the Carleton College Off-Campus Studies Faculty Workshop, Northfield, MN.

Twombly, S. B., Salisbury, M. H., Tumanut, S. D., & Klute, P. (2012). *Study abroad in a new global century: Renewing the promise, refining the purpose* (ASHE higher education report 38(4)). San Francisco, CA: Jossey-Bass.

Tyler, A. (1985). *The accidental tourist.* New York, NY: Knopf.

Ungar, S. J. (2016, March–April). The study-abroad solution: How to open the American mind. *Foreign Affairs, 95*(2), 111–123.

University of Michigan. (2018). *Science Learning Center.* Retrieved from https://lsa.umich.edu/slc

University of Minnesota. (2009). *Undergraduate student learning and development outcomes: Twin Cities.* Retrieved from https://policy.umn.edu/education/undergradlearning

University of Minnesota Learning Abroad Center. (2018). Curriculum integration papers and events. Retrieved from https://umabroad.umn.edu/professionals/curriculumintegration/

University of Minnesota Pre-Health Student Resource Center. (2018). *Global ambassadors for patient safety.* Retrieved from https://www.healthcareers.umn.edu/courses-and-events/online-workshops/global-ambassadors-patient-safety

University of Wisconsin Office of Residential Life. (n.d.). *Residential life.* Retrieved June 15, 2017, from http://www.housing.wisc.edu/reslife

Vande Berg, M. (2007). Intervening in the learning of U.S. students abroad. *Journal of Studies in International Education, 11,* 392–399.

Vande Berg, M., Connor-Linton, J., & Paige, R. M. (2009). The Georgetown Consortium project: Interventions for student learning abroad. *Frontiers, 18,* 1–31.

Vande Berg, M., Paige, R. M., & Hemming Lou, K. (Eds.). (2012). *Student learning abroad: What our students are learning, what they're not, and what we can do about it.* Sterling, VA: Stylus.

Walton, W. (2009). *Internationalism, national identities, and study abroad: France and the United States, 1890–1970.* Stanford, CA: Stanford University Press.

Wanger, W. (Producer), & Siegel, D. (Director). (1956). *Invasion of the body snatchers.* [Motion picture]. USA: Walter Wanger Productions.

Walton, W. (2009). *Internationalism, national identities, and study abroad: France and the United States, 1890–1970.* Stanford, CA: Stanford University Press.

Wexler, B. (2006). *Brain and culture.* Cambridge, MA: MIT Press.

Willis Allen, H. (2010). Language-learning motivation during short-term study abroad: An activity theory perspective. *Foreign Language Annals, 43*(1), 27–49.

Wolf, M. (2007). *Proust and the squid: The story and science of the reading brain.* New York, NY: HarperCollins.

Yale University. (2015, October 12). Yale-NUS celebrates opening of its permanent campus. *YaleNews.* Retrieved from https://news.yale.edu/2015/10/12/yale-nus-celebrates-opening-its-permanent-campus

Zauzmer, J. (2018, April 12). Holocaust study: Two-thirds of millennials don't know what Auschwitz is. *Washington Post.* Retrieved from https://www.washingtonpost.com/news/acts-of-faith/wp/2018/04/12/two-thirds-of-millennials-dont-know-what-auschwitz-is-according-to-study-of-fading-holocaust-knowledge/

Zoeylola. (2012, September 24), List of funny travel complaints [Online forum comment]. Retrieved from https://www.tripadvisor.com/ShowTopic-g240327-i395-k5786375-A_list_of_Funny_Travel_Complaints-Puerto_Morelos_Yucatan_Peninsula.html

AAC&U. See Association of American Colleges and Universities
academic advisers
  off-campus training for, 53
  shifting, 52
  study away guidance by, 51–52
academic disciplines
  experiential learning supported by, 99
  faculty desire for, 70
  global centers and, 161
  global citizenship with, 116–17
  student hiatus from, 58
  students and, 63
academic objectives
  financial, practical eclipsing, 29
  integrative learning including, 32
  personal growth as separate from, 35–36
The Accidental Tourist (Tyler), 83
accountability, x
ACTFL. See American Council on the Teaching of Foreign Languages
administrators, vii, 7, 52, 153–54
advising
  academic, 51–53
  pathways, 54–55, 76
  planning and, 55
  reintegration from preparation, 65
  study abroad, 34
AIEA. See Association of International Education Administrators
American Council of Education
  on assessment, 113
  internationalization by, 3
  Internationalization Toolkit of, 19n3

American Council on the Teaching of Foreign Languages (ACTFL), 89, 115
assessment, x, 18
  ePortfolios, 120–25
  formative, 119, 122
  global centers for, 162
  global networks for, 120
  integrative, 62, 120–21, 124
  intercultural competence, 116
  language proficiency or accuracy, 115–16
  of metacognitive abilities, 120–21
  methods of, 113, 125n1
  of off-campus study, 112–13
  program needs in, 125
  quantitative over qualitative, 40–41, 114, 125n3
  reflection essays for, 119, 122–23, 163
  resources advocated by, 137
  by self-reporting, 114
Association of American Colleges and Universities (AAC&U), viii, 4–6
  global and intercultural rubrics, 111
  on high-impact practices, 98
  intentional learners and, 15–16
  on liberal education, 30–31
  VALUE rubric, 31, 116, 121, 123
Association of International Education Administrators (AIEA), 2, 8, 20n8, 28, 158
Association of International Educators (NAFSA), 3, 28, 42n6, 136

Bates College, 157, 160

Bauman, Z., 109
Beloit College, 54–55, 67
best practices
    cultural mentoring as, 119, 126n8
    IES Abroad and language, 115–16
    sharing and adapting, 137
Brewer, E., 3, 56, 95n2
bridging capital, 98

capstone projects, 6, 46, 106, 117, 124
careers, 39
    alumni and international, 136
    connections to, 76
    ePortfolios and, 70
    experiences noted for, 162, 164n2
    internships connecting, 106
    language and interpreter, 84
    liberal education for, 108
    off-campus study relating to, 76–77,
        152–53
    study abroad for, 77, 102, 108
Carleton College, 126n7
    autobiographical essay, 122
    faculty and, 35, 53
    field trips and, 60n1
    global coaching programs, 101
    Growing Up Cross-Culturally, 56
    independent research at, 59–60
    intercultural contact course, 67,
        77n1
    internships at, 106–7, 155
    Lisbon photography and, 123–24
    pathways advising, 54
    predeparture consultations by, 50–51
    student, professor comments via,
        19n1
    winter break model of, 48
Carnegie Foundation, 98
CEFR. See Common European
    Framework of Reference for
    Languages
civic engagement
    classroom and society in, 108
    community and, 101–2

democracy connections with, 109
liberal education and, 97–98
multiplier effect of, 102
off-campus and, 97, 109
paternalism and ethics in, 101
over service-learning, 19n5
short-term limitations for, 139
study abroad impacting, 100, 102
support for, 150
CLAC. See cultures and languages
    across the curriculum
climate change, 73, 164
Club Med, 83, 91
cognitive dissonance, 67, 81
COIL. See Collaborative Online
    International Learning
collaborative assignments
    high-impact practices, 82
    science departments and, 151–52
collaborative internationalization, 142
Collaborative Online International
    Learning (COIL), 5, 144
collaborative projects, 6
colonial gaze, 83, 87
Common European Framework of
    Reference for Languages (CEFR),
    115
common experiences, 5–6, 82
communications, x, 58, 86
community-driven outcomes, 101–2
comparative study, 13–14
complex competencies, 120
complexity, 135–36
conceptual frameworks, 36
confirmation bias, 79–80
Connecticut College, 68, 161
consortium-based programs, 11
Council on International Educational
    Exchange, 28, 125n6
creative travel writing class, 68, 73
credits
    ePortfolios and granting of, 124
    translation of, 10, 16, 27, 33
    cross-disciplinarity, See
        interdisciplinarity

cross-discipline teams, 1
  interdisciplinarity in, 74–76
  skills and knowledge in, 72
cross-regional lives, 1
cultural connections, 1, 17, 72, 117
  blindness regarding, 79–80
  Club Med lacking, 91
  ease of, 91–92
  effect of modest levels of, 92
  homestays, service-learning for, 93
  hosts and, 18, 37
  island programs, 81–82
  language and, 73, 86, 89
  misunderstandings, 88–89
  from off-campus study, 6–7
  study abroad and courses on, 56
  technology and loss of, 143
cultural difference, x, 1–2, 5, 13–15,
      17, 18, 38, 56, 80–95, 107, 109,
      116, 120, 125n1, 139. See also
      dissonance
cultural gaps, 39, 69, 88–89, 91, 113,
      125n2
  engaging, 119, 126n9
  friction in, 144–46
  gender pronouns, safe spaces in, 145
  global citizenship and, 17
  study abroad and, 106, 110n3
cultural grammars
  behavior, practices, expressions, 90
  in interdisciplinarity, 92–93
  learning, 111–12
cultural mentoring, 118–19, 126n8
cultures and languages across the
      curriculum (CLAC), 73, 78n5
Cunningham, K., 3, 56, 95n2
curriculum, 2
  ePortfolios and, 70
  faculty and integration of, 156–57
  formal, informal, hidden, 78n4
  hidden, 83
  integration, 41, 56, 121, 156–57
  multiple skills in, 31–32
  off-campus for home, 73
  after off-campus study, 62–63

off-campus leading to on-campus, 71
post-off-campus and university,
      62–63
reflection essays connecting, 119,
      122–23, 163
scaffolding, 51

debriefing, 41, 104, 126n8
departmental territorialism, 130,
      133–35
departure preparation, 16, 45–60. See
      also predeparture work
DeWinter, U., 27, 41n1
diachronic integration, 41
difference, 80–95. See also cultural
      difference
digital presentation skills, 70
direct matriculation, 12
disintegration, 146
dislocation, ix–x, 2, 94
  of comfort zones, 83
  cultural grammars and, 90
  cultural integration for, 81
  dissonance from, 13–15
  from home, 81
  immersion for, 139
  perspective shift from, 13
  rift straddled in, 46–47
  straddling cultures and, 90
  study away with, 139
  technology neutralizing, 143
dissonance, 13–15, 18, 67, 81, 126n10,
      127, 143
DIS Study Abroad in Scandinavia
  cultural ethics, 99–100
  faculty seminar with, 53
  field trips and, 60n1
  geography knowledge, 57
  practicum by, 104
  on psychological challenges, 118
  student, professor comments via,
      19n1
diversity, 5, 14, 23–24, 35, 38, 42n5,
      76, 119–20, 124, 140

education. See also liberal education
  globalization influencing, vii
  off-campus requirement in, 24
  off-campus study for, 3, 8
  undergraduate, 3, 19n2, 125
embedded programs, 12, 33, 47–50,
  101–102
employers, 107–8
end-of-program activities, 67
entrepreneurship, 98–99, 102
ePortfolios, xi
  curricula to careers in, 70
  disparate experience in, 17
  essays, field trips, home stays in, 124
  evidence curated into, 69–70
  extracurricular activities in, 40–41,
    114, 125n4
  global centers with, 162–63
  global learning documented in, 70,
    78n3
  as integrative assessment, 120-25
  learning across context, 121
Erasmus Programme, 23, 42n2
essays
  application, 54–55
  autobiographical, 122
  ePortfolios for, 124
  photography, film, drawing, 123,
    124, 127n12
  postprogram reflection, 67
  project description, 51
  reflection, 119, 122–23, 162
ethics
  captive species and, 99–100
  of community engagement, 101
  global citizenship, 17–18
  of off-campus study, 140–41
  preparation concern for, 46
European Language Portfolio, 78n3
experiential learning, ix, 2, 9, 98–99
extracurricular activities, 40–41, 114,
  125n4

faculty, 21, 42n3, 54, 70

accommodation by, 71–72
bottom-up change by, 154
Carleton College, 19n1, 35, 53
connections not made by, 36
curriculum integration involving,
  156–57
customization and resistance by, 71
development of, 136
expectations of foreign, 145
extra work for, 64
fellows and independent research,
  59–60
global centers involving, 159–60
inexperience of, 130, 132–33
isolation of, viii–ix
off-campus and, vii, 52–53, 72
programs led by, 133
reflection essays and, 119, 122–23,
  163
on concern for standards, 134
on student changes, 72
students circumventing, 147
study abroad experiences, 60n3
study abroad led by, 11
three-pronged approach involving,
  155
travel seminars for, 133
Fair Trade Learning movement, 27,
  102–3
fellowships. See internships
field trips, ix, 50–51, 99, 111
  Carleton, DIS Study Abroad with,
    60n1
  documenting via ePortfolio, 124
  model for short-term programs,
    47–50
  preparations for, 47, 65
finances
  academics limited by, 29
  aid availability on, 24
  as hurdle or obstacle, 70, 130–31
  off-campus, 131, 132
  study abroad and away, 7, 22
  third-party programs and, 26–27
  universities and, 26, 136, 154

FIU. See Florida International
    University
FLAC. See foreign languages across the
    curriculum
Florida International University (FIU),
    157, 162–63
foreign languages across the curriculum
    (FLAC), 73–74, 78n5, 159
formative assessment, 119, 122
Forum on Education Abroad, 28, 113
Fulbright program, 23

Generations Study Abroad, 4
geography ignorance, 57
global centers
    academic majors not at, 161
    for assessment, 162
    as bridge, 159
    ePortfolios in, 162–63
    faculty and, 157–60
    small departments into, 160–61
    universities and, 157, 161
global citizenship, ix, 97, 104–5, 107, 131
    academics and interdisciplinarity in,
        116–17
    cultural differences and, 17
    ePortfolios documenting, 70, 78n3
    intercultural competence with, 116
global engagement, 131, 157
globalization, vii, 16, 101, 140, 168
Global Learning Medallion, 162–63
Global Liberal Arts conferences,
    158–59
global networks, 101, 103, 120
global problems, 73–75, 163
Goldberg, Rube, 149, 164n1
Goldilocks zone, 15, 47, 81
Gordon College, 127n12
Goucher College, 33
Growing Up Cross-Culturally, 56

Higher Education Consortium for
    Urban Affairs (HECUA), 50,
    55–56

high-impact practices, viii, 6, 56, 76,
    82, 98, 102, 112, 140
    AAC&U on, 98
    civic engagement as, 102
    learning communities, common
        experiences, collaboration, 82
    multiplier effect of, 5, 38, 76, 102,
        131, 149
    research on, 19n6
home campus, 5, 13–14
    dislocating from, 81
    integration designed by, 41
    international activities on, 137
    judgments based on, 145
    off-campus and, 2, 6–7, 17, 73
    students and changing, 39, 93
    third-party understanding of, 28
homecoming steps, 14, 16–17
homestays, 93, 124
hosts
    cultural connections with, 37
    relationships with, 18
    study abroad and away with, 139
hybrid programs, 11, 37

IDI. See Intercultural Development
    Inventory
IES Abroad
    internships, service-learning projects,
        106
    language best practices, 115–16
IFE. See Institute for Field Education
IIE. See Institute of International
    Education
immersion, x
    classroom difference to, 115
    for dislocation, 139
    language benefit from, 84, 137–38
    seminar for, 72
independent studies, 59–60, 71
Institute for Field Education (IFE),
    50–51
Institute of International Education
    (IIE), 4, 20n10, 141

institutions. See universities
integration, 164. See also reintegration
  commitments to, 19
  curricula, 56, 121
  curriculum and cocurriculum,
    156–57
  diachronic and synchronic, 41
  dislocation from cultural, 81
  FLAC for, 73–74
  global centers for, 157
  multidisciplinary, 38, 92–93
  off-campus and outsider, 27–28
  of off-campus experience, viii, 150,
    152–53
  social barriers to, 43n9
  sources on, 91, 95n7
  of students, 92
  study abroad and, 78n4, 125
integrative assessment, 62
  of complex competencies, 120
  ePortfolios in, 120–5
  integrative learning in, 121
integrative learning, 20n12, 21, 63
  academic, personal development in,
    32
  American education with, 61
  challenges for, 34–35
  education core as, 45
  shortcomings of, 39–40, 43n9, 43n11
  immediate relevance of, 37–38
  for intentional learners, 31
  multiple skills in, 31–32
  off-campus study for, 3, 15–16, 29,
    36, 45, 163
  study abroad with, 100–101
  weak connections in, 35–36
intentionality, viii, 2, 123
intentional learners
  integrative learning for, 31
  learning communities, 43n10
  off-campus and, 15–16
intercultural competence, 4–5, 18, 66,
    70, 93, 108, 113, 122, 162
  assessing, 114, 116-20

Carleton College course, 67, 77n1
  core, 114
  crucial, 117
  employers' desire for, 107
  psychosocial, cognitive, personal,
    moral, 118
  sensitivity in, 12n9, 119
  service-learning in, 118, 125n6
Intercultural Development Inventory
    (IDI), 126n8
intercultural lives, 1, 103
interdisciplinarity, 23, 72–73
  cross-discipline teams, 74–76
  cultural learning in, 92–93
  global citizenship with, 116–17
  using for global problems, 73–74
International and Global Studies
    Colloquium, 75
internationalization, vii, x
  American Council of Education, 3,
    19n3
  of faculty, 52
  of home campus, 137
  NAFSA on, 136
  senior officer for, 158
  three-pronged approach for, 155
International Partnerships for Service
    Learning (IPSL), 101
internships, 104
  abroad demand, 105
  career goals and, 106
  collaboration for, 155
  connections and languages from, 6
  domestic and abroad, 23
  employers on, 107–8
  ePortfolios for, 124
  experience building and, 17
  IES Abroad, 106
  interconnected learning, 106, 110n3
  off-campus study and, 10, 152–53
  research projects after, 107
  support for, 150
IPSL. See International Partnerships for
    Service Learning

island programs
American experience in, 11
culture problematic in, 81–82
numerical targets for, 40
winter break model as, 49–50

knots, 74–76

language acquisition, viii–ix, 90
abroad for, 22
assessing, 115–16
consideration of, 41n1
culture connections and, 89
culture similarity to, 73
hardwired versus, 86–87
immersive, 84, 137–38
internships and, 6
interpreter career and, 84
nonverbal, 17, 86
off-campus and, 87–88, 161
preparatory courses, 55
requirements, 56–57
short-term programs in, 138
strictures known in, 84–85
thought shaped by, 85–86, 89,
95nn4–5
virtual exchanges in, 144
learning
challenge balancing, 20n11
across context, 121
doing after, 98
ePortfolios and global, 70, 78n3, 121
by error, 89
from extracurricular, 40–41, 114,
125n4
intercultural, 114, 116
internships for, 106, 110n3
language acquisition and, 17
measuring, 113–14
not transferred, 36
parts and wholes for, 61
personal growth and, 111–12
reflection for, 121

learning communities, 6, 38, 43n10, 82
Leask, B., 73, 78n4
liberal education, vii, 21, 24, 31, 36
American expression of, 42n8
careers justifying, 108
definition of, 29–30, 32–34
civic education in, 97–98
links to integrative education, 34–35
non-U.S. universities on, 30
off-campus accomplishing, 29, 39,
125
Lincoln Commission Fellowship Act, 24
liquid modernity, 109
literature studies, 22
long-term programs, viii, 10, 12, 132,
137

Marquette University, 67
Massachusetts Institute of Technology,
29–30
McCullough, David, 21–22
medium-term programs, 9, 11–12, 24,
26, 50, 68, 138
metacognitive abilities, 120–21
Middlebury College, 75, 161
mission statements, 32–33
Modern Language Association, 56–57,
89
Mount Holyoke, 75, 157, 159–60, 162
multidisciplinary integration, 38,
92–93
multimedia storytelling, 68
multiplier effect, 76, 102

NAFSA. See Association of
International Educators
naïve realism
combating student, 93
examples of, 95n1
experience of, 80
National Assessment of Educational
Progress, 57
Northwestern University, 157, 162

off-campus study, 5–6, 28. See also
    study abroad and study away and
    specific topics
    arguments applied in, 19n4
    complexities in, 24–25
    definition of, 8, 10–11
    future of, 18
    ideals of, 12–13
    unrealized potential, 50, 149–50
off-campus study advisory committees,
    53
on-campus learning, 5
The Onion, 83
otherness
    outsider as, 27–28, 38–39
    study away offering less, 140

Palmer, P., 31–32, 34, 121
pathways advising, 54–55, 76
peninsula programs, 11, 37
personal growth, 2
    from challenges, 38–39
    integration and barriers to, 43n9
    integrative learning and, 32
    learning and, 111–12
    nonacademic skill, qualities, 66
    off-campus for, 61–62
    students documenting, 121
    study abroad for, 4, 22
    university offices for, 35–36
postprogram opportunities, 50
practica, ix, 103–5. See also internships
predeparture work, 3, 49
    Carleton College and, 50–51
    Connecticut College, 68
    early, 45–46
    project description essay in, 51
    reintegration after, 65
    as shepherding, 64
preparatory courses, 16, 46, 56
    field trips and, 47, 65
    languages, discipline-specific as, 55
prereading courses, 50, 60n2
pressure points, 129–30

professors. See faculty
programs, 23, 42n2. See also study
    abroad and study away and third-
    party programs
    activities for end of, 67
    assessing needs of, 125
    consortium-based, 11
    course year, 12
    embedded, 12, 33, 47–50, 101–102
    faculty-led, 133
    formats, 137–38
    global coaching, 101
    global problems, 75
    hybrid, 11, 37
    immersion, 72
    island, 11, 40, 49–50, 81–82
    language immersion, 84, 137–38
    long-term (year-long), viii, 10, 12,
        132, 137
    medium-term (quarter or semester),
        9, 11–12, 24, 26, 50, 68, 138
    Marquette reentry, 67
    peninsula, 11, 37
    predeparture work after, 50
    in semester or two quarters, 12
    short-term (eight weeks or less),
        9, 12, 15, 17, 24, 40, 50, 82,
        137–38, 246
projects. See also research projects
    capstone, 6, 46, 106, 117, 124
    senior thesis, 71
    study abroad, 17, 48, 50–51, 58
Purdue University, 67–68

reciprocity, 17–18, 102–3
reentry activities, 3, 67–68
reflection, ix, 103
    electives, social events for,
        66–67
    essay, 119, 122–23, 162
    guiding principles, 127n11
    learning from, 121
    reentry seminars for, 67–68
    storytelling for, 68–69

Rehearsing Change program, Ecuador, 101–2
reintegration, viii
    Connecticut College, 68
    idiosyncratic needs in, 64–65
    personal growth in, 66
    as process, 65, 67
    after study abroad, 58–59, 64
research projects, 27
    after internships, 107
    after study abroad, 17, 58, 61, 71, 94
    study abroad including, 17, 48, 50–51, 58
Rhodes scholars, 22
Rumbley, L., 27, 41n1

Salisbury, M., 116, 119, 125
Sanford, N., 20n11, 47
Sapir, Edward, 85, 95nn4–5
Scholar Ship, 83, 95n3
School for International Training, 51
science, 50
Senator Paul Simon Study Abroad Act (2017), 4, 24, 136
senior international officer, 2–3, 8, 20n8, 153, 158
senior thesis projects, 71
service-learning, 10, 76–77
    civic engagement over, 19n5
    with communities, 6
    culture connections from, 93
    domestic and abroad, 23
    IES Abroad, 106
    intercultural competence from, 118, 125n6
    universities interested in, 158
    short-term programs, 9, 12, 15, 17, 24, 40, 50, 82, 137–38, 246
Sideli, K., 26–27
skills and knowledge, 70–71
Skype, x, 143
social media, x, 142–44
Soka University of America, 33, 132, 158

standards, 28, 115, 134
State University of New York, 144
Stohl, Michael, 52, 133
storytelling, 68–69
students, viii–ix, 1
    academic changes for, 63
    Carleton College, 19n1
    comfort zones, 83
    courses added by, 135, 147n1
    electronic gallery of, 124
    entrepreneurship for, 98–99
    faculty on changes in, 72
    growth documented by, 121
    homeland changing for, 39, 93
    identities of, 119, 126n10
    integration of, 92–93
    knots and groups of, 74
    missions for, 98, 110n2
    multidisciplinary work for, 92–93
    naïve realism of, 93
    off-campus cobbled by, 146–47
    off-campus increasing, 135
    out of sync, 63
    performance gaps and, 77n2
    reciprocity and foreign, 103
    research by, 27
    skill transference by, 34
    study abroad and, 4–5, 23–24, 42n4, 131
study abroad, 1–2, 4–5. See also study away and off-campus study.
    advising, 34
    careers justifying, 77, 102, 108
    civic preparation in, 100, 102
    communications during, 58
    costs for students, 131
    cultural assumptions and, 106, 110n3
    culture, country courses before, 56
    curricula integration of, 78n4
    disciplines transformed by, 21
    diversity appreciation and, 119–20
    dominance of European destinations in, 141

employers on, 107–8
faculty experiences, 60n3
as high-impact practice, viii, 140
hosts and, 139
hype of, 40
integration sources for, 91, 95n7
with integrative learning, 100–101
marketing claims on, 103
numbers for, 7
participation in, 20n7
performance gaps in, 77n2
personal initiative for, 22
practicum fitting, 105
projects during, 17, 48, 50–51, 58
reintegration after, 58–59, 64
research projects after, 17, 58, 61,
    71, 94
Rhodes scholars with, 22
Soka, Goucher requiring, 33
student, destinations in, 23–24,
    42n4
study away and, 116, 125n5, 139–40
uberization of, 146–47
undergraduate education integrating,
    125
value proven, 40–41, 114, 125n3
virtual, 144
study away, 1–2, 7
    academic advisers guiding, 51–52
    dislocation in, 139
    diversity for, 23, 42n5
    domestic/international under, 20n9
    faculty experiences, 60n3
    as high-impact practice, viii, 140
    with hosts, 139
    locus lack for, 156
    numbers in, 24
    study abroad and, 116, 125n5,
        139–40
summative assessments, 122
survey comments, 19n1
sustainability, 48
synchronic integration, 41

systems thinking, 42n7

technology, x, 142–44
theoretical tools, 36
third-party programs, 150. See also Fair
    Trade Learning movement
    budget cuts and, 26
    conversations with, 59
    development of, 25–26
    island or peninsula, 11
    nonprofit and for-profit, 27
    preparation recommended by, 55
    students communicating with, 27
    universities and, 26, 28
threading, 74
three-pronged approach, 155–56
transfer of learning, 36
transformative learning, x, 6, 45, 69,
    81, 95n2
transparency, x, 84–85, 102
Tyler, Anne, 83

undergraduate education, vii, 1, 6
    off-campus study and, 3, 19, 19n2
    study abroad integrated in, 125
UNICollaboration, 144
universities
    bottom-up alternative for changing,
        154
    classes outsourced from, 133–34
    collaboration and, 136–37, 150–51
    deans, provost involvement, 153
    department clustering at, 151–52
    differences in foreign, 26–27
    diversity and, 35, 119–20
    finances and, 26, 136
    funding gaps and, 154
    global centers at, 157–162
    international conferences by, 159
    leadership support at, 136–37
    lost opportunities for, 64
    off-campus study and, 29, 47

after off-campus study and, 62–63
preparation recommended by, 55–56
pressure points for, 130
relational approach for, 156
for service-learning, 158
student comfort zones and, 83
students circumventing, 147
third parties for, 26, 28
University of Delaware, 22
University of Minnesota, 65–66
University of Wisconsin, 157, 161
university specialization, 7

virtual collaboration, 144

Wesleyan University, 157, 160
Whorf, Benjamin Lee, 85, 95nn4–5
winter break models, 50
word clouds, 32–33
writing-intensive courses, 6, 17

Yale University, 157, 159, 161–62

Zajonc, A., 29, 31–32, 34, 121

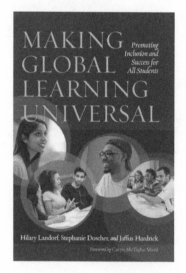

Making Global Learning Universal

Promoting Inclusion and Success for All Students

Hilary Landorf, Stephanie Doscher, and Jaffus Hardrick

Foreword by Caryn McTighe Musil

"At a moment when terms like diverse, interconnected, and global have become, in the authors' words, 'politically charged dynamite,' this book argues persuasively that making global learning universal is essential to student success in an increasingly interconnected world. Organized thoughtfully in three sections that include cogent definitions, exemplary promising practices, and assessment and program evaluation, this publication is required reading for those committed to exploring global literacy in the primary, secondary, and tertiary educational sectors." —*Gil Latz, PhD; Associate Vice Chancellor for International Affairs, Professor of Geography, and Affiliated Professor of Philanthropic Studies; Indiana University-Purdue University Indianapolis*

This book is copublished with NAFSA.

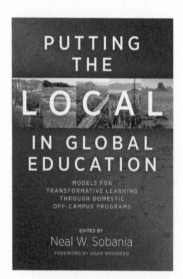

Putting the Local in Global Education

Models for Transformative Learning Through Domestic Off-Campus Programs

Edited by Neal W. Sobania

Foreword by Adam Weinberg

"The time has come for all international educators to consider more seriously how we actively bridge global learning with the local, domestic context. *Putting the Local in Global Education* is a critical read for those educators who seek to ensure that global learning is accessible for all students—not just those who are able to study abroad." —*Gayle Woodruff*, Director, Curriculum and Campus Internationalization, University of Minnesota

This book presents both the rationale for and examples of "study away," an inclusive concept that embraces study abroad while advocating for a wide variety of domestic study programs, including community-based education programs that employ academic service-learning and internships.

Community-Based Global Learning

The Theory and Practice of Ethical Engagement at Home and Abroad

Eric Hartman, Richard C. Kiely, Christopher Boettcher, and Jessica Friedrichs

Foreword by Rafia Zakaria

"Global learning is full of paradox, straddling intention and ambiguity. It is more important than ever to encourage the basic human impulse to connect with people across boundaries. Yet we also have a responsibility to introduce young people to a harsh reality—that 'making a difference' is actually quite difficult. Hartman and colleagues' book is a beacon and a guide for how we can support all who are beginning the lifelong journey of understanding how social transformation happens." —*Jennifer Lentfer*, Director of Communications, Thousand Currents

22883 Quicksilver Drive
Sterling, VA 20166-2019

Subscribe to our e-mail alerts: www.Styluspub.com

Also available from Stylus

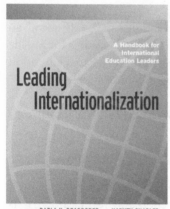

Leading Internationalization

A Handbook for International Education Leaders

Edited by Darla K. Deardorff and Harvey Charles

Foreword by E. Gordon Gee

Afterword by Allan E. Goodman

"This is one of the most comprehensive, if not the most comprehensive, collection of essays on international higher education leadership. This book builds very well on the AIEA Standards of Professional Practice of senior international officers. A must-have on the desk for everyone in the field, both in the United States and beyond." —*Markus Laitinen, President, European Association for International Education (EAIE)*

This resource is a vital starting point for anyone in a senior leadership role in higher education, as well as for anyone desiring to understand more about this key leadership position essential to higher education institutions in developing institutional global capacity and in educating global-ready graduates.

(Continues on preceding pages)